THE HOME WINEMAKER'S COMPANION

Secrets, Recipes, and Know-How for Making 115 Great-Tasting Wines

GENE SPAZIANI,
Past President of the American Wine Society,
AND ED HALLORAN

STOREY
BOOKS

*The mission of Storey Publishing is to serve our customers
by publishing practical information that encourages personal independence
in harmony with the environment.*

Edited by Brad Ring, Dan Callahan, and Marie Salter
Copyedited by Doris Troy
Cover design by Meredith Maker
Front cover photograph © Janet Kerr, Envision
Spine and back cover photographs © Artville
Text design and production by Susan Bernier
Line drawings by Randy Mosher; decorative drawings by Laura Tedeschi
Indexed by Nan Badgett/Word•a•bil•i•ty

The information in this book is true and complete to the best of our knowledge. All recommendations are made without guarantee on the part of the authors or Storey Publishing. The authors and publisher disclaim any liability in connection with the use of this information. For additional information, please contact Storey Publishing, 210 MASS MoCA Way, North Adams, MA 01247

Storey books are available for special premium and promotional uses and for customized editions. For further information, please call 1-800-793-9396.

Printed in the United States by Von Hoffmann
10 9 8 7 6 5 4

Library of Congress Cataloging-in-Publication Data

The home winemaker's companion : secrets, recipes, and know-how for making 115 great-tasting wines / Gene Spaziani and Ed Halloran.
    p. cm.
  Includes index.
  ISBN 1-58017-209-1 (alk. paper)
  1. Wine and wine making—Amateurs' manuals. I. Spaziani, Gene. II. Halloran, Edward John.
TP548.2 .H65 2000
641.8'72—dc21   00-037046

CONTENTS

PREFACE iv

ACKNOWLEDGMENTS v

1 Getting Started 1

2 Essential How-tos 21

3 Wine from Kits 26

4 Wine from Concentrates 33

5 Wine from Juices 70

6 White Wine from Grapes 122

7 Red Wine from Grapes 161

8 Wine from Fruit 198

9 Sparkling and Fortified Wines 215

10 Troubleshooting 231

APPENDIXES 238

Winemaking Record 239

Fermentation Data/Bottling Data 240

Wine Evaluation 241

Competitions 245

Suppliers and Equipment 247

GLOSSARY 254

INDEX 260

PREFACE

*May our wine brighten the mind and
strengthen the resolution.*

— Traditional Toast

THIS BOOK WAS WRITTEN WITH YOU IN MIND, and we hope it will bring a new and exciting dimension to your home winemaking. We've included information and recipes for novice and experienced winemakers and expect this book will quickly become an invaluable addition to your winemaking library.

By paring down the art of winemaking to its simplest form and demystifying what actually is a fairly straightforward process, we hope to encourage a lifelong interest in the winemaking hobby. As technology continues to improve, the opportunities for making excellent wine get better and better. If you follow our recommendations and instructions and embrace the discipline of patience, you will be richly rewarded.

HOW TO USE THIS BOOK

Begin by reading the first two chapters in their entirety. They will provide you with a good overview of the process of making wine and later will serve as ready reference tools.

Next, read the introductory pages of chapters 3 through 7. They've been designed to walk you through the entire spectrum of winemaking, from the simple (using kits) to the most complex (producing red wine from grapes). Subsequent chapters deal with more advanced issues.

Choose a method, based on your comfort level with the procedures required to produce the wine. Then carefully follow the instructions in the recipe.

Generally speaking, people who balk at making wine from grapes do so because they're afraid of what they call "all that science." Actually, checking specific gravity and acid and sugar content doesn't require a degree in chemistry. We'll show you how it's done, and your wines will be even better because you'll be able to exercise more control over them from start to finish.

People from every walk of life have been making wine for a long while, and you can too. Good luck!

ACKNOWLEDGMENTS

WE'RE PARTICULARLY GRATEFUL to our friend, Phil Anger, who brought us together and enabled us to make this book a reality.

Early on, we were encouraged by Sarah Kennedy and Herb Cohen, and we were aided enormously by Brad Ring and Dan Callahan, who literally helped us to map out the book.

Marie Salter joined us late in the game but, together with Doris Troy, tightened the text, making for a smoother read.

Our wives, Isabel Spaziani and Maria Cristina Halloran, supported us throughout the publication process. Maria proofread rough copy and took photographs to assist the illustrators. Isabel typed our drafts and the final manuscript, and she prepared memorable meals whenever it was necessary for the two far-flung winemakers to work together.

We're also grateful to the following people for their suggestions and support: Ray Corsini, Carmen Spagnola, Ginny Della Mura, Bonnie Pease, Cathy Surface, Charles Stephenson, Jim Bobbitt, Sante Isopo, Gordon Gribble, Frank Lipski, Bob Szaro, Tom Mannello, Jon Haight, Tony DiNicola, Armand Brandi Kucinskas, Andy Gambardella, Bob Landino, Dan Kucinskas, Joe Cory, Glen Lemaire, Ricardo Quental, Cameron Beard, Angel, Joe and Renée Nardone, Bill Halliwell, Ray Hartung, Tom Pelick, Doug Moorehead, Tess Szamatulski, Larry McCulloch, Bill Hopkins, Howard Bursen, Harry McWatters, Phyllis Hands, Barbara Shenfish, Ron Binz, Igor Cadmus, Jeff Williams, Anne Cofone, David Gimbel, Terry Akre, Wanda and Bob Stretch, Amy Neurenberg, Tim Merrick, Parker Carlson, Nick Prior, Bob Slaktowicz, Gerard Takiguchi; Gene's daughters, Raina, Resa, and Rhonda; his son, Gene III; Uncle Jack Spaziani; and grandsons Jake McTigue and E. J. Spaziani IV.

Obviously, we weren't alone in this venture and, if we left anyone out, we apologize. The fact is, every wine lover we've ever met has taught us something of value.

Gene's lifelong love of winemaking was inspired by his grandfather, Igino, and his father, Americo. His mother, Theresa, who died while this book was being written, also encouraged him.

DEDICATION

To my grandfather, Igino Spaziani, who used to lead our family
winemaking process like a symphony conductor,
barking out orders and directing traffic. The wonderful
memories of those days are still fresh in my mind,
though sixty years have passed. Every year, I dedicate
a batch of rich, hearty red wine to my grandfather's memory,
because he inspired and encouraged me to become a winemaker.

—Gene Spaziani

To Kirsten, Bill, and Hannah Pearson. In the
words of the old English toast,
"May your love be like a good wine and grow stronger with time."

—Ed Halloran

GETTING STARTED

Good company, good wine,
good welcome make good people.

—Shakespeare (1564–1616)

OUR GOAL IS TO ASSIST YOU in the process of making wine. We will present a simple method for attaining quality results with easy-to-understand recipes. Although experienced winemakers rarely use recipes, people who are just starting out find that if they follow instructions carefully, they will make good wines from the outset.

Modern technology makes it easy to make high-quality wines, as new methods for preserving freshly crushed grape juices, either by blast-freezing or through various pasteurization processes, enable them to remain stable and usable for a long period.

Wine, by the way, can be made from any number of things besides grapes, including a variety of other fruits and vegetables. Depending on where you live, many of the raw materials for winemaking may be available locally from vineyards, farms, wholesalers, and retailers.

Whether you make your wine from scratch or a kit, from juices or concentrates, you'll find that making your own wine is easy and fun!

Novices have produced excellent wines by using kits. These provide the necessary ingredients and instructions, and make it a simple matter for first-timers to create delightful wines. We'll explore this approach in chapter 3.

WINE FROM YOUR GARDEN? YES!

You can produce a first-rate wine from many vegetables. Tomatoes, for example, make a delightful blush wine, and anyone who drinks it without knowing what it is will think it was made from grapes. (See page 210 for recipe.)

Using juices or concentrates also will enable you to produce wonderful wines. Thanks to the preservation techniques we mentioned earlier, it is possible for home winemakers to make wines from all of the world's great grape regions. There are separate chapters devoted to these methods.

Of course, the ultimate experience comes when you make wine from scratch. This requires more work, but the satisfaction you'll get makes it worth the effort.

DON'T BE AFRAID!

The process of making wine is simple, and we'll walk you through it one step at a time. This book is designed to meet the needs of many people — from novices to experienced winemakers eager to learn a few new techniques.

Some people will discover that they already know a great deal about the process, because they've learned how to brew their own beers and ales. Winemaking is the logical next step for home brewers, because they already have a lot of the equipment they will need and have learned the importance of cleanliness and patience.

Cleanliness is critical when you're making wine, and you'll find that if you follow our suggestions for keeping your work area, equipment, and bottles squeaky clean, you'll avoid many of the problems caused by unwanted bacteria and foreign matter.

Patience is also important. It's quite natural to want to taste your wine as soon as possible, but Mother Nature needs to be allowed time to work — alone! Often, the best thing to do is simply to stay away from your wine and let it develop on its own. In fact, oftentimes all you have to do is step back and let nature take its course.

EIGHT STEPS TO WINEMAKING

Winemaking is a fairly simple process and can be accomplished in eight steps:

1. Choose grapes.
2. Crush grapes.
3. Strain juice into fermentor.
4. Inoculate juice with yeast.
5. Allow wine to ferment. Be patient!
6. Rack wine (that is, move the wine to new containers as needed). Be patient!
7. Bottle wine.
8. Age wine. Be patient!

As you can see, during fermentation, between rackings, and after bottling, all you have to do is let the wine "work" by itself.

Using kits, juices, or concentrates lets you skip the pressing and crushing steps, which is why many beginners feel more comfortable with these winemaking methods. Some winemakers never get beyond these methods, because they enjoy producing their wines with relative ease. There's nothing wrong with this: Regardless of the method, every winemaker puts his or her own stamp on the finished product, and it's this variation that makes making and tasting wines such a delightful experience.

A BRIEF HISTORY OF WINEMAKING

According to Greek legend, Dionysus (Roman Bacchus), the son of Zeus, made the first wine on Mount Nysa in what is now Libya.

According to the Egyptians, Osiris was the inventor; the Bible credits Noah with developing the art of grape growing and winemaking after the Flood.

For thousands of years wine has served as a tonic, a soporific, a tranquilizer, an elixir, a daily beverage, a food, and an important element in religious ceremonies. The Roman legions brought the vine to England, Germany, France, and Belgium. The Roman influence carries on today, and its viticultural and winemaking processes are legendary.

As Christianity spread throughout the world, so too did wine. Church leaders required it for religious rites and understood the food value of wine. Monks became vintners, and laypeople followed in their footsteps.

Even in the Americas, the Church's influence was felt: A Dominican missionary, Padre Junipero, is credited with bringing the first grapevines to California from Spain.

It wasn't until the 1860s that the miracle of winemaking was explained. The French scientist Louis Pasteur clarified the process of fermentation and identified organisms he called *fermints* as the stimuli for fermentation. Thanks to his efforts, winemakers now knew what happens when grape juice starts to change color, begins to bubble, and eventually turns into wine.

Thomas Jefferson, himself a winemaker, once said, "I think it is a great error to consider a heavy tax on wines as a tax on luxury. On the contrary, it is a tax on the health of our citizens." Recent medical studies would seem to concur, suggesting that wine — red wine in particular — promotes good health by lowering cholesterol and moderating conditions that can lead to heart disease.

After centuries of making wine, modern technology has taken a lot of the guesswork out of the process, and we are now producing the finest wines ever made.

EQUIPMENT

Earlier, we used the term *kit* when we talked about ingredients for making wine. Now it's time to look at another type of kit: the equipment you'll need to turn your ingredients into wine.

Becoming a home winemaker requires a small financial commitment for basic equipment. Over time, you may decide to experiment with different varieties of wine (including champagnes) and in greater quantities. In that case, you'll need to purchase additional equipment. If,

WINEMAKING EQUIPMENT

Basic Equipment

- Primary fermenting vessel, 6.5- to 7.5- gallon (25–28 L)
- 1 or 2 Glass or plastic carboys, 5-gallon (19 L)
- Siphon
- Stirring spoons or paddles
- 2 Bottle brushes
- Fermentation locks (air locks)
- Carboy bungs (rubber stoppers)
- 3 Funnels
- Measuring cups
- Hydrometer (saccharometer)
- Hydrometer jar
- Thermometer (floating)
- Acid test kit
- Bottles
- Corks or caps

Advanced Equipment

- Vinometer
- Wine thief
- Bottle sterilizer/rinser
- Crusher or stemmer-crusher
- Presses
- Bottle closures
- Bottle corkers

however, you opt to continue making wine from juices and concentrates, the basic kit will serve you well for many years.

Pay a visit to your local wine supply store. Staff there are likely to have put together one or more basic winemaking kits, or they can create one to meet your specific needs. They're also a good source of information concerning equipment that you may not want to purchase at this point in your winemaking career, but that may be available for a small rental charge or even on loan from other winemakers.

For example, stemmer-crushers, which are used by people who make grape wine from scratch, are relatively expensive. Generally speaking, winemakers use these devices for only a few hours a year, so they're usually willing to share.

In any event, when you're starting out, it's best to purchase just the items you'll actually need for your first winemaking project. Therefore, we urge you to talk it over with a knowledgeable person at the wine supply store so you can put together a basic list.

The great thing about the equipment you acquire is that you can use it again and again. And if you've been brewing your own beer, you already have most of what you need!

THE ESSENTIALS: BASIC EQUIPMENT

Let's take a closer look at what you'll need to get started. You may already have some of these items on hand. We've included alternative equipment where possible.

PRIMARY FERMENTOR. You'll probably use either a 6- to 7.5-gallon (23–28 L) glass carboy or a food-grade plastic pail in sizes ranging from 6 to 32 gallons (23–121 L). You'll need a container that's larger than the amount of wine you plan to make in order to allow for foaming and expansion. Stainless-steel and enamel containers with no cracks are also acceptable.

pail

GLASS OR PLASTIC CARBOYS. You'll need at least one 5- to 7-gallon (19–27 L) carboy for aging and racking your wine. Two containers would be better because you're going to have to lift and handle them when they're filled with wine, and this can be cumbersome and awkward. You may even want to consider 3-gallon (11 L) glass carboys for greater ease in handling.

glass carboy

SIPHON. A 6-foot (1.8 m) piece of ⅜-inch (0.95 cm) or ½-inch (1.3 cm) polyvinyl tubing will do nicely. A J-tube is another type of siphon. There are also bottling siphons that can do the job — these are inexpensive and efficient, as they will pick up virtually every drop of wine.

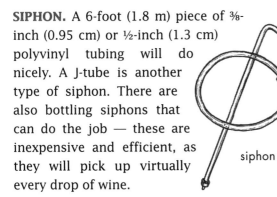

siphon

STIRRING SPOON OR PADDLE. These are particularly helpful when you are making a red wine (more on this later). Spoons or paddles should be of food-grade plastic, stainless steel, or wood. If you have a lathe, you can turn out your own paddles at minimal cost.

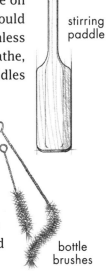

stirring paddle

BOTTLE BRUSHES. You'll need two, one for carboys and the other for bottles. They should have nylon bristles and heavy-gauge wire handles. You can then bend them to reach into tight corners and realign them as necessary.

bottle brushes

FERMENTATION LOCK. This device may also be called an air lock, bubbler, water seal, or fermentation trap. Whatever the name, it serves a dual purpose — to allow gas to escape during fermentation and to keep air from getting to the wine. This lock fits into the carboy bung.

  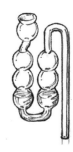

air lock   water seal   fermentation trap

CARBOY BUNG (RUBBER STOPPER). This is a rubber stopper with a hole drilled through it to allow for the insertion of the fermentation lock. The bung is made of sulfur-free, pure gum rubber, and is usually sold in combination with a fermentation lock. You'll need several of these units.

carboy bung

FUNNELS. Buy several plastic or polypropylene funnels. A large one, 12 inches (30 cm) across, used with a strainer, will help you to fill carboys or barrels. You should also have one that measures 7 inches (17.8 cm) across, and a smaller funnel with an outside diameter of ¼ inch (6 mm). We'll discuss their uses later. Funnels are readily available at the super-market, hardware store, and wine supply shop.

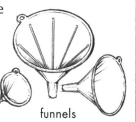

funnels

MEASURING CUPS. You probably already have a standard-size measuring cup in your kitchen, but you'll also need at least a ½-gallon (1.9 L) cup. There are times when you'll find the larger one particularly useful, especially if you're making red wine from grapes and have to scoop the must into a pressing container.

measuring cup

HYDROMETER (SACCHAROMETER). This is a necessity for all winemakers. The hydrometer eliminates guess-work and ensures accuracy. It measures the sugar content of the juice and describes the potential alcohol content. There are a number of different types, but we advocate purchasing one that measures the sugar percentage (Brix temperature; see page 22), alcohol potential, and specific gravity.

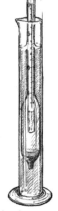

hydrometer in jar

HYDROMETER JAR. The hydrometer floats inside this container, which contains either wine or must. The jar is cylindrical and can be made of glass or plastic. Graduations will be marked in milliliters (100 mL, 250 mL, 500 mL, for example).

FLOATING THERMOMETER. A mercury column and scale encased in a ¾-inch (1.9 cm) glass cylinder, the thermometer floats upright in liquid and is used to measure the temperature of wine.

hydrometer jar

ACID TEST KIT. After the test for sugar content, the test for acidity is the most important measurement a winemaker takes. Although it is a relatively simple procedure, many home wine-makers object to learning how to do it and find myriad excuses to avoid it. Perhaps they are intimidated by the fact that chemistry is involved. Whatever the case, without determining the amount of acidity, a winemaker is prone to make one mistake after another.

It is important to perform this test because your sugar and acid counts should be in harmony before you inoculate for fermentation. It is very difficult to make adjustments later. A complete acid test kit is reasonably priced, and worth every penny! Most kits include a 25 mL burette with a pinchcock; a 5 mL pipette, burette stand, and clamp; 16 ounces (474 mL) of N/10 sodium hydroxide; 1 ounce (30 mL) of phenolphthalein; and a set of instructions.

acid test kit

You should also purchase a 250 mL Erlenmeyer flask to hold your samples. A 250 mL Pyrex beaker is also handy, and you'll need a supply of distilled water in order to perform the tests. Buy a gallon (3.8 L) bottle (they're usually cheapest at the supermarket) and keep it with your testing gear.

Erlenmeyer flask

Pyrex beaker

BOTTLES. Generally speaking, we recommend using the bottle type traditionally used for the wine you're going to produce (see page 10 for illustrations of standard bottles). Still, there really aren't any hard-and-fast rules, so you can be flexible. The main thing is to make sure that your bottles are properly cleaned and sanitized before filling them (see page 10) and that they are tightly sealed.

CORKS OR CAPS. Corks, either plastic or natural, are perfectly fine for sealing your bottles. For that matter, so are plastic-capped push corks and screw caps, unless you're making champagne! (See page 9 for more on bottle closures.)

ADVANCED EQUIPMENT

You'll need to purchase most of the equipment that follows from a reliable wine supply store or, if you're lucky, perhaps at reduced cost from a home winemaker who's having a going-out-of-business sale. In either case, whether new or used, make sure that the equipment you buy is in good shape. And be sure to tell your friends and relatives that advanced winemaking equipment makes a great gift!

VINOMETER. This is an inexpensive instrument for measuring alcohol content. Strictly speaking, it isn't necessary, but we believe that you'll find it useful to know what your wine's final alcohol count is.

vinometer

WINE THIEF. This is an inexpensive gadget that allows you to lift samples out of barrels, carboys, and other containers. It's a good thing to have on hand.

BOTTLE STERILIZER/RINSER. This unit consists of a water reservoir (we recommend using a sulfur dioxide solution) and a spring-loaded pump. A screen filters out foreign matter from the recirculating liquid. To operate, push down the bottle several times while it is placed over the pump mechanism. Do this just prior to filling your bottles.

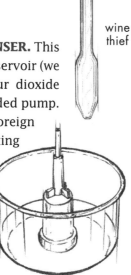

wine thief

bottle sterilizer/rinser

CRUSHER.
If you decide to make wine from fresh grapes, you'll have to crush and press them in order to obtain their juice. Creative individuals have made their own devices, but if you don't have a lot of grapes to deal with, you can always do it by hand.

When dealing with a large amount of grapes, options are to purchase this relatively expensive equipment, rent it, or use a friend's.

There are a number of crushers on the market. Our favorite, the flywheel type, usually has a stainless-steel hopper and is about 48 inches (1.2 m) long.

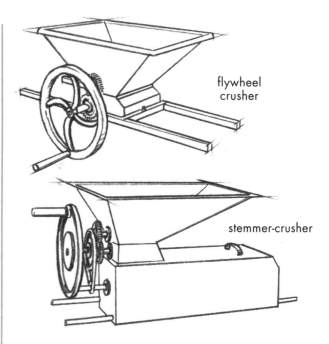

flywheel crusher

stemmer-crusher

Fruit crushers can also do the job, and more than one winemaker has acquired his at a garage sale. Or you may decide to purchase the upscale stemmer-crusher. This electrified unit crushes greater quantities in a short period. Grapes are placed in the trough, crushed, and dropped into a container underneath while unwanted stems are dispensed out the back of the machine.

PRESSES. Basket presses have been around for many years. In fact, a used one that was more than 100 years old when it was replaced served the Spaziani household well for decades.

These days, bladder presses are coming into vogue (see page 127). They're larger and more expensive than basket presses, but they're highly efficient and should last for years.

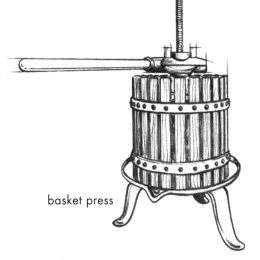

basket press

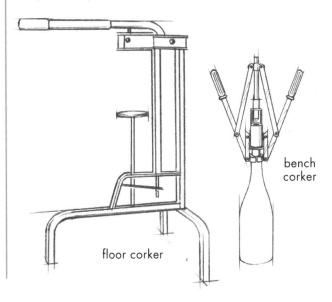

floor corker

bench corker

CAUTION

Never reuse a cork once it's been pulled from a bottle. Doing so is an invitation to disaster: Once a cork has been in a bottle for any length of time, it loses its elasticity and is vulnerable to oxidation problems. This can ruin your wine.

Either way, look into purchasing a used press. Generally speaking, the only reason to replace one is to move up to a larger unit. Presses are needed for just a few hours a year, so second-hand ones tend to be in excellent condition.

BOTTLE CLOSURES. If you intend to drink all of your wine within one year, plastic-top corks are perfectly fine. They're easy to insert; in fact, you can do it by hand.

With access to the proper bottles, you can save time and money by using screw caps. Otherwise, spend the money and buy good-quality corks. Trying to save on corks can cost you a great deal in the long run; cheap corks tend to leak and will ruin the wine. If you use regular wine corks, you'll have to acquire an insertion device.

plastic-top cork

cork stopper

BOTTLE CORKERS. Hand corkers earn mixed reviews. Some people swear by them; others swear at them. We recommend a floor or a bench model, as it will function efficiently with minimal effort on your part. After more than 15 years, the Portuguese floor-model corker we use still works flawlessly. A four-piece plastic compression head squeezes the cork evenly on all sides, the bottle stand locks in place, and cork depth is adjustable.

Broods of Bottles

Home winemakers are constantly dealing with acquiring, cleaning, and storing bottles. Our cellars and garages are filled with bottles of all shapes and sizes. They've been scrounged from restaurants, wineries, tasting rooms, and friends. This can be something of a pain, but it beats buying new bottles all the time, which is expensive, and shipping charges alone may exceed the cost of the bottles.

If you're a resourceful scrounger, it's particularly important to keep your word and pick up the empties on the appointed day and at the designated hour. Even though friends may be flexible, empty bottles are a hazard and create space problems in restaurants and wineries.

Bottle Cleaning

If your donors will rinse out the used bottles for you, so much the better, but you still must clean the bottles at home. Start by rinsing them to get rid of accumulated debris, fungus, and other undesirables. (If any of this material solidifies, it will be difficult to clean and sanitize your bottles.) Then soak the bottles in cold water to which 1 tablespoon (15 mL) of chlorine bleach per gallon has been added. A dash of sal soda also helps. When the bottles have been properly soaked and you have scraped off the old labels, rinse each bottle thoroughly with hot water. Let dry before placing them in storage.

When it is time to fill the bottles, first rinse them in hot water. Sanitize each bottle, using your bottle sanitizer/washer with a potassium metabisulfite powder solution (see page 28). Then shake free any excess liquid before bottling. Allow for approximately ½ inch (1.3 cm) between the wine and the bottom of the cork once it's been inserted.

Types of Bottles

Different regions of the world use specifically shaped and colored bottles to identify the wine's origin. Bordeaux bottles have sharp shoulders and use colored glass to indicate the type of wine in the bottle.

Burgundy bottles have sloping shoulders, and several colors are used.

Most German wines are made in the area of the Rhine River or along the Moselle. In both cases, they use tall, slender bottles. There are two colors of glass, brown for the Rhine region and green for Moselles. German-style bottles are also used in the Alsace region of France.

The most common size today is the 750 mL (25.4 oz) bottle. Other sizes are the

Bordeaux   burgundy   German

375 mL   750 mL   1.5 L

1.5 L (50.7 oz) and the 375 mL (12.7 oz) half bottle. These are particularly good for wine left over during the bottling process.

Some winemakers prefer using even larger jugs. They may hold a gallon (3.8 L) or more, and they're fine — provided, of course, that the wine is consumed soon after the jug has been opened.

BOTTLES AND THE WINES THEY HOLD

What follows are the most commonly used bottle types listed by region of origin. These pairings are only general guidelines; the ultimate decision as to which bottle to use is yours.

Bordeaux Bottles
- Cabernet Franc
- Cabernet Sauvignon
- Gamay
- Grenache
- Malbec
- Merlot
- Sauvignon Blanc
- Zinfandel

Burgundy Bottles
- Chardonnay
- Marsanne
- Petite Sirah
- Pinot Blanc
- Pinot Noir
- Syrah
- Viognier

German Bottles
- Gewürztraminer
- Johannisberg Riesling
- Muller-Thurgau
- Sylvaner

INGREDIENTS

"You can't make good wine from poor grapes . . . you must have good grapes to make good wine." We've heard this statement over and over from the world's best winemakers. On the other hand, as a lot of people can tell you from experience, it is possible to make bad wine from good grapes, and quite a few of us, learning gradually through trial and error, have done that many times.

Happily, thanks to better raw materials and the increased dissemination of the craft's secrets, today's home winemakers are producing first-rate drinks.

Your goal should be to make a quality wine, not merely a drinkable one. And this should be the goal set by first-time winemakers, not just veterans, as the ready availability of top-drawer juices and concentrates makes the use of inferior ingredients inexcusable.

Field grape picking, pressing, and freezing techniques now stabilize juices for protracted periods, and the same is true for improved pasteurization processes. Thus, the North American winemaker today has easy access to juices and concentrates from all over the world. The fact that these ingredients remain stable makes it possible for the home winemaker to produce wine at his own convenience, rather than being restricted to harvesttime.

Traditionally, California has been the source for most of our fresh grapes. That's changing, however, as more wineries throughout North America are selling grapes to the general public.

Finally, whether you're going to use grapes, juices, concentrates, fruits, or vegetables to make your wine, get the best ingredients you can afford. That way, the likelihood for success will increase.

If you haven't decided yet what wine to make, look at our recipes in the chapters dealing with juices, concentrates, and grapes. Find one or two that appeal to you, then begin your search for ingredients. A local wine supply store or a fruit wholesaler is a good place to start.

BASIC SUPPLIES

We will address the issue of ingredients in greater detail a bit later in this chapter when we look at basic winemaking steps. What follows is a list of supplies you should have on hand.

- Potassium metabisulfite powder (alternatively, Campden tablets)
- Acid blend
- Natural grape tannin
- Yeast nutrient (Fermaid; Scott Laboratories, Petaluma, CA)
- Pectic enzyme
- Wine yeast
- Soda ash (sal soda)
- Bentonite
- Drifine isinglass powder (Cellulo Company, Fresno, CA)
- Gelatin powder
- Silica gel (kieselsol)

POTASSIUM METABISULFITE POWDER. Purchase the food-grade version of this powder. It's your best friend — it inhibits molds and bacteria and serves as an antioxidant and general cleansing agent.

More shops are carrying sodium bisulfite, which does the same job. We've heard reports that it can, on rare occasions, impart an unwanted flavor. It's important to remember that commercial wineries use potassium metabisulfite, and we suggest that you follow their example.

CAMPDEN TABLETS. These perform the same tasks as potassium metabisulfite, only they come in a solid form. You'll need to crush the tablets before adding them to your wine.

ACID BLEND. This powder is a combination of tartaric, malic, and citric acids, usually in a 40-40-20 ratio. You'll need this to make acid adjustments, particularly if you have California grapes or juice, which have a tendency to require acid before fermentation.

NATURAL GRAPE TANNIN. Add ½ teaspoon (1 g) to 5 gallons (19 L) of wine to assist in clarifying most fruit, honey, vegetable, and white wines. Red wines don't require additional tannins; nature has already provided them with an ample supply.

YEAST NUTRIENT (FERMAID). This powder, made by Scott Laboratories, contains diammonium phosphate, yeast hulls, folic acid, magnesium sulfate, niacin, and calcium pantothenate. It's used to nourish yeast and help its action.

PECTIC ENZYME LIQUID (RAPIDASE VINO SUPER). This helps wines to settle and conditions them to filter more easily. Normal usage is 1.5 to 3 drops per gallon (3.8 L). *Note:* 1 mL (⅕ tsp) = approximately 20 drops.

WINE YEAST. Never use brewer's or baker's yeast. Purchase commercial yeast designed specifically for winemaking. Your wine supply source will tell you which yeast is best for the wine you're making. In most cases, a 5-gram foil packet will help to ferment up to 6 gallons (23 L) of wine.

SODA ASH (SAL SODA). This is an excellent, inexpensive, alkaline cleaning agent for equipment, bottles, and wine stains. Don't buy the scented kind as it may taint the wine.

FINING AGENTS. Although they aren't mandatory at the outset, you'll probably need them down the road. Following is a list of some we've used with success.

◆ **Bentonite** (powder): This clay corrects hazes and attracts positively charged particles. It will also reduce protein stability. Mix 1 or 2 grams per gallon (3.8 L) with a little water and then thin with wine before stirring it into your batch. After mixing, let the bentonite

SHOPPING TIP

Many supplies have a limited shelf life. We recommend buying only the quantities you need.

mixture sit for several hours before immersing it in wine. Rack the wine at least once. Filter wine before bottling.

◆ **Drifine isinglass** (powder): This is used primarily to clarify white and sparkling wines. Isinglass is a traditional proteinaceous fining product. It's easy to prepare and you'll use 0.015 to 0.07 grams per gallon (3.8 L).

◆ **Gelatin** (powder): This is used as a fining agent and flavor enhancer. Gelatin removes tannins from red wines and helps to soften them. It should be used on wines that are less than a year old. With white wines, it is recommended that you add an equal amount of grape tannin to prevent a haze. The suggested amount is 0.5 to 1.0 grams per gallon (3.8 L). Unflavored, store-bought gelatin may be used for these purposes.

◆ **Silica gel** (kieselsol): Used alone, this product removes colloidal hazes, but we suggest using it in conjunction with bentonite and gelatin to provide more compact lees. The shelf life for silica gel is about 1 year. Order only what you expect to use within that time to ensure product stability and effectiveness.

BEGIN AT THE BEGINNING: HINTS TO HELP YOU GET STARTED

Now that you've got your equipment and supplies, it's time to have some fun! Good wine starts with selection of the right ingredients, which may seem a daunting task at first. Be sure to seek help when you need it.

◆ **Purchase the best ingredients you can afford.** Starting with top-of-the-line grapes (or juices or concentrates), while not an iron-clad guarantee that you'll make a first-rate wine, greatly increases the likelihood that you'll turn out a product you'll be proud of.

◆ **Band together with other winemakers.** Doing this can assist you in two ways. First, you'll have more help when it comes to selecting the best grapes for the wine you want. Second, by making your purchases together, you'll stand a better chance of getting your ingredients at a lower price. (Contact local wine supply stores, fruit wholesalers, and the American Wine Society for help locating active winemakers in your area.)

◆ **Don't make wine the old-fashioned way.** Until relatively recently, home winemaking was a hit-or-miss situation. Typically, improper sanitation and storage caused wines gradually to turn into vinegar. Today, we know a lot more about what's needed to produce high-quality wines, and if you carefully follow the instructions in this book, you shouldn't have any problems.

◆ **Read this book.** Pay particular attention to the text that follows: It gives an overview of the process of making white and red wines from grapes. It may seem complex at first, but feel free to review the instructions as often as necessary before and during the winemaking process. And recall that experience is our greatest teacher.

◆ **Use proper sanitation.** While in this text we'll explore making wine from scratch, the rules of proper sanitation always apply, whether you're using grapes, a kit, juices, or concentrates. (See page 21 for more information.)

◆ **Take your time.** The beauty of winemaking is that you don't have to rush. Take a few moments to review the recipe you've selected before you begin working, and as you proceed take additional time to refresh your memory and check your progress. Trust us — the wine is willing to wait!

WINEMAKING BASICS

This section is explicit because we want it to serve as your principal reference once you're actually making wine. By following our instructions, the risk for problems is greatly reduced if not totally eliminated, and a pleasing beverage is the final result. New winemakers are cautioned not to deviate from these instructions, experiment, or heed the advice of old-timers whose approach to winemaking stands in sharp contrast to our own. Our methods yield consistently good results.

The winemaking process is simple and natural. We start with raw materials (kits, concentrates, juices, and fresh grapes) and guide them to their destiny — wine. Mother Nature does most of the work, and we gently guide her through the process. In the chapters that follow, you'll find recipes for all kinds of delightful wines. Familiarize yourself with these basic steps before you make wine.

SANITIZING AND SETTING UP YOUR EQUIPMENT

Even before you bring home your grapes, properly sanitize all of your equipment. (See page 28 for complete instructions.)

Arrange your equipment for maximum efficiency and ease of use. Place it in such a way that physical effort, such as lifting or reaching, is minimized. Keep your equipment close together and situate it in order of use, for example, crusher, press (if making white wine), and fermentation vessel, with a hose nearby to aid in cleaning.

WHITE OR RED?

Some people prefer to drink white wines, while others favor red wines. Your personal taste can help you choose which wine to make. White wines can be consumed earlier than reds, usually within one year of the vintage. So if you are eager and lack patience, white wine may be a good choice for you. Red wines require longer aging before drinking — typically two years after the vintage — a fact that might discourage some. Either way, if you choose to use fresh grapes, you'll need to make the wine in the fall of the year the grape crop is harvested. (See pages 122–130 for more on grapes.)

TESTING THE JUICE

Once you've gathered a sufficient quantity of grapes, it's time to crush them. If you're making red wine, you'll keep everything you crush except the stems. Skins and pulp go right into the fermentation container along with the juice. The skins and pulp provide color, character, and complexity. If you're making white wine, you'll crush the grapes and then press them until only the juice remains. There is no place for skins and pulp in white wine.

Before going any further, analyze the juice for sugar and acid counts. These counts tell you exactly what you've got to work with. Almost invariably, you'll have to make some adjustments. (Instructions for performing these evaluations and adjustments appear on pages 36–38.)

As a rule, California grapes have sufficient or even a high sugar count, but their acids are usually less than ideal. Thus, you may need to lower the sugar count and raise the acid level.

Grapes grown in the eastern and northern regions of North America usually have a high acid count and low sugar levels.

Resign yourself to the fact that you're likely to have to make one or more adjustments each time you make wine. After you've taken the juice to the desired levels, it's time to proceed.

ADDING SULFUR DIOXIDE

The juice that's now sitting in your fermentation container(s) has undesirable wild yeasts and organisms growing in it. If you don't eliminate these undesirable elements now, they can cause the wine to develop off-odors and off-tastes, ruining it completely.

Adding potassium metabisulfite, either in powdered form or as crushed Campden tablets, will release sulfur dioxide (SO_2), which rids your juice of the undesirable elements.

Because the recipes in this book call for specific amounts of potassium metabisulfite, it is critical that you know exactly how much juice you have on hand so that you can add just the right amount. If you add too little, some wild yeasts and organisms are apt to survive. Add too much, and your wine will have an off-odor.

Let the wine settle for at least 24 hours. If you're making a white wine, once the settling period is over, rack the juice into another sanitized fermenting vessel, leaving the debris in the first container. You'll have a cleaner must (that is, your soon-to-be-fermented juice) and will be more likely to produce a crisp and complex wine.

YEAST

For white wines, use only one yeast type per batch of wine, at least during your early days as a winemaker. Follow the recipe directions carefully. Once the mixture of yeast, sugar, and warm water (as explained in the recipe) has begun to swell and gives off a strong aroma (usually within 30 minutes), pour it into your must and stir it. Then cover the container with a cloth and let Mother Nature do her thing.

For red wines, you'll need to add pectic enzyme to your must before putting in the yeast. The pectic enzyme helps the wine to settle and makes it easier to press out after fermentation. Follow the recipe's directions closely, and stir the pectic enzyme into the container(s), swabbing the sides as you do so. Then follow the same yeast inoculation procedures given above for white wines.

After you've gained some experience, you may want to experiment with different yeasts (see pages 40–42 for a list of available yeasts). This will enable you to make a variety of wines out of the same batch of must. The key here is to take good notes, so you'll have a record of which yeast went into a given container. (See page 239 for a sample winemaking record.) In time, as you perfect your techniques, you'll develop your own recipes.

FERMENTATION

Once the must has been inoculated with yeast, the fermentation process begins within a few hours. The grape sugars in the must will be attacked by the yeast and the juice converted to equal amounts of alcohol and carbon dioxide gas.

As fermentation takes place, there will be a great deal of frothing and bubbling. The carbon dioxide will rise above the juice and act as a preservative. Keep your vessel covered with a plastic sheet or a fermentation lock to prevent the must from coming in contact with outside air — oxygen and wine can combine to produce acetic acid, which produces a pungent odor. If this happens, put the wine bottles away because you are now perfectly positioned to distribute "designer" vinegar.

WHITE WINES

Many whites benefit from a malolactic, or secondary, fermentation. Chardonnays, for example, usually taste better if they are inoculated with a malolactic culture. It will give your wine a softer, buttery quality.

There are several cultures available. They vary a bit, particularly in terms of when during the main fermentation process you should add them. Read and follow the package instructions carefully!

Generally, the fermentation process takes about a week to complete. Nature's timetable is different according to the type of grape. The yeast you use, the temperature, and other atmospheric conditions may also influence the rate of fermentation.

Taking a Hydrometer Reading. Once the bubbling has stopped and the wine begins to clear, it's time to take specific gravity readings with a hydrometer. Begin by drawing off some of the wine, then put it into the hydrometer cylinder. Insert the hydrometer and take the reading at the point where it floats. If your reading is 1.000 specific gravity or lower, fermentation has ended. You are now ready to rack the wine into a properly sanitized storage container. We recommend a 5-gallon (19 L) glass carboy.

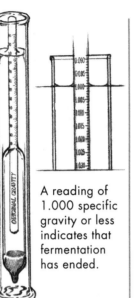

A reading of 1.000 specific gravity or less indicates that fermentation has ended.

Racking the Wine. Crush and dissolve half a Campden tablet per gallon (3.8 L) of wine, or ½ teaspoon (3.1 g) of potassium metabisulfite powder or 2½ teaspoons (25 mL) of potassium metabisulfite solution per 5 gallons (19 L) of wine for the first racking.

Siphon off everything but the sediment from the fermentation container into a clean carboy. Seal it with a fermentation lock and store in a cool or even cold (but not freezing) area; this will enable you to cold-stabilize the wine. Temperatures between 40 and 50 degrees Fahrenheit (5–10°C) are ideal for wine storage.

The stabilization process causes white crystals, or tartrates, to form on the bottom of the carboy. Tartrates must be eliminated by reracking. We recommend that potassium metabisulfite be added at each racking. *Note:* If your wine

is inadvertently subjected to freezing temperatures for a protracted period, the wine is likely to freeze, expanding and therefore cracking your carboys.

Check the wine periodically. When sediment accumulates on the bottom, rack the wine into another container. Each time you do so, add approximately 25 percent less of the potassium metabisulfite agent. Three or four rackings during a 7- to 9-month period should bring your wine to readiness for bottling.

If your wine exhibits a haze or appears cloudy, use one of the fining agents we discussed earlier (see page 13).

Tasting and Sweetening the Wine. Taste the wine. If you're satisfied, it's ready for bottling. To sweeten, you can add sugar to taste, but you'll also need to add potassium sorbate and potassium metabisulfite to ensure that the wine won't begin to ferment again and blow off the corks. (See chapter 10 for tips on avoiding exploding bottles.)

Potassium sorbate is a yeast inhibitor. Add 1 to 1¼ grams per gallon (3.8 L) or 2½ teaspoons (7.5 g) per 5-gallon (19 L) carboy. Also add either 3 crushed Campden tablets or ¼ teaspoon (1.4 g) of potassium metabisulfite powder to the carboy before bottling.

RED WINES

We suggest that you subject your red wines to a malolactic, or secondary, fermentation. This softens and eliminates the harshness from the wine and expedites the aging process. Specific yeast cultures are available for this. The process is the same as the one described above for white wines. As always, follow package instructions carefully.

Forcing and Pressing. With red wines, you've got another important responsibility when it comes to handling the must during fermentation: You have to force the skins, pulp, and stems back to the bottom of the container twice daily, either by pushing down with your hands or by using a paddle or stick.

Once the fermentation process has run its course, the cluster of grapes, skins, and pulp you've been dealing with will sink to the bottom. Take a specific gravity reading with a hydrometer. If it's below 1.010 specific gravity, you'll have to make a stylistic decision.

Many winemakers will immediately press out the must and start the aging process. For more color and complexity, though, we suggest leaving the wine on the lees for an additional 2 to 3 weeks before pressing and bottling. Many winemakers believe that this is a dangerous practice because the wine may oxidize, so they press anywhere from 8 days to 2 weeks after fermentation.

Experiment by pressing at different times and recording the results. That way, you'll be able to determine what works best for you.

In any event, during and after fermentation, be sure that the container is covered with plastic, a cotton ball, or a fermentation lock (but can still breathe) to protect your wine from foreign matter, particularly flying gnats.

PRESSING WINE

In order to separate wine from the must, the must must be pressed or squeezed. A basket press is ideal, but any effective device will do. When using a basket press, line the outside wall with wire or plastic mesh to help trap foreign matter inside the press. We're only interested in the wine — the juice — not skins, pulp, stems, or seeds.

If you don't have access to a basket press, you can press the wine by hand using a clean piece of cheesecloth or a nylon stocking. Pour the must into the cloth and twist until all juice is removed.

When you're ready to rack the wine, press it out with a winepress or by hand. All you want now is the wine itself, no solids.

Racking and Storage. Rack the wine into a properly sanitized 5-gallon (19 L) carboy that has already received 5 crushed Campden tablets or ½ teaspoon (3.1 g) potassium metabisulfite powder.

When the carboy is filled, fit it with a fermentation lock (with potassium metabisulfite solution in it) inserted into a rubber stopper.

Store the wine in a cozy corner of your cellar or in a closet. In a month or so you'll see sediment settling at the bottom of the carboy, as the wine will have begun to clear. Rack it into a sanitized carboy (leaving the sediment behind), to which a standard amount of potassium metabisulfite has been added.

During the next 6 to 9 months, rack the wine five or six times. This will aerate it, which is a very good thing.

LET YOUR WINE BREATHE

When wine is fermenting, carbon dioxide and other gases develop. These gases must dissipate into the atmosphere or they will become part of the finished product. Aerating wine during racking ensures a wine free of foul odors and tastes.

After a few rackings, the wine should look bright and clear; red wines rarely require a fining agent. If the wine does require fining, whip up one egg white with some wine and put it directly into the carboy. After a few weeks, when the wine has cleared, rack it into another sanitized carboy with some potassium metabisulfite.

Bottling and Waiting. When it's ready for bottling, take the time to select the right type of container. (See bottle descriptions and recommendations on pages 10–11.) Once bottled, let the wine stand for a week or so, then store it upside down or on its side for a least a year before you drink it. The waiting is downright agonizing for winemakers, but trust us, it's worth it! In fact, if you've got the discipline to do so, we suggest that you age your reds for 2 years before you drink them.

ESSENTIAL HOW-TOS 2

THE INSTRUCTIONS IN THIS CHAPTER are extremely important and must be followed precisely to produce a quality finished wine. We can't overemphasize the value of the sanitation procedures you must faithfully practice and the testing procedures you must learn. All are necessary activities that can be easily mastered.

 KEEP IT CLEAN

Contamination will destroy your wine. Therefore, it's important that you keep work area, equipment, and bottles scrupulously clean. A simple solution of plain (unscented) bleach, tap water, and a dash of sal soda will do the job quite nicely.

1. Add 1 tablespoon (15 mL) of bleach to each gallon (3.8 L) of cold water. (Do *not* add any other cleaning agent or mix with hot water, as hazardous fumes may result.)
2. Add a dash of sal soda to each gallon of water-bleach solution.
3. Scrub equipment well to eliminate foreign matter and bacteria.

4. After thoroughly scrubbing the items you're cleaning, soak them in the solution for at least 30 minutes.
5. Rinse thoroughly, at least twice, with piping-hot water.

 DETERMINING SPECIFIC GRAVITY AND SUGAR PERCENTAGE

The hydrometer and hydrometer jar are important tools that will help you measure the sugar content of the juice and, thus, the potential alcohol content of the wine. These measurements will alert you to any adjustments that are needed during fermentation. Reading a hydrometer is simple.

1. Sanitize all equipment (see page 28).
2. Fill the hydrometer jar with wine to three-fourths of its capacity, and put the hydrometer into the jar. The hydrometer will float clear from the bottom of the jar and be suspended in the liquid. At this point, you'll be able to determine the Brix or sugar percentage.

3. Rotate the jar to the alcohol percentage side. If your Brix reading was 20, you'll have an alcohol reading of 11.5 percent. You determine this by multiplying the Brix number by 0.575. Staying with our sample reading, the specific gravity is 1.080.

4. Take a specific gravity reading throughout the fermentation process until it reaches 1.000. At this point, you'll know that all of the sugar has fermented and that the process is complete.

TESTING FOR ACID CONTENT

The ideal acidity of a finished wine ranges from 0.55 to 0.85 percent expressed as tartaric acid. (Fresh juice totals are higher because some acidity is lost during fermentation.) The approaches for testing white and red wines vary slightly, but the materials and equipment are the same. If you find that acidity is below the minimum acceptable range (0.55 percent), you'll add an acid blend to bring it up to an acceptable level (see page 37).

Materials and Equipment

Burette
Pipette
Sodium hydroxide
Beaker or glass container, 250 mL (8.5 oz)
Distilled water
Wine sample to be tested
Sterile eyedropper
Phenolphthalein indicator
Paper and pen to record testing process

WHAT IS THE BRIX SCALE?

The Brix, or Balling scale, is a numerical range from −10 to 40 degrees that indicates the percentage of sugar content in a liquid. The Brix count multiplied by 0.575 indicates the eventual alcohol content of the juice. For example, a Brix reading of 21 degrees generates a final alcohol content of 12 percent.

21 x 0.575 = 12 percent

Testing White Wines or Juices

1. Sanitize all equipment (see page 28).

2. Fill the burette with sodium hydroxide.

3. Using the pipette, put a 5-mL sample of the wine or juice into the beaker or glass container.

4. Add 100 mL (3.5 oz) of distilled water to the sample.

5. Add 5 drops of phenolphthalein indicator.

6. Place the wine sample container under the burette. Record the sodium hydroxide level in the burette before you begin testing.

7. Start running sodium hydroxide into the sample by turning the valve at the bottom of the burette. This will cause the sample to turn pink.

8. Stir the sample; the pink color will begin to disappear quickly. As you approach the end point of the test, the pink color will take longer to fade. The end point is the first, faint pink blush that will not fade within 20 seconds. On reaching the end point, record the level of sodium hydroxide in the burette.

9. Subtract the first reading from the amount in step 6 to determine the milliliters of the sodium hydroxide used.

10. Calculate the percentage of acidity expressed as tartaric acid.

Milliliters of sodium hydroxide x 0.15 = percentage of acidity expressed as tartaric acid. For example, 0.5 mL sodium hydroxide x 0.15 = 0.075 or 7.5% acidity.

Testing Red Wines or Juices

This process is similar to that used for testing white wines with one major exception: Phenolphthalein indicator is *not* added as early in the process for red wines as it is for whites.

1. Sanitize all equipment (see page 28).
2. Fill the burette with sodium hydroxide.
3. Using the pipette, add a 5-mL sample of the wine or juice to the beaker or glass container.

4. Add 100 mL (3.5 oz) of distilled water to the sample.

5. Place the wine sample container under the burette. Record the sodium hydroxide level in the burette before you begin testing.

6. Start running sodium hydroxide into the sample. This will cause the red pigments in the sample to deepen in color.

7. Stir the sample; the deep red pigments should change to blue or green.

8. Add 5 drops of phenolphthalein indicator to the sample.

9. Stir the sample; the blue or green color will begin to disappear quickly. As you approach the end point of the test, the blue or green color will take longer to fade. The end point is the first, faint color that will not fade within 20 seconds. On reaching the end point, record the level of sodium hydroxide in the burette.

Note: If the sample is deeply pigmented, dilute it with 50 mL (1.7 oz) of distilled water. This won't skew the results.

10. Subtract the first reading from the amount in step 5 to determine the milliliters of the sodium hydroxide used.

11. Calculate the percentage of acidity expressed as tartaric acid.

Milliliters of sodium hydroxide x 0.15 = percentage of acidity expressed as tartaric acid.

RACKING THE WINE

Racking is the process of moving wine from one container to another as it ages. This enables you to clarify the wine by leaving any sediment behind in the container you're racking from.

Materials and Equipment

Primary container of wine
Secondary container(s), size of primary
   container or larger
Siphon tube
Waste container (optional; not needed if
   working near sink)

1. Sanitize the siphon tube and secondary container(s). (See instructions on page 21 for the proper technique.)
2. Position the primary container of wine so it is at least twice as high as the secondary container.
3. Fill the siphon tube with water, holding a thumb over either end of the tube.
4. Immerse one end of the tube in the liquid in the primary container to just above the sediment.
5. Take your thumb away from the bottom end of the siphon tube and allow the tube to drain into the waste container until the water in the tube is replaced with wine. (If you're doing this near a sink, simply let the water go down the drain.)

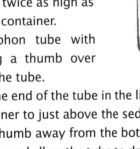

primary container

secondary container

Now, cap the bottom of the tube with your thumb.
6. Hold the bottom end of the tube over the secondary container and remove your thumb.
7. Allow the wine to flow freely into the secondary container.
8. If the flow stops before you've racked everything but the residue in the primary container, repeat steps 3 through 6.

OAKING WINE

Many wines benefit from the addition of an oak flavor. Rather than going to the expense of purchasing oak barrels, you can use oak chips or Oak-Mor granular white oak (Cellulo Company, Fresno, CA), both of which are available at wine supply stores. It's really up to you how much oak taste you want in your wine, but remember that too much oaking can mask a wine's unique characteristics. Err on the side of caution.

Materials and Equipment

Oak chips or Oak-Mor granular white oak
Cheesecloth bag (optional)

1. Sanitize all equipment (see page 28).
2. Measure 2 to 3 tablespoons of oak chips (36.4–54.6 g) or Oak-Mor (7.4–11.1 g) for each 5 gallons (19 L) of wine. Go light at first; it is always possible to add more oak later in the aging process.
3. Add oak in one of two ways:
   a. Pour the oak chips directly into your container; they will settle to the bottom as part of the sediment and be left behind the next time you rack the wine. *Or,*

b. Put the oak chips into a secured cheesecloth bag. Place the bag in your original container, where it will settle to the bottom. Throw away the bag after the next racking.

4. Taste wine before the next racking. If you are satisfied with oak flavor, rack the wine. If you want more oak flavor, add oak chips as before and re-evaluate at next racking.

BOTTLING WINE

Your racking experience will come in handy when it's time to bottle the wine, because the principles are the same ones you used earlier.

Materials and Equipment

Bottles, 26 750-mL (25.4 oz) bottles for each 5 gallons (19 L) of wine
Siphon tube
Waste container (optional; not needed if working near sink)

1. Sanitize bottles and siphon tube (see page 21).
2. Place a carboy of wine on a counter, table top, or shelf. Gravity aids this process, so always place the carboy at a level higher than the sink or waste container.
3. Fill the siphon tube with water, sealing both ends of the tube with your thumbs.
4. Immerse the top end of the tube in the carboy, just above sediment.
5. Hold the bottom end of the tube over the sink or a waste container.

6. Release your thumb from the bottom end of the tube and drain the water into the sink or a waste container. When wine begins to flow through the tube, place a thumb over the open end.
7. Position the bottom end of the tube over the first bottle.
8. Release your thumb and fill the bottle to within ½ inch (1.3 cm) of where the cork's bottom will be when it's been rammed home, or, if you're using screw caps, to just below the rim of the bottle.
9. When the bottle is sufficiently full, place thumb over end of tube and move on to the next bottle.
10. If the flow stops, repeat steps 3 through 6.

CAPPING AND CORKING TIPS

If you are using plastic caps to seal your wine, soak the caps in boiling water for at least 15 minutes prior to use; this sanitizes the caps and helps to protect the wine. Because metal caps tend to rust, we recommend plastic over metal.

You can set the depth of insertion on most corking devices. A cork is easiest to remove when its top is flush with the lip of the bottle, so that should always be your goal. Floor and table corkers are relatively easy to use, whereas hand corkers are tricky and more strenuous.

WINE FROM KITS

If God forbade drinking,
would He have made wine so good?

—Cardinal Richelieu (1585–1642)

KITS REPRESENT THE EASIEST AND FASTEST way to produce wine at home. With all the premeasured and prebalanced ingredients included in one package, kit winemaking defines simplicity. There used to be a certain trade-off between this simplicity and the quality and diversity of the wine you could produce with a kit. But thanks to improved technology, kits now enable the home winemaker to make a decent version of just about any type of wine.

The initial development of kits took place in Canada, where high taxes caused citizens to look for affordable alternatives to commercial wines. Improved technology, combined with a recent boom in the winemaking hobby in the United States, has resulted in kit manufacturers rolling out a wide variety of wines from all over the world. In addition to standard table wines, exotic varieties now come in kits, as do ports, sherries, and ice wines. Kit manufacturers don't confine themselves to grape wines, either; there is an extensive assortment of fruit wine and cider kits on the market as well. The increased demand for kits has also improved the quality of the ingredients, resulting in consistently better wines than kits of the past could produce. The options available continue to expand and improve. Just ask your local winemaking supply retailer about the latest selection of kits.

SELECTING YOUR FIRST KIT

It's important to consider how long a given wine needs to age before it's ready for consumption. Although some kit makers promise wine that will be ready in a month or so, remember that they're providing basic table wines. These beverages are fine, but they lend themselves to everyday use rather than special occasions.

Many fledgling winemakers start out with one of the table wines, and they're quite happy that a month or so after they bring home their kits they're able to quaff a wine they've made. If it's drinkable — and it probably is — they're satisfied. The ironic thing is that with a little more planning and patience, they could have produced a better-quality wine, one suitable for special gifts and major events.

You have the whole world to choose from when it comes to selecting a kit. Taking the time to plan for a holiday or other occasion that's a year or more away will enable you to produce a special wine for it. Making wines that require a longer aging period calls for patience, but the wait is really worth it.

Whatever wine you choose for your first attempt, we urge you to pass on the 1-gallon (3.8 L) kits, because with only a little more effort on your part you can produce a lot more wine. Many kits are in the 5-gallon (19 L) range, and this is a useful size because it yields a nice supply, enabling you to give bottles as gifts and also to enjoy the wine on your own.

Note: Many wine supply stores sell basic equipment packages, which they may refer to as kits. Keep in mind that these are usually just equipment starter sets and are unlikely to contain any winemaking ingredients. Before purchasing a kit, be sure you know exactly what it contains.

FROM GRAIN TO GRAPES

Many people who have been using brewing kits to produce their own beer have also tried winemaking. Their first experience tends to be a positive one, because winemaking with a kit is really so simple. Homebrewers also already have most of the equipment required for winemaking, so the transition from brewing beer to winemaking is relatively smooth.

WHAT'S IN YOUR KIT

In a kit you'll receive a combination of juices and concentrates that have been carefully balanced and blended according to specialized recipes. The juice is packed in a sterile container from which the air has been removed. The kit will also include yeast, yeast nutrients, fining agents (to help your wine become clear), and, if appropriate, wood chips to impart an aged flavor.

WHAT'S NOT IN YOUR KIT: EQUIPMENT YOU NEED

Even with a well-supplied kit, you'll need some basic equipment to make wine. Happily, this will not be a major investment, and you may already own some items. (See chapter 1 for more information about equipment.)

- Primary plastic fermenting vessel, 5–7 gallon (19–27 L)
- Glass or plastic carboy, 5 gallon (19 L)
- Siphon tube
- Stirring spoon or paddle
- Fermentation lock (air lock)
- Carboy bung (rubber stopper)
- Funnel
- Measuring cup
- Hydrometer (saccharometer)
- Hydrometer jar
- Bottles
- Corks (traditional or push top)

MAKING KIT WINE

Your kit package contains a full set of instructions that address the type of wine you will make, but it's useful to review beforehand the steps typically followed by kit makers. In the discussion that follows, we've added some special advice to help make your kit wine sparkle.

THREE KEYS TO WINEMAKING SUCCESS

If you have these three things, your wines — whether made from a kit or from scratch — are guaranteed to please your palate:

- Sanitary equipment
- The best ingredients
- Patience

SANITIZING THE EQUIPMENT

The most important thing any winemaker can do to help his or her wine turn out great is to sanitize all equipment thoroughly and properly. Poorly cleaned equipment is the leading cause of contaminated homemade wine. Sanitize all equipment that will touch the wine or juice by rinsing it with a metabisulfite solution:

1. Put 3 tablespoons (56 g) of potassium metabisulfite into a 1-liter (33.8 oz) jug of hot water — 85°F (29°C) — to make a reusable sanitizing solution. It will last up to 6 months, if kept tightly sealed. (Store at room temperature.)
2. Rinse all equipment thoroughly in the solution.
3. After sanitizing, rinse equipment with cold water.

PREPARING THE MUST

After sanitizing the equipment, it is time to mix together the ingredients that will eventually ferment to become wine. The main ingredient in your wine is water. Tap water is perfectly fine unless it has an unusual taste, such as of chlorine. Boiling tap water eliminates the taste of chlorine and will also kill off any unwanted organisms if your water is from a well. Fifteen minutes at a rolling boil should do the trick. Remember to let the boiled water cool to room temperature before using it to make wine.

1. Sprinkle the package of bentonite enclosed with the kit in approximately 2 cups (475 mL) of warm water. Mix to form a slurry.

2. Pour the bag of concentrate into the primary fermentor. Be sure to rinse out the remaining concentrate with hot water so none is wasted.

3. Fill the primary fermentor to the 23-liter mark (for 23-L kits) with cool water. The temperature of the must in the fermentor should be between 72° and 77°F (22°–25°C).

4. Using a hydrometer, check the specific gravity. It should be between 1.074 and 1.080. (For more information on using a hydrometer, see chapter 2).

5. Sprinkle the contents of the yeast additive package onto the surface of the must.

6. Place the lid on the primary fermentor. Insert a rubber bung with an air lock half filled with water. This will help prevent contamination.

7. Place the primary fermentor in an elevated area that maintains a temperature of 72° to 77°F (22°–25°C) to work for approximately 8 days, or until the specific gravity on the hydrometer is 1.010 or lower.

SECONDARY FERMENTATION

This step is needed only if the specific gravity of the must is 1.010 or lower. At this point, the must is about halfway to becoming wine, thanks to fermentation.

1. With the sterilized tube, siphon (or rack) the fermenting wine from the primary fermentor into a carboy, leaving behind the sediment. If the carboy is not full, top up within 2 inches (5 cm) of the bottom of the air lock with water that has been boiled, then cooled to room temperature.

2. Reinsert air lock and rubber bung into carboy.

3. Place in a location where the temperature will be a consistent 72° to 77°F (22°–25°C) to allow the fermentation to finish — 4 to 7 days, or until the specific gravity is below 0.0998.

STABILIZING AND CLEARING

The wine is now fermented, but it still needs to be stabilized and cleared before bottling. This will help the wine to look and taste its best when you uncork your creation.

1. Remove and discard 1 cup (240 mL) of wine from the carboy to allow for later additions. (To make this process easier, discard the contents of the test cylinder after measuring the specific gravity above, which will make room for later additions. Remember, the specific gravity reading on the thermometer should be below 0.0998.)

2. Add the kit's package of potassium metabisulfite and potassium sorbate to ½ cup (120 mL) of water. Stir to dissolve. This mixture will help stabilize the wine by killing off any yeast or other organisms still alive and active. This step is also called *sulfiting.*

3. Slowly add the potassium metabisulfite/sorbate mixture to the carboy and stir well with a sanitized long-handled plastic spoon.

4. Mix the kit's isinglass in ½ cup (120 mL) of cool water. This mixture will help clear the wine of any cloudiness.

5. Add the isinglass mixture to the carboy, stirring well to ensure a complete blend. Replace the air lock and rubber bung.

6. Twice daily for the next 3 days, vigorously stir the wine in the carboy with a long-handled plastic spoon to remove dissolved gases. After stirring, place the wine in an elevated area to allow clearing (approximately 10 days) and to prepare for racking.

BOTTLING

Once the wine is fully cleared, you may proceed with bottling. *Never* bottle a cloudy wine. If the wine is cloudy, leave it for an additional period to clear. As discussed in chapter 1, always choose bottles to match the type of wine you're making. This will help you "sell" your wine by making it appear more authentic in the eyes of your guests.

1. Sanitize all equipment (see page 28).
2. Siphon or filter (optional) the wine into a primary fermentor. Depending on your preference, you may wish to sweeten or adjust the wine at this time (contact your retailer for more details).
3. Fill a sanitized container with tepid water and ¼ teaspoon (1.4 g) of potassium metabisulfite powder. Mix well. Soak corks in sulfite solution for 20 minutes. Thoroughly rinse the corks with hot water before inserting them into bottles.
4. Use a siphon hose to transfer the wine into bottles, leaving 1 inch (2.5 cm) to the bottom of the cork.
5. Insert corks by hand if using push-top-style corks or with a hand-corking machine.
6. Leave bottles standing upright for 1 week (this allows the cork face to dry) prior to laying

CORK CONSIDERATIONS

Push-top corks are available at most wine supply stores and are much easier for hand-corking than are traditional ones. The slightly tapered cork has been glued to a round plastic cap. It looks similar to the type of cork you would find in a sherry or port bottle. Hand-corkers, used to insert traditional corks, are reasonably priced but physically grueling after just a few bottles. Table-style corking machines are much easier to work, but also much more expensive, and not really recommended for kit winemakers.

wine bottles on their side for storage. Keep the wine in a temperature-controlled environment around 70°F (21°C) and out of direct sunlight for 2 to 3 months prior to consumption.

LABELING

While the wine is maturing, give some thought to how you'll label your bottles. Computers make it possible for you to design highly personalized labels. They will greatly enhance the value of your wine if you choose to give it as a gift because there's nothing like receiving

Personalize your wines with creative labels.

a bottle of wine that has been labeled expressly for the recipient. Plus, the labels will help keep track of your inventory as you make different styles of wine.

FINE-TUNING THE KIT WINE

Kits are designed to produce wines with a minimum of effort. They are carefully formulated so that you'll create a drinkable wine every time. As you grow more experienced and your palate becomes more discerning, though, you're likely to detect variations from one batch of wine to another, even though you're using the same brand of kit. There are any number of reasons for these variations to occur, but they usually manifest themselves as sugar and acid imbalances.

Altered sugar and acid counts probably won't ruin your wine, but they can keep it from reaching its full potential. Although checking your wine's chemistry may seem like a daunting task, it really is rather easy to do. (See pages 21–23 for an explanation of the process). Taking a little extra time to balance the sugar and acid counts can help you transform a good wine into a great one!

USING KITS FOR BLENDING

Many people, particularly those with limited time and space, confine their winemaking efforts solely to kits. This is fine because new kits are coming out virtually every day, enabling kit aficionados to produce a bounty of different wines. Keep in mind, though, that you don't have to make kit wines one at a time. It's possible to come up with variations by combining various kit wines. See the chart on the next page for a few ideas to get you started.

We subscribe to the European philosophy that the blending of wines usually improves them, as long as you have the right combinations. Blend your kits using a ratio of 20 to 80 percent or 25 to 75 percent to create new and exciting flavors to add to your wine inventory. The art of wine blending has been practiced for hundreds of years and follows no rigid guidelines. Here, as elsewhere in winemaking, experience will be your greatest teacher.

A SAMPLE BLEND

You can blend wines to suit your taste. Blending is done after the wines are made and in their final stage of aging. For example, take 20 percent or 1 gallon (3.8 L) of Merlot, and siphon it into an empty, sanitized 5-gallon (19 L) carboy. Then fill the balance of the carboy with Cabernet Sauvignon. Next, take the residuals of the Cabernet Sauvignon (approximately 1 gallon [3.8 L]) and siphon them into the remnants of Merlot. You now have a Cabernet Sauvignon–dominated blend and a Merlot-dominated blend.

Over time, through experimentation and comparing notes with other winemakers, you'll develop your own variations. That's one of the great things about winemaking — whether you use kits or fresh grapes, you will continue to learn and grow as a winemaker. In the process, you'll produce wines with increasingly greater character and complexity.

GREAT KIT COMBINATIONS*

COMBINATION	COMMENTS
Cabernet Sauvignon and Merlot	A blend of about 20 percent Merlot with 80 percent Cabernet Sauvignon will add softness and character; adding 20 percent Cabernet Sauvignon to 80 percent Merlot will add some body and flavor. Each blend will be improved. (Cabernet Franc could be substituted for either of the above.)
Sauvignon Blanc and Semillon	These two white favorites have traditionally blended well using the 20:80 ratio.
Riesling and Gewürztraminer	Blending these spicy white varieties at the 20:80 ratio results in a great partnership.
Pinot Blanc or Chenin Blanc and Riesling or Gewürztraminer	This flexible pairing group has a long track record of producing excellent and complex blends using our standard formula.
Syrah and Pinot Noir	This is a favorite blend of ours with consistent results.
Zinfandel and Syrah	America's great red grape meets a growing favorite in this pleasing blend.
Syrah and Cabernet Sauvignon	We've had excellent success with this combination.

* A 20:80 blending ratio is recommended by some kit producers. We suggest that you experiment with different percentages, but only after you have used the 20:80 ratio, which works well.

WINE FROM CONCENTRATES 4

While wine and friendship crown the board, we'll sing the joys that both afford.

—John Dyer (1700–1758)

CONCENTRATES HAVE COME A LONG WAY from old days when producers often used poor-quality grapes for the juice and then heated them to the point of caramelization, thereby greatly lowering the concentrate's winemaking potential. Today, however, in a highly competitive market, you're able to purchase a broad range of first-rate juices. Concentrated grape juices are now readily available from all of the world's great wine regions. As a result, you'll be able to make just about any type of wine you desire, at a reasonable cost per bottle.

ADVANTAGES OF USING CONCENTRATES

While it's great fun to select grapes at a vineyard or wholesaler and take them through the process, step-by-step, until you have a first-class wine, we understand that not everyone has the time, money, or inclination to do this. If you feel this way, concentrates may be a reasonable compromise. And, given the variety of concentrates available from all over the globe, they'll allow you to make wines that just a few years ago would have been out of the reach of most people, because the grapes are available only in one particular place and only at harvesttime.

Today's concentrates allow you to have a lower cost per bottle than fresh grapes. The fruit used for the juice is picked at full ripeness, not prematurely, as some fresh grapes are. Further, the concentrate is free of sediment and pulp, and it is processed so that it has no wild yeasts or other organisms, which can cause spoilage.

PURCHASING CONCENTRATES

Wine supply stores carry a variety of concentrates, and they are also able to secure others for you. We recommend purchasing the best available concentrates. Be wary of those preserved with sulfites, as they tend to be somewhat less desirable and seem to deteriorate more rapidly. Be particularly careful with concentrates sold in tin cans, as the acids in the juice may eat away at the metal, causing leakage. Always ask your suppliers to sell you the freshest concentrates available and make sure that they'll back up the sale with a guarantee to replace any concentrates that turn out to be spoiled.

It's possible to buy as little as 1 gallon (3.8 L) of concentrate, but we urge you to select a larger quantity, as you'll find that it takes just a little more time and effort to make a lot more wine.

WHAT ARE CONCENTRATES?

The process of creating a concentrate is simple. Fresh grape juice is slowly heated in a vacuum to remove excess water and to preserve the original fruitiness and other positive qualities of the juice. The juice is reduced to approximately one third of its original volume, and its sugar and acid content are also concentrated. Those counts will come down to acceptable levels when you add the water volume called for in a recipe.

EQUIPMENT AND SUPPLIES

You'll need some basic equipment and extra supplies to make wine from concentrate (see chapter 1 for more information on equipment).

◆ Primary plastic fermenting vessel, 5–7 gallon (19–27 L)
◆ Glass or plastic carboy, 5 gallon (19 L)
◆ Siphon tube
◆ Stirring spoon or paddle (plastic preferred)
◆ Fermentation lock (air lock)
◆ Carboy bung (rubber stopper)
◆ Funnel
◆ Measuring cup
◆ Hydrometer (saccharometer)
◆ Hydrometer jar
◆ Bottles
◆ Corks (traditional or push top)
◆ Potassium metabisulfite powder or Campden tablets
◆ Sugar
◆ Commercial wine yeast
◆ Yeast nutrient
◆ Fining agent (to clarify wine)
◆ Acid blend

GETTING STARTED

Many beginners simply follow the instructions listed on the can of concentrate, hope for the best, and drink the results. We urge you to read and follow the advice given in the next section, to increase the likelihood that you'll come up with a first-rate wine, rather than leaving things to chance. What we're suggesting here isn't all that hard to do, and it can make a significant difference in terms of results. When you've read these instructions, you'll be ready to try one of the recipes.

One of the most important things any winemaker can do to help his or her wine turn out great is to sanitize all equipment thoroughly and properly. Poorly cleaned equipment is the leading cause of contaminated homemade wine. Sterilize all equipment that will touch the wine or juice by rinsing it with metabisulfite solution (see box at right).

DILUTING THE CONCENTRATE

Boil the water for your wine at least 15 minutes. This helps remove any organisms or chemicals that could contribute off-flavors to the wine. Let the water cool to room temperature before using. When making a 5-gallon (19 L) batch, always fill the fermenting container with less water than the recipe calls for. Start with 3 or 3½ gallons (11–13 L), add the rest of the ingredients, then complete the water addition up to the 5 gallons (19 L) to create the must. Check the specific gravity with a hydrometer to ensure that the proper levels mentioned on the can of concentrate are achieved. See chapter 2 for more information on using a hydrometer.

SUGAR AND ACID TESTING

Processing a grape juice concentrate back to its regular volume by adding water is explained

SANITIZING EQUIPMENT

The need to sanitize all equipment that comes in contact with your wine cannot be overstated. Here is a method we use with success.

Potassium metabisulfite powder
Hot water
Jug

1. Put 3 tablespoons (56 g) of potassium metabisulfite into a 1-liter (33.8 oz) jug of hot water — 85°F (29°C) — to make a reusable sanitizing solution. It will last up to 6 months, if kept tightly sealed. (Store at room temperature.)
2. Rinse all equipment thoroughly in the solution.
3. After sanitizing, rinse with cold water.

by the concentrate supplier, but because of possible flaws in the process, it is best to test your final volume before fermentation. More times than not, adjustments will have to be made before you add yeast for fermentation. Testing is relatively simple and adjustments are easy to make, so don't try to make wine without testing it first. Give yourself the best possible chance of making a quality wine — don't gamble with your grape juice!

Sugar Test. The reason for making a sugar test is to determine what the eventual alcohol content will be. If the sugar is too low, the alcohol will be too low, and the possibility of wine becoming unstable is greater with low alcohol levels. Sugar counts that are too high can also cause problems: Most yeast strains cannot ferment the grape juice beyond 14 percent. As a result, when the fermentation reaches that point, the higher alcohol content will kill the yeast and stop the fermentation, leaving a high alcohol count and a high residual sugar count. The result will be a high-alcohol sweet wine, which is undesirable. You are the master of your wine's destiny, so do what yields the best result.

There is a recommended sugar range to which you should adhere in order to make quality wine. The sugar percentage is called degrees Brix, or degrees Balling, and you will see either term used whenever reference is made to grape sugar.

Traditionally, red wines have had more alcohol because of longer aging, more body structure, and more complexity. A high-alcohol white wine is not desirable, as too much alcohol disturbs the balance of most white wines, which are very delicate.

DEGREES BRIX RANGES

White Wines: 19–22 degrees Brix, which will eventually have an alcohol count of 10.9–12.6%

Red Wines: 20–24 degrees Brix, which will eventually have an alcohol count of 11.5–13.8%

The measuring device for testing the degrees Brix is the hydrometer. For convenience and efficiency, we recommend that you use a hydrometer that shows degrees Brix, alcohol, and specific gravity readings. You also need a hydrometer jar to hold the juice when you are measuring degrees Brix. This jar size can range from 3.5 to 8.5 ounces (100–250 mL).

If you add sugar, retest the juice to make sure that the sugar has done its job. Also, be sure that the newly added sugar has dissolved completely and is not resting at the bottom of the carboy in a white mass. If the sugar hasn't dissolved completely, your reading won't be accurate. Once you are satisfied with the sugar count, it's time to test the acid count.

Acid Test. If you've ever had a flat or flabby wine, you've tasted a wine with little or no acid backbone. Such a wine has no crispness and limited longevity. Acids are an important part of wine, as they interact with the alcohol during the aging cycle to produce fruitiness and bouquet.

DETERMINING ALCOHOL CONTENT

To determine alcohol content, multiply degrees Brix by 0.575. For example:

19 degrees Brix x 0.575 = 10.9% alcohol

BALANCING A MUST

JUICE ACID LEVEL (PERCENT)	ACID NEEDED TO RAISE 1 GALLON OF JUICE TO 0.7 PERCENT
0.40	11.4 g (1½ tsp*)
0.45	9.5 g (1¼ tsp)
0.50	7.6 g (1 tsp)
0.55	5.7 g (¾ tsp)
0.60	3.8 g (½ tsp)
0.65	1.9 g (½ tsp)
0.70	0.0

All teaspoon measurements are heaping.

Several organic acids are present in wine, but the most important are citric, tartaric, malic, and succinic.

Acid blends are popular, and most wine supply stores will have various blends available. The blending acid percentages vary and are not that important. Most of the needed acid blends have each of the basic acids in them; when necessary, order an acid blend and use it. Always check the results to determine effectiveness.

The procedures for testing white and red wines for acid count are described in detail in on pages 22–23, but the adjustment procedures are not. We are constantly looking for a happy balance between acid balance and pH counts. When acid counts are high (as is the case with a number of eastern wines), the pH counts are

GUIDE TO RAISING DEGREES BRIX

Raising the sugar count (degrees Brix) is fairly easy. Note that 2 ounces (56.7 g) of sugar raises the sugar count in 1 gallon (3.8 L) of juice by 1 degree Brix.

1. Compute the needed increase in degrees Brix:

Desired degrees Brix – current degrees Brix = needed increase

For example, 21° Brix – 16° Brix = 5° Brix

2. Multiply the needed increase by the number of gallons to be adjusted to arrive at the total increase in degrees Brix needed.

For example, for a 5-gallon carboy:
5 x 5 = 25

3. Multiply this total by 2 ounces (56.7 g) to arrive at total sugar needed.

25 x 2 = 50 oz or 3 lbs 2 oz or 1.4 kg of sugar

usually low. The opposite is also true: When acid counts are low (as in many California wines), the pH counts are high.

A Happy Acid Balance? Acids too high will produce a sour wine, and wines with acids too low will make a flabby, bodiless drink. The best wines have a happy balance with acid numbers in the 0.55 to 0.85 range.

Through the years, we have never worried too much about pH because pH works opposite the acid balances. When we balance the acid, the pH always seems to adjust automatically. We suggest that you adjust the acid and not worry about the pH count.

The specific gravity ranges that we are looking for are 1.070 to 1.090 for white wines and 1.090 to 1.098 for red wines. They can be determined by measuring the juice or must with a hydrometer.

The easiest method to lower high acids counts is to add water and dilute the juice or must. The same procedure is used to lower high sugar counts. With the lowering of high acids you must also add sugar as you dilute the acid count. With the lowering of high sugar counts with water, you will have to watch the acid counts, check again, and adjust when finished.

EAST MEETS WEST

As you become more experienced, you will find that a blend of eastern wines with western wines, of like character and variety if possible, often can balance out naturally, as the eastern higher-acid wines pick up the lower-acid western wines. This is also true of the sugar counts.

CHOOSING A YEAST

Any home winemaker who expects to produce a quality wine with a minimum amount of effort has to use a yeast culture for fermentation. Modern technology allows us to select from a wide range of options when choosing the yeast. Each commercial yeast culture performs its fermentation task in a different manner and has been developed to maximize the potential of each variety of grape juice. There are yeasts that eat up much of the malic acid, if you like, and others that retain the fruitiness of the wine. Some will ferment totally dry and others will leave some residual sugar, and on and on. The varieties are endless and readily available in most wine supply stores.

New strains of yeast are continually in development. Your wine supply store will keep up with newly developed strains of yeast, and staff will be able to make helpful recommendations. See the chart on pages 40–42 for a list of some commonly available commercial yeast cultures.

DRY YEAST HYDRATION

Yeast hydration allows for a more vigorous and healthy fermentation. Simply place a cup of lukewarm preboiled water in a sanitized bowl, add a teaspoon (6.2 g) of sugar, stir, then add the package of wine yeast and let sit for about 30 minutes. The yeast should start working by foaming, bubbling, and giving off a wonderful yeasty aroma. Add the yeast to the diluted concentrate juice in the primary fermentor.

The Primary Fermentation

This is the magic of winemaking: the wonderful, stimulating action that converts the grape juice to wine. The first two weeks of the primary fermentation should be done in a cool, dry location away from direct sunlight. The fermentation container should be secured so as not to allow any foreign matter to get inside, yet there should be enough room to allow for bubbling and foaming without letting any juice or wine to escape the container. Glass carboys are ideal. Seal with a plastic fermentation lock inserted in the jug with a rubber stopper.

There are several varieties of yeasts that, while efficient in carrying out their winemaking responsibilities, do not cause a lot of foaming or bubbling action in the fermentation container. Instead, they do their job by turning the juice into a gray, cloudy mass. These varieties are recommended for some wines. Consult your wine supply store for more information.

Racking

Racking is the transfer of wine from one container to another, leaving unwanted sediment behind. The lees, or sediment, can cause off-flavors and off-odors in your wine if left in contact for a long period. Racking allows your wine to fall free and clear and maintains its quality. You'll use a sanitized siphon tube to transfer the wine from a primary fermentor to the secondary fermentor. Place the secondary fermentor lower than the primary to allow gravity to help the process. Racking is done several times in the life of your wine. (See page 24 for instructions.)

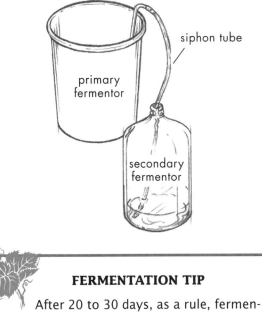

siphon tube

primary fermentor

secondary fermentor

SOME COMMERICAL YEAST STRAINS

NAME	QUALITY	RECOMMENDED USE
Gist-brocades Fermiblanc	Slow fermenting and low foaming, which brings out fruitiness and floral notes	Recommended for fruity-style wines
Gist-brocades Fermivin	A good general-purpose yeast strain for quick starting with low foam production; has high alcohol tolerance	Recommended for both red and whie wines
Gist-fermirouge	A quick-starting yeast with low foam production, low volatile acid production; enhances aromatic aromas in reds and improves mouth feel, as it softens harshness in young wine	Good for high acid red wines; retains aromas and color
Lallamand K1-V116	Low-foaming yeast has a "killer" factor[a] and is tolerant of high temperatures; capable of fermenting up to 20% alcohol	An excellent general-purpose yeast for both white and red wines
Lalvin EC-1118	A low-foaming strain with a high killer factor[a]; good for restarting stuck fermentation[b]; imparts a citrus flavor	Good for both white and red wines
Lalvin L2056	Retains varietal aromas and flavors and has good alcohol tolerance and low SO_2; maintains good color stability	Good for quick-to-market reds; early-drinking reds
Lalvin 71B-1122	Produces fruity wines and metabolizes more malic acid during fermentation than other strains	Good for wines with a high acid count like Seyval Blanc and Vidal Blanc
Lalvin Wadenswil 27	Good for cool fermentation of white wines; produces little heat, which is excellent for reds; has low glycosidase production, so little color is lost during fermentation	Good for both white and red wines
Red Star Côtes des Blancs	Formerly known as Epernay 2; slow fermenting, low-foaming yeast that brings out a lot of floral and fruity notes in wine; won't go as high in alcohol as most of the other yeasts, especially with a cool fermentation	Good for fruity-style wines
Red Star Montrachet	Vigorous yeast with high SO_2 and alcohol tolerance; tends to foam more than most strains and to produce slightly more buttery wines	Good general-purpose yeast for red and white wines

NAME	QUALITY	RECOMMENDED USE
Red Star Pasteur Champagne	Moderately vigorous with high SO_2 alcohol tolerance; fairly neutral; cold tolerant	Good for still or sparkling wines and fairly good with stuck fermentation[b]
Red Star Pasteur Red	A strong, even fermenter; produces full-bodied wines with fairly complex flavors	Good for the Cabernet family of grapes
Red Star Premier Cuvée	Formerly known as Pris de Mousse; like Pasteur Champagne yeast, a *Saccharomyces bayanus* strain that ferments over a wide temperature range; imparts a subtle, citruslike flavor	Good with white and red wines; good for both sparkling and still wines; good for restarting stuck or sluggish fermentation[b]
Wyeast Assmannhausen	Red wine yeast from Germany; ferments slower than most red wine strains; enhances vinifera character in French-American hybrids; color tolerant	Best for German reds, Riesling, red varietals, Merlot, red French-American hybrids
Wyeast Bordeaux	Produces distinctive, intense berry–graham cracker nose, jammy, rich, very smooth complex profile; slightly vinous; well suited for higher sugar content musts	Use for French Cabernet, Pinot Noir, Merlot, Petite Sirah, Rioja, Valdepenas, and Syrah
Wyeast Chablis	Produces extreme profile, high-ester formation with bready, vanilla notes; allows fruit character to dominate aroma and flavor profile; finishes slightly sweet and soft	For fruity white wines, Chardonnay, Chablis, ciders, Gewürztraminer, Chenin Blanc, Pinot Gris
Wyeast Chianti	Rich, big, bold, well-rounded profile; nice soft fruit character with dry, crisp finish	Best for Barolo, Barbera, Barbaresco, Nebbiolo, Chianti, Valpolicella, Sangiovese
Wyeast Eau de Vie	A good choice for alcohol tolerance and stuck fermentation[b]; produces a clean, dry profile; low ester and other volatile aromatica; 21% alcohol tolerance	Excellent for cordials, grappa, barley wine, eau de vie, single malts

chart continues on page 42

SO_2 = *Sulfur dioxide.*

[a] *The* killer factor *is a yeast's ability to kill all unwanted bacteria during fermentation, thus eliminating any potential unwanted odors or flavors from the wine.*

[b] *Occasionally, wine will start fermenting and then stop before fermentation is complete, hence* stuck fermentation. *See page 232 for possible solutions.*

NAME	QUALITY	RECOMMENDED USE
Wyeast Mead, Dry	Used in many award-winning meads; low foaming with little or no sulfur production; use additional nutrients as recommended in recipe for mead making	For mead, fruit mead, herbal mead, dry ciders, and cysers
Wyeast Mead, Sweet	Leaves 2–3% residual sugar in most mead; rich fruity profile complements fruit-mead fermentation; use additional nutrients for mead making	Best for ciders; cysers; fruit wines; ginger ale; cherry, raspberry, and peach wines
Wyeast Rudischeimer	Produces distinct Riesling character; rich flavor, creamy, fruity profile with nice dry finish and a hint of Riesling sweetness in the aftertaste	Best for Rhine wines, fruity ciders, Riesling, ice wine
Wyeast Sake #9	Used in conjunction with Koji for making a wide variety of Asian jius (rice-based beverages); full-bodied profile with true sake character	Best with sake, Nigori, Dai Gingo, fruit, plum wine, rice beer
Wyeast Steinberg	Classic German yeast from the Rheingau district; produces full-bodied wines with great depth, dry smoky characteristics with a sharp finish	For Riesling, Sylvaner, Moselles, Liebfraumilch, and Muller-Thurgau

SECONDARY FERMENTATION

This will be accomplished after you rack your wine into a clean container right after the primary fermentation. Depending on the wine type, the winemaker might induce or stimulate a second fermentation by *yeast inoculation,* or adding a new yeast strain. If left alone, most wines will automatically go through the second fermentation. This stage of fermenting softens the wine and makes it more pleasant to drink.

STABILIZING

Your wine is now fermented, but it still needs to be stabilized to help with proper aging. *Sulfiting,* or adding potassium metabisulfite to the wine, will kill off unwanted yeast and other organisms that could ruin your wine with off-flavors and smells. This sultfite comes in two main forms: Campden tablets and potassium metabisulfite powder. For a 5-gallon (19 L) batch, we find that using five Campden tablets or ½ teaspoon (3.1 g) potassium metabisulfite powder at each racking after fermentation is complete usually does the trick. Crush the Campden tablets to a powder before putting them in the carboy.

CLARIFYING AND FINING

It is recommended that all wines made from grape juice concentrates be clarified by adding a fining agent after the secondary fermentation is completed. Fining makes the wine sparkle and clear itself of any protein matter, yeasts, and any other foreign matter. There are several types of fining agents available in today's market. Check with your wine supply store for recommendations.

WINE AGING

Unlike wines made from fresh grapes and fresh juices, wines from grape juice concentrates and wine kits do not require long aging before drinking. The chemical makeup of concentrates allows for early drinking, which is an additional incentive for making wines from concentrates. As soon as the wine has been clarified after its fermentation, it is ready for bottling. Allow a few weeks after bottling before drinking to give the wine an opportunity to settle from bottle shock and into its new environment.

BOTTLING

After the fermentation, clarifying, and fining procedures have been completed and the wine is clear and is sparkling, it is ready for bottling. With concentrates, bottling occurs about 60 days from when the yeast was first added to the must. Do *not* bottle before the above procedures have been completed and the wine is clear. Premature bottling causes all kinds of problems. Be patient! It will be worth the wait.

If you don't want to invest money in a corker device, we suggest using the push-top corks available at most supply shops. When filling the sanitized bottles with the siphon hose,

CORK CONSIDERATIONS

Push-top corks are available at most wine supply stores and are much easier for hand-corking than are traditional ones. The slightly tapered cork has been glued to a round plastic cap. It looks similar to the type of cork you would find in a sherry or port bottle. Hand-corkers, used to insert traditional corks, are reasonably priced but physically grueling after just a few bottles. Table-style corking machines are much easier to work, but also much more expensive, and not really recommended for kit winemakers.

leave about ½ inch (1.3 cm) of space between cork and wine.

A WORD ABOUT OUR RECIPES

Generally speaking, experienced winemakers don't follow rigid recipes. That way, they can deal with variables. The recipes we've provided are designed to create wines that you'll enjoy drinking yourself and sharing with others. Over time, you should experiment a little and develop your own variations. Keep notes on everything you do when you make wine. With good records, you'll know what works and can go back and replicate past successes.

White Wine from Chenin Blanc Grape Concentrate

This refreshing wine is clean, crisp, and dry. Originally from the Loire region of France, it now flourishes in California. This versatile wine can be made in a soft sweet style or crisp and dry. It is always fruity with a distinctive bouquet of apples and honey. It is pleasant with fish, white meats, and medium cheese or served as an aperitif.

Yield: 5 gallons (19 L)

1 can (96 oz; 2.8 L) Chenin Blanc concentrate
5¾ cans (16.3 L) water
5 cups (1.1 kg) sugar
3 teaspoons (8.8 g) yeast nutrient
4 teaspoons (13.6 g) bentonite
2 teaspoons (28.8 g) acid blend
1 package (5 g) Wyeast Chablis yeast
15 Campden tablets or 1½ teaspoons (9.3 g) potassium metabisulfite powder

1. Sanitize all equipment.

2. Put the concentrate, water, sugar, yeast nutrient, bentonite, and acid blend into a clean 6- or 7-gallon (23–27 L) fermentation container. Stir well, making sure that all ingredients are dissolved.

3. Dissolve the yeast in 1 cup (240 mL) of the above mixture, then add to the fermentation container and mix well. Place in a cool, dry location.

4. Stir daily until fermentation starts, then stop and let it rest.

5. After 3 or 4 days, if there are no bubbles or gas (evidence of fermentation), warm the container to about 75°F (24°C) until surface bubbles appear. Continue stirring the contents once a day. Remove to a cool location as soon as fermentation starts.

6. Fermentation is complete when bubbling stops and sediment forms in the bottom of the container. Specific gravity should read 1.000 or less.

7. Allow the wine to settle out 1 to 2 weeks after fermentation is complete.

8. Crush to a powder 5 Campden tablets or use ½ teaspoon (3.1 g) potassium metabisulfite powder and put into a sanitized 5-gallon (19 L) glass carboy before racking. Repeat at each racking.

9. Rack. Siphon off the top clear wine into the 5-gallon (19 L) carboy, being careful not to disturb the heavy sediment. Discard the sediment.

10. Rack in 3 weeks, and again in 3 months after that. The wine should be crystal clear and ready for bottling.

11. Sanitize 26 750-mL (25.4 oz) bottles, fill them, and insert closures. Wait 3 months, then taste your wine. 🍇

WHITE WINE FROM EMERALD RIESLING GRAPE CONCENTRATE

This spicy hybrid, developed by the University of California, Davis, features Riesling flavors tempered with crispness and fruitiness. A softer version of the German Riesling, the Emerald Riesling balances spiciness with good fruit and makes an enjoyable summer wine; well-suited for Asian dishes, light foods, and barbecues.

Yield: 5 gallons (19 L)

- 1 can (96 oz; 2.8 L) Emerald Riesling concentrate
- 5¾ cans (16.3 L) water
- 5 cups (1.1 kg) sugar
- 3 teaspoons (8.8 g) yeast nutrient
- 4 teaspoons (13.6 g) bentonite
- 2 teaspoons (28.8 g) acid blend
- 1 package (5 g) Red Star Côtes des Blancs yeast
- 15 Campden tablets or 1½ teaspoons (9.3 g) potassium metabisulfite powder

1. Sanitize all equipment

2. Put the concentrate, water, sugar, yeast nutrient, bentonite, and acid blend into a clean 6- or 7-gallon (23–27 L) fermentation container. Stir well, making sure that all ingredients are dissolved.

3. Dissolve the yeast in 1 cup (240 mL) of the above mixture, then add to the fermentation container and mix well. Place in a cool, dry location.

4. Stir daily until fermentation starts, then stop.

5. After 3 or 4 days, if there are no bubbles or gas (evidence of fermentation), warm the container to about 75°F (24°C) until surface bubbles appear.

Continue stirring the contents once a day. Remove to a cool location as soon as fermentation starts.

6. Fermentation is complete when bubbling stops and sediment forms at the bottom of the container. Specific gravity should read 1.000 or less.

7. Allow the wine to settle out 1 to 2 weeks after fermentation is complete. No further mixing is required.

8. Crush to a powder 5 Campden tablets or use ½ teaspoon (3.1 g) potassium metabisulfite powder and add to a sanitized 5-gallon (19 L) glass carboy before racking. Repeat at each racking.

9. Rack. Siphon off the top clear wine into the 5-gallon (19 L) carboy, being careful not to disturb the heavy sediment. Discard the sediment.

10. Rack in 3 weeks, and again in 3 months after that. The wine should be crystal clear and ready for bottling.

11. Sanitize 26 750-mL (25.4 oz) bottles, fill them, and insert closures. Wait 3 months, then taste your wine. 🍇

WHITE WINE FROM FRENCH COLOMBARD GRAPE CONCENTRATE

Enjoy this wine in its youth. Aromas of fresh fruit prevail while, on the palate, the wine tastes crisp and clean. A nice touch of acidity carries the wine to a long finish. This is an easy-drinking white wine with a lot of character and complexity. It goes well with many foods, but it shines with fish and poultry.

Yield: 5 gallons (19 L)

- 1 can (96 oz; 2.8 L) French Colombard concentrate
- 5¾ cans (16.3 L) water
- 5 cups (1.1 kg) sugar
- 3 teaspoons (8.8 g) yeast nutrient
- 4 teaspoons (13.6 g) bentonite
- 2 teaspoons (28.8 g) acid blend
- 1 package (5 g) Lallamand K1-V116 yeast
- 15 Campden tablets or 1½ teaspoons (9.3 g) potassium metabisulfite powder

1. Sanitize all equipment.

2. Put the concentrate, water, sugar, yeast nutrient, bentonite, and acid blend into a clean 6- or 7-gallon (23–27 L) fermentation container. Stir well, making sure all ingredients are dissolved.

3. Dissolve the yeast in 1 cup (240 mL) of the above mixture, then add to the fermentation container and mix well. Place in a cool, dry location.

4. Stir daily until fermentation starts, then stop.

5. After 3 or 4 days, if there are no bubbles or gas (evidence of fermentation), warm the container to about 75°F (24°C) until surface bubbles appear. Continue stirring the contents once a day. Remove to a cool location as soon as fermentation starts.

6. Fermentation is complete when bubbling stops and sediment forms in the bottom of the container. Specific gravity should read 1.000 or less.

7. Allow the wine to settle out 1 to 2 weeks after fermentation is complete.

8. Crush to a powder 5 Campden tablets or use ½ teaspoon (3.1 g) potassium metabisulfite powder and add to a sanitized 5-gallon (19 L) glass carboy before racking. Repeat at each racking.

9. Rack. Siphon off the top clear wine into the 5-gallon (19 L) carboy, being careful not to disturb the heavy sediment. Discard the sediment.

10. Rack in 3 weeks, and again in 3 months after that. The wine should be crystal clear and ready for bottling.

11. Sanitize 26 750-mL (25.4 oz) bottles, fill them, and insert closures. Wait 3 months, then taste your wine. 🍇

White Wine from Gewürztraminer Grape Concentrate

This wine is light straw in color, with aromas of spice and cloves. It is well balanced with a long, tingling finish. Very spicy, the wine offers a frontal attack on your taste buds. When well aged, it becomes truly distinctive. Historically popular in Alsace, France, this wine's spiciness complements a variety of culinary specialties, including Asian, Thai, Cajun, and Mexican foods.

Yield: 5 gallons (19 L)

- 1 can (96 oz; 2.8 L) Gewürztraminer concentrate
- 5¾ cans (16.3 L) water
- 5 cups (1.1 kg) sugar
- 3 teaspoons (8.8 g) yeast nutrient
- 4 teaspoons (13.6 g) bentonite
- 2 teaspoons (28.8 g) acid blend
- 1 package (5 g) Red Star Côtes des Blancs yeast
- 15 Campden tablets or 1½ teaspoons (9.3 g) potassium metabisulfite powder

1. Sanitize all equipment.

2. Put the concentrate, water, sugar, yeast nutrient, bentonite, and acid blend into a clean 6- or 7-gallon (23–27 L) fermentation container. Stir well, making sure that all ingredients are dissolved.

3. Dissolve the yeast in 1 cup (240 mL) of above mixture, then add to the fermentation container and mix well. Place in a cool, dry location.

4. Stir daily until fermentation starts, then stop.

5. After 3 or 4 days, if there are no bubbles or gas (evidence of fermentation), warm the container to about 75°F (24°C) until surface bubbles appear. Continue stirring the contents once a day. Remove to a cool location as soon as fermentation starts.

6. Fermentation is complete when bubbling stops and sediment forms in the bottom of the container. Specific gravity should read 1.000 or less.

7. Allow the wine to settle out 1 to 2 weeks after fermentation is complete.

8. Crush to a powder 5 Campden tablets or use ½ teaspoon (3.1 g) potassium metabisulfite powder and add to a sanitized 5-gallon (19 L) glass carboy before racking. Repeat at each racking.

8. Rack. Siphon off the top clear wine into the 5-gallon (19 L) carboy, being careful not to disturb the heavy sediment. Discard the sediment.

10. Rack in 3 weeks, and again in 3 months after that. The wine should be crystal clear and ready for bottling.

11. Sanitize 26 750-mL (25.4 oz) bottles, fill them, and insert closures. Wait 3 months, then taste your wine. 🍇

WHITE WINE FROM GREY RIESLING GRAPE CONCENTRATE

This grape variety is not a member of the Riesling family and is named improperly. There is no spiciness to it; its character is closer to either Chenin Blanc or Sauvignon Blanc. This is an interesting variety: The wine is crisp with good acidity and fruit flavors. Aromas of citrus and melon add to its complexity. It is an excellent match for most fish and poultry dishes.

Yield: 5 gallons (19 L)

- 1 can (96 oz; 2.8 L) Gray Riesling concentrate
- 5¾ cans (16.3 L) water
- 5 cups (1.1 kg) sugar
- 3 teaspoons (8.8 g) yeast nutrient
- 4 teaspoons (13.6 g) bentonite
- 2 teaspoons (28.8 g) acid blend
- 1 package (5 g) Red Star Côte des Blancs yeast
- 15 Campden tablets or 1½ teaspoons (9.3 g) potassium metabisulfite powder

1. Sanitize all equipment.

2. Put the concentrate, water, sugar, yeast nutrient, bentonite, and acid blend into a clean 6- or 7-gallon (23–27 L) fermentation container. Stir well, making sure that all ingredients are dissolved.

3. Dissolve the yeast in 1 cup (240 mL) of the above mixture, then add to the fermentation vessel and mix well. Place in a cool, dry location

4. Stir daily until fermentation starts, then stop.

5. After 3 or 4 days, if there are no bubbles or gas (evidence of fermentation), warm the container to about 75°F (24°C) until surface bubbles appear. Continue stirring the contents once a day. Remove to a cool location as soon as fermentation starts.

6. Fermentation is complete when bubbling stops and sediment forms in the bottom of the container. Specific gravity should read 1.000 or less.

7. Allow the wine to settle out 1 to 2 weeks after fermentation is complete.

8. Crush to a powder 5 Campden tablets or use ½ teaspoon (3.1 g) potassium metabisulfite powder and add to a sanitized 5-gallon (19 L) glass carboy before racking. Repeat at each racking.

9. Rack. Siphon off the top clear wine into the 5-gallon (19 L) carboy, being careful not to disturb the sediment. Discard sediment.

10. Rack in 3 weeks, and again in 3 months after that. The wine should be crystal clear and ready for bottling.

11. Sanitize 26 750-mL (25.4 oz) bottles, fill them, and insert closures. Wait 3 months, then taste your wine. 🍇

WHITE WINE FROM JOHANNISBERG RIESLING GRAPE CONCENTRATE

Fruity yet floral, this German-style wine has a clean, tart flavor. Although light in color, it boasts a full-bodied texture. Slight oaking of this wine brings out an exciting bouquet and flavor. Usually served dry, it can be sweetened without disturbing the overall quality. A social wine, it also complements a light meal or cheese tray.

Yield: 5 gallons (19 L)

- 1 can (96 oz; 2.8 L) Johannisberg Riesling concentrate
- 5¾ cans (16.3 L) water
- 5 cups (1.1 kg) sugar
- 3 teaspoons (8.8 g) yeast nutrient
- 4 teaspoons (13.6 g) bentonite
- 2 teaspoons (28.8 g) acid blend
- 1 package (5 g) Red Star Côtes des Blancs yeast
- 15 Campden tablets or 1½ teaspoons (9.3 g) potassium metabisulfite powder

1. Sanitize all equipment.

2. Put the concentrate, water, sugar, yeast nutrient, bentonite, and acid blend into a clean 6- or 7-gallon (23–27 L) fermentation container. Stir well, making sure that all ingredients are dissolved.

3. Dissolve the yeast in 1 cup (240 mL) of the above mixture, then add to the fermentation container and mix well. Place in a cool, dry location.

4. Stir daily until fermentation starts, then stop.

5. After 3 or 4 days, if there are no bubbles or gas (evidence of fermentation), warm the container to about 75°F (24°C) until surface bubbles appear. Continue stirring the contents once a day. Remove to a cool location as soon as fermentation starts.

6. Fermentation is complete when bubbling stops and sediment forms in the bottom of the container. Specific gravity should read 1.000 or less.

7. Allow the wine to settle out 1 to 2 weeks after fermentation is complete.

8. Crush to a powder 5 Campden tablets or use ½ teaspoon (3.1 g) potassium metabisulfite powder and add to a sanitized 5-gallon (19 L) glass carboy before racking. Repeat at each racking.

9. Rack. Siphon off the top clear wine into the 5-gallon (19 L) carboy, being careful not to disturb the sediment. Discard the sediment.

10. Rack in 3 weeks, and again in 3 months after that. The wine should be crystal clear and ready for bottling.

11. Sanitize 26 750-mL (25.4 oz) bottles, fill them, and insert closures. Wait 3 months, then taste your wine. 🍇

WHITE WINE FROM LIEBFRAUMILCH GRAPE CONCENTRATE

This wine is easy to make and provides a delightful blend of Rieslings with a fruity aroma and clean taste. It is well balanced as either a dry, crisp wine or a medium sweet wine. It has a soft spiciness that blends well with Asian, Thai, and Mexican dishes. This wine is best enjoyed young (within 1 year of bottling).

Yield: 5 gallons (19 L)

- 1 can (96 oz; 2.8 L) Liebfraumilch concentrate
- 5¾ cans (16.3 L) water
- 5 cups (1.1 kg) sugar
- 3 teaspoons (8.8 g) yeast nutrient
- 4 teaspoons (13.6 g) bentonite
- 2 teaspoons (28.8 g) acid blend
- 1 package (5 g) Red Star Côtes des Blancs yeast
- 15 Campden tablets or 1½ teaspoons (9.3 g) potassium metabisulfite powder

1. Sanitize all equipment.

2. Put the concentrate, water, sugar, yeast nutrient, bentonite, and acid blend into a clean 6- or 7-gallon (23–27 L) fermentation container. Stir well, making sure that all ingredients are dissolved.

3. Dissolve the yeast in 1 cup (240 mL) of the above mixture, then add to the fermentation container and mix well. Place in a cool, dry location.

4. Stir vessel daily until fermentation starts, then stop.

5. After 3 or 4 days, if there are no bubbles or gas (evidence of fermentation), warm the container to about 75°F (24°C) until surface bubbles appear. Continue stirring the contents once a day. Remove to a cool location as soon as fermentation starts.

6. Fermentation is complete when bubbling stops and sediment forms in the bottom of the container. Specific gravity should read 1.000 or less.

7. Allow the wine to settle out 1 to 2 weeks after fermentation is finished.

8. Crush to a powder 5 Campden tablets or use ½ teaspoon (3.1 g) potassium metabisulfite powder and add to a sanitized 5-gallon (19 L) glass carboy before racking. Repeat at each racking.

9. Rack. Siphon off the top clear wine into the 5-gallon (19 L) carboy, being careful not to disturb the sediment. Discard sediment.

10. Rack in 3 weeks, and again in 3 months after that. The wine should be crystal clear and ready for bottling.

11. Sanitize 26 750-mL (25.4 oz) bottles, fill them, and insert closures. Wait 3 months, then taste your wine. 🍇

WHITE WINE FROM PINOT BLANC GRAPE CONCENTRATE

Pinot Blanc is often mistaken for Chardonnay because of its rich, full-bodied flavor and slightly weedy aroma. Subtle undertones of peach round out this wine. Pinot Blanc can stand on its own and it also is an excellent blending wine. The high concentration of solid acids adds crispness and body. It can be drunk young and with a wide variety of foods, including many fish and poultry dishes and hard cheeses.

Yield: 5 gallons (19 L)

1	can (96 oz; 2.8 L) Pinot Blanc concentrate
5¾	cans (16.3 L) water
5	cups (1.1 kg) sugar
3	teaspoons (8.8 g) yeast nutrient
4	teaspoons (13.6 g) bentonite
2	teaspoons (28.8 g) acid blend
3	tablespoons (11.1 g) Oak-Mor
1	package (5 g) Red Star Montrachet yeast
15	Campden tablets or 1½ teaspoons (9.3 g) potassium metabisulfite powder

1. Sanitize all equipment.

2. Put the concentrate, water, sugar, yeast nutrient, bentonite, acid blend, and Oak-Mor into a clean 6- or 7-gallon (23–27 L) fermentation container. Stir well, making sure that all ingredients are dissolved.

3. Dissolve the yeast in 1 cup (240 mL) of the above mixture, then add to the fermentation container and mix well. Place in a cool, dry location.

4. Stir daily until fermentation starts, then stop.

5. After 3 or 4 days, if there are no bubbles or gas (evidence of fermentation), warm the container to about 75°F (24°C) until surface bubbles appear. Continue stirring the contents once a day. Remove to a cool location as soon as fermentation starts.

6. Fermentation is complete when bubbling stops and sediment forms in the bottom of the container. Specific gravity should read 1.000 or less.

7. Allow the wine to settle out 1 to 2 weeks after fermentation is complete.

8. Crush to a powder 5 Campden tablets or use ½ teaspoon (3.1 g) potassium metabisulfite powder and add to a 5-gallon (19 L) glass carboy before racking. Repeat at each racking.

9. Rack. Siphon off the top clear wine into the sanitized 5-gallon (19 L) carboy, being careful not to disturb the sediment. Discard sediment.

10. Rack in 3 weeks, and again in 3 months after that. The wine should be crystal clear and ready for bottling.

11. Sanitize 26 750-mL (25.4 oz) bottles, fill them, and insert closures. Wait 3 months, then taste your wine. 🍇

WHITE WINE FROM PINOT CHARDONNAY GRAPE CONCENTRATE

This full-bodied wine will please the sophisticated palate with its crisp, green-apple bouquet and hearty, deep flavor. It is one of the finest wines on the market, if you value depth. Oaking is necessary to bring out the natural vanilla aroma. This wine improves with age and goes well with most shellfish and chicken dishes. Everyone should have this in his or her wine cellar.

Yield: 5 gallons (19 L)

1	can (96 oz; 2.8 L) Pinot Chardonnay concentrate
5¾	cans (16.3 L) water
5	cups (1.1 kg) sugar
3	teaspoons (8.8 g) yeast nutrient
4	teaspoons (13.6 g) bentonite
2	teaspoons (28.8 g) acid blend
3	tablespoons (11.1 g) Oak-Mor
1	package (5 g) Red Star Montrachet yeast
15	Campden tablets or 1½ teaspoons (9.3 g) potassium metabisulfite powder

1. Sanitize all equipment.

2. Put the concentrate, water, sugar, yeast nutrient, bentonite, acid blend, and Oak-Mor into a clean 6- or 7-gallon (23–27 L) fermentation container. Stir well, making sure that all ingredients are dissolved.

3. Dissolve the yeast in 1 cup (240 mL) of the above mixture, then add to the fermentation container and mix well. Place in a cool, dry location.

4. Stir daily until fermentation starts, then stop.

5. After 3 or 4 days, if there are no bubbles or gas (evidence of fermentation), warm the container to about 75°F (24°C) until surface bubbles appear. Continue stirring the contents once a day. Remove to a cool location as soon as fermentation starts.

6. Fermentation is complete when bubbling stops and sediment forms in the bottom of the container. Specific gravity should read 1.000 or less.

7. Allow the wine to settle out 1 to 2 weeks after fermentation is complete.

8. Crush to a powder 5 Campden tablets or use ½ teaspoon (3.1 g) potassium metabisulfite powder and add to a sanitized 5-gallon (19 L) glass carboy before racking. Repeat at each racking.

9. Rack. Siphon off the top clear wine into the 5 gallon (19 L) carboy, being careful not to disturb the sediment. Discard sediment.

10. Rack in 3 weeks, and again in 3 months after that. The wine should be crystal clear and ready for bottling.

11. Sanitize 26 750-mL (25.4 oz) bottles, fill them, and insert closures. Wait 3 months, then taste your wine. 🍇

WHITE WINE FROM PREMIUM CHABLIS GRAPE CONCENTRATE

This full-flavored wine is smooth, clean, and well balanced. It usually has a Chardonnay base, with complementary varieties added for complexity. It is a clean wine with citrus and melon flavors and a lingering aftertaste. Due to its crowd-pleasing nature, it is the perfect wedding wine. It's also an excellent poolside companion and is well suited for most fish and poultry dishes.

Yield: 5 gallons (19 L)

- 1 can (96 oz; 2.8 L) Premium Chablis concentrate
- 5¾ cans (16.3 L) water
- 5 cups (1.1 kg) sugar
- 3 teaspoons (8.8 g) yeast nutrient
- 4 teaspoons (13.6 g) bentonite
- 2 teaspoons (28.8 g) acid blend
- 3 tablespoons (11.1 g) Oak-Mor
- 1 package (5 g) Red Star Montrachet yeast
- 15 Campden tablets or 1½ teaspoons (9.3 g) potassium metabisulfite powder

1. Sanitize all equipment.

2. Put the concentrate, water, sugar, yeast nutrient, bentonite, acid blend, and Oak-Mor into a clean 6- or 7-gallon (23–27 L) fermentation container. Stir well, making sure that all ingredients are dissolved.

3. Dissolve the yeast in 1 cup (240 mL) of the above mixture, then add to the fermentation container and mix well. Place in a cool, dry location.

4. Stir daily until fermentation starts, then stop.

5. After 3 or 4 days, if there are no bubbles or gas (evidence of fermentation), warm the container to about 75°F (24°C) until surface bubbles appear. Continue stirring the contents once a day. Remove to a cool location as soon as fermentation starts.

6. Fermentation is complete when bubbling stops and sediment forms in the bottom of the container. Specific gravity should read 1.000 or less.

7. Allow the wine to settle out 1 to 2 weeks after fermentation is complete.

8. Crush to a powder 5 Campden tablets or use ½ teaspoon (3.1 g) potassium metabisulfite powder and add to a sanitized 5-gallon (19 L) glass carboy before racking. Repeat at each racking.

9. Rack. Siphon off the top clear wine into the 5-gallon (19 L) carboy, being careful not to disturb the sediment. Discard sediment.

10. Rack in 3 weeks, and again in 3 months after that. The wine should be crystal clear and ready for bottling.

11. Sanitize 26 750-mL (25.4 oz) bottles, fill them, and insert closures. Wait 3 months, then taste your wine. 🍇

WHITE WINE FROM SAUVIGNON BLANC GRAPE CONCENTRATE

Enjoy one of the most popular and widely grown vinifera grapes in the world. Straw yellow in color with a hint of young leaves, the bouquet of this wine captures the essence of green grass in springtime with a dash of bell pepper. A montage of flavors astonishes the palate: gooseberries, tropical fruit, and asparagus leading to a long, lingering aftertaste. Partner this wine with shellfish, grilled white meats, Southwestern, and Tex-Mex dishes.

Yield: 5 gallons (19 L)

1 can (96 oz; 2.8 L) Sauvignon Blanc concentrate
5¾ cans (16.3 L) water
5 cups (1.1 kg) sugar
3 teaspoons (8.8 g) yeast nutrient
4 teaspoons (13.6 g) bentonite
2 teaspoons (28.8 g) acid blend
1 package (5 g) Lalvin EC-1118 yeast
15 Campden tablets or 1½ teaspoons (9.3 g) potassium metabisulfite powder

1. Sanitize all equipment.

2. Put the concentrate, water, sugar, yeast nutrient, bentonite, and acid blend into a clean 6- or 7-gallon (23–27 L) fermentation container. Stir well, making sure that all ingredients are dissolved.

3. Dissolve the yeast in 1 cup (240 mL) of the above mixture, then add to the fermentation container and mix well. Place in a cool, dry location.

4. Stir daily until fermentation starts, then stop.

5. After 3 or 4 days, if there are no bubbles or gas (evidence of fermentation), warm the container to about 75°F (24°C) until surface bubbles appear. Continue stirring the contents once a day. Remove to a cool location as soon as fermentation starts.

6. Fermentation is complete when bubbling stops and sediment forms in the bottom.

7. Allow the wine to settle out 1 to 2 weeks after fermentation is complete.

8. Crush to a powder 5 Campden tablets or use ½ teaspoon (3.1 g) potassium metabisulfite powder and add to a sanitized 5-gallon (19 L) glass carboy before racking. Repeat at each racking.

9. Rack. Siphon off the top clear wine into the 5-gallon (19 L) carboy, being careful not to disturb the sediment. Discard sediment.

10. Rack in 3 weeks, and again in 3 months after that. The wine should be crystal clear and ready for bottling.

11. Sanitize 26 750-mL (25.4 oz) bottles, fill them, and insert closures. Wait 3 months, then taste your wine. 🍇

White Wine from Vino Blanc Grape Concentrate

This is a pleasant generic wine made from a blend of several white varieties. It is crisp yet soft on the palate with plenty of fruit, featuring apple, pineapple, and melon. It then gives way to a crisp, clean finish. This wine is ideal with light foods and snacks.

Yield: 5 gallons (19 L)

1	can (96 oz; 2.8 L) Vino Blanc concentrate
5¾	cans (16.3 L) water
5	cups (1.1 kg) sugar
3	teaspoons (8.8 g) yeast nutrient
4	teaspoons (13.6 g) bentonite
2	teaspoons (28.8 g) acid blend
1	package (5 g) Red Star Premier Cuvée yeast
15	Campden tablets or 1½ teaspoons (9.3 g) potassium metabisulfite powder

1. Sanitize all equipment.

2. Put the concentrate, water, sugar, yeast nutrient, bentonite, and acid blend into a clean 6- or 7-gallon (23–27 L) fermentation container. Stir well, making sure that all ingredients are dissolved.

3. Dissolve the yeast in 1 cup (240 mL) of the above mixture, then add to the fermentation container and mix well. Place in a cool, dry location.

4. Stir daily until fermentation starts, then stop.

5. After 3 or 4 days, if there are no bubbles or gas (evidence of fermentation), warm the container to about 75°F (24°C) until surface bubbles appear. Continue stirring the contents once a day. Remove to a cool location as soon as fermentation starts.

6. Fermentation is complete when bubbling stops and sediment forms in the bottom of the container. Specific gravity should read 1.000 or less.

7. Allow the wine to settle out 1 to 2 weeks after fermentation is complete.

8. Crush to a powder 5 Campden tablets or use ½ teaspoon (3.1 g) potassium metabisulfite powder and add to a sanitized 5-gallon (19 L) glass carboy before racking. Repeat at each racking.

9. Rack. Siphon off the top clear wine into the 5-gallon (19 L) carboy, being careful not to disturb the sediment. Discard sediment.

10. Rack in 3 weeks, and again in 3 months after that. The wine should be crystal clear and ready for bottling.

11. Sanitize 26 750-mL (25.4 oz) bottles, fill them, and insert closures. Wait 3 months, then taste your wine. 🍇

White Wine from Niagara Grape Concentrate

This popular native American (Labrusca) wine is found in the eastern and northern United States and Canada. A "grapey" flavor is characteristic of this variety — a distinct grape aroma is recognized immediately on pouring it into a glass. It is not considered a sophisticated wine; rather, it is one for quaffing during the summer months while picnicking or just lounging around.

Yield: 5 gallons (19 L)

1 can (64 oz; 1.9 L) Niagara Grape concentrate
9 cans (17 L) water
8 cups (1.1 kg) sugar
3 teaspoons (8.8 g) yeast nutrient
4 teaspoons (13.6 g) bentonite
2 teaspoons (28.8 g) acid blend
1 package (5 g) Red Star Côtes des Blancs yeast
20 Campden tablets or 2 teaspoons (12.4 g) potassium metabisulfite powder

1. Sanitize all equipment.

2. Put the concentrate, water, sugar, yeast nutrient, bentonite, and acid blend into a clean 6- or 7-gallon (23–27 L) fermentation container. Stir well, making sure that all ingredients are dissolved.

3. Dissolve the yeast in 1 cup (240 mL) of above mixture, then add to the fermentation vessel and mix well. Place in a cool, dry location.

4. Stir daily until fermentation starts, then stop.

5. After 3 or 4 days, if there are no bubbles or gas (evidence of fermentation), warm the container to about 75°F (24°C) until surface bubbles appear. Continue stirring the contents once a day. Remove to a cool location as soon as fermentation starts.

6. Fermentation is complete when bubbling stops and sediment forms in the bottom of the container. Specific gravity should read 1.000 or less.

7. Allow the wine to settle for 1 to 2 weeks after fermentation is complete.

8. Crush to a powder 5 Campden tablets or use ½ teaspoon (3.1 g) potassium metabisulfite powder and add to a sanitized 5-gallon (19 L) glass carboy before racking. Repeat at each racking.

9. Rack. Siphon off the top clear wine into the 5-gallon (19 L) carboy. Be careful not to disturb the sediment. Discard sediment.

10. Rack in 3 weeks, and again in 3 months after that. The wine should be crystal clear and ready for bottling.

11. Sanitize 26 750-mL (25.4 oz) bottles, fill them, and insert closures. Wait 3 months, then taste your wine. 🍇

RED WINE FROM BARBERA WINE CONCENTRATE

This makes a great wine to serve with pizza and pasta dishes. It is a rich and full-bodied red with a fruity bouquet. The wine acids match up well with the acidity in tomatoes and tomato sauces. These grapes are from Italy and those areas to which Italian immigrants brought the vine and their culinary traditions.

Yield: 5 gallons (19 L)

- 1 gallon (3.8 L) Barbera wine concentrate
- 2 gallons (7.6 L) hot water (75°–80°F; 23°–27°C)
- 2 gallons (7.6 L) cold water (45°–55°F; 7°–10°C)
- 5¾ cups (1.3 kg) sugar
- 6½ teaspoons (29.9 g) yeast nutrient
- 1½ teaspoons (4.2 g) grape tannin
- 1 package (5 g) Wyeast Chianti yeast
- 20 Campden tablets or 2 teaspoons (12.4 g) potassium metabisulfite powder

1. Sanitize all equipment.

2. Put the concentrate, water, sugar, yeast nutrient, and tannin into a clean 6- or 7-gallon (23–27 L) fermentation container. Stir well, making sure that all ingredients are dissolved.

3. Test for sugar and acid counts. Make adjustments if necessary.

4. When the juice temperature is between 65° and 75°F (18°–8°C), draw out a cup (240 mL) of juice and dissolve the yeast in it. Let stand for 30 minutes, then add to the fermentor and stir well.

5. Keep the fermentation container covered with either a fermentation lock or a sheet of plastic loosely applied to allow gas to escape.

6. Stir at least daily to assist the fermentation.

7. After the second day, check the must daily. As soon as the specific gravity drops to 1.030 (8 degrees Brix), the must is ready for the first racking.

8. Add to a sanitized container 5 Campden tablets (crushed to a powder) or ½ teaspoon (3.1 g) of potassium metabisulfite powder. Rack the old wine into the new container, leaving the fermentation debris behind. Secure the container with a fermentation lock.

9. Rack at least three more times (once a month or so) until the wine is clear. When the wine clears, leave it in the container another 3 months to age.

10. To ensure that all fermentation has ceased and that the wine has achieved the required clarity, place a lighted candle behind it and look through the jug. If your wine is hazy or cloudy, or if any bubbles are present, empty the air lock and refill with fresh potassium metabisulfite solution. Store, undisturbed, for 2 more months, then test again.

11. Sanitize 26 750-mL (25.4 oz) bottles, fill them, and insert closures. Wait 6 months, then taste your wine. 🍇

RED WINE FROM BAROLO WINE CONCENTRATE

This is a full-bodied wine with high tannins and a rich flavor. Plum and berry flavors add complexity. This wine needs additional aging to soften the tannins, but the wait is well worth it. The Barolo concentrates from Italy are interesting to explore, as the Italians have been able to retain the varietal characteristics of this grape. The wine goes well with steak and prime rib.

Yield: 5 gallons (19 L)

1	can (96 oz; 2.8 L) Barolo wine concentrate
5¾	cans (16.3 L) cold water
8	cups (1.8 kg) sugar
3	teaspoons (8.8 g) yeast nutrient
⅓	ounce (9.5 g) bentonite
2	teaspoons (28.8 g) acid blend
1	package (5 g) Red Star Pasteur Red wine yeast
20	Campden tablets or 2 teaspoons (12.4 g) potassium metabisulfite powder

1. Sanitize all equipment.

2. Put the concentrate, water, sugar, yeast nutrient, bentonite, and acid blend into a clean 6- or 7-gallon (23–27 L) fermentation container. Stir well to make sure all ingredients are dissolved.

3. Dissolve the wine yeast in 1 cup (240 mL) of the above mixture, then add to the grape juice and stir well. Place in a cool, dry location.

4. Mix the concentrate daily.

5. After 3 or 4 days, if there is no evidence of fermentation, warm the container to about 75°F (24°C) until bubbles appear. Stir the contents daily, and remove to a cool location when fermentation starts.

6. Fermentation is complete when bubbling stops and sediment forms in the bottom of the container. After 20 to 30 days, as a rule, fermentation takes less time at 80°F (27°C) than at 60°F (13°C). Specific gravity should read 1.000 or less.

7. Allow the wine to settle out 1 to 2 weeks after fermentation is complete. Do not mix.

8. Add to a sanitized 5-gallon (19 L) glass carboy 5 Campden tablets (crushed to a powder) or ½ teaspoon (3.1 g) potassium metabisulfite powder.

9. Rack. Siphon off the top clear wine into the 5-gallon (19 L) carboy, being careful not to disturb the sediment. Discard sediment.

10. Rack the wine three or four more times over the next 5 to 6 months, or until the wine is crystal clear. When the wine clears, it is ready for bottling.

11. Sanitize 26 750-mL (25.4 oz) or 13 1.5-L (50.8 oz) bottles, then fill them and insert closures. Leave about ½ inch (1.3 cm) of space between cork and wine. Wait 6 months, then taste your wine. 🍇

RED WINE FROM CABERNET SAUVIGNON WINE CONCENTRATE

This king of red wines is the great wine of Bordeaux, France, and the most popular red in California. A full-flavored, aggressive, medium dark red wine, it has a smoky taste with a touch of spice and berries. A hint of violet is present in the bouquet. It ages well and blends nicely with most other red wines. It is an excellent companion to red meats.

Yield: 5 gallons (19 L)

- 1 can (96 oz; 2.8 L) Cabernet Sauvignon concentrate
- 5¾ cans (16.3 kg) cold water
- 7½ cups (1.7 kg) sugar
- 3 teaspoons (8.8 g) yeast nutrient
- ⅓ ounce (9.5 g) bentonite
- 2 teaspoons (28.8 g) acid blend
- 1 package (5 g) Red Star Pasteur Red wine yeast
- 20 Campden tablets or 2 teaspoons (12.4 g) potassium metabisulfite powder

1. Sanitize all equipment.

2. Put the concentrate, water, sugar, yeast nutrient, bentonite, and acid blend into a clean 6- or 7-gallon (23–27 L) fermentation container. Stir well, making sure that all ingredients are dissolved.

3. Dissolve the wine yeast in 1 cup (240 mL) of tepid water with a teaspoon (6.2 g) of sugar dissolved in it. After 30 minutes, add the yeast to the fermentation vessel and stir well. Place in a cool, dry location.

4. Stir the mixture daily.

5. After 3 or 4 days, if there are no bubbles or gas (evidence of fermentation), warm the container to about 75°F (24°C) until surface bubbles appear. Continue stirring the contents once a day. Remove to a cool location as soon as fermentation starts.

6. Fermentation is complete when bubbling stops and sediment forms in the bottom of the container. Specific gravity should read 1.000 or less.

7. Allow the wine to settle out 2 to 3 weeks after fermentation is complete. Do not mix.

8. Add to a sanitized 5-gallon (19 L) glass carboy 5 Campden tablets (crushed to a powder) or ½ teaspoon (3.1 g) potassium metabisulfite powder.

9. Rack. Siphon off the top clear wine into the 5-gallon (19 L) carboy, being careful not to disturb the sediment. Discard sediment.

10. Rack the wine three or four more times over the next 5 to 6 months, or until the wine is crystal clear. When the wine clears, it is ready for bottling.

11. Sanitize 26 750-mL (25.4 oz) or 13 1.5-L (50.8 oz) bottles, then fill them and insert closures. Wait 6 months, then taste your wine. 🍇

RED WINE FROM GAMAY BEAUJOLAIS WINE CONCENTRATE

This wine is made in a fruity style ideal for early consumption. Medium colored and medium bodied, the wine features flavors of raspberry and cassis accompanied by an aroma of bell pepper. It is low in tannins and soft on the palate. Served slightly chilled, its fruitiness is heightened. This is an easy-drinking red wine, ideal for many occasions. A potential companion to many different menus, this wine is a great summer special for a patio party featuring finger foods.

Yield: 5 gallons (19 L)

2	cans (46 oz; 1.4 L) Gamay Beaujolais concentrate
11½	cans (15.6 L) cold water
8	cups (1.8 kg) sugar
3	teaspoons (8.8 g) yeast nutrient
⅓	ounce (9.5 g) bentonite
2	teaspoons (28.8 g) acid blend
1	package (5 g) Red Star Côtes des Blancs yeast
20	Campden tablets or 2 teaspoons (12.4 g) potassium metabisulfite powder

1. Sanitize all equipment.

2. Put the concentrate, water, sugar, yeast nutrient, bentonite, and acid blend into a clean 6- or 7-gallon (23–27 L) fermentation container. Stir well, making sure that all ingredients are dissolved.

3. Dissolve the yeast in 1 cup (240 mL) of the above mixture. Let sit for 30 minutes, then add to fermentation vessel and stir well. Place in a cool, dry location.

4. Stir the mixture daily.

5. After 3 or 4 days, if there are no bubbles or gas (evidence of fermentation), shake the container and place in a warmer environment. Continue mixing every day.

6. Fermentation is complete when bubbling stops and sediment forms in the bottom of the container. Specific gravity should read 1.000 or less.

7. Allow the wine to settle for 1 to 2 weeks after fermentation. Do not mix anymore.

8. Crush to a powder 5 Campden tablets or use ½ teaspoon (3.1 g) potassium metabisulfite powder and put into a sanitized 5-gallon (19 L) glass carboy before racking. Repeat at each racking.

9. Rack. Siphon off the top clear wine into the 5-gallon (19 L) carboy, being careful not to disturb the sediment. Discard sediment.

10. Rack the wine three or four more times over a period of 4 to 6 months, until the wine is crystal clear and ready for bottling.

11. Sanitize 26 750-mL (25.4 oz) bottles, fill them, and insert closures. Wait 3 months, then taste your wine. 🍇

RED WINE FROM MERLOT WINE CONCENTRATE

Merlot is a smooth, rich wine with a medium dark color and a blackberry and currant taste. A hint of green olive and violets heightens its complexity. This softer, easier-to-drink red wine has captured the fancy of wine buffs and currently ranks behind Cabernet Sauvignon as a favorite red. Its ideal companion is lamb, but it also matches beautifully with most cheeses and meat casseroles.

Yield: 5 gallons (19 L)

1	can (96 oz; 2.8 L) Merlot wine concentrate
5¾	cans (16.3 L) cold water
8	cups (1.8 kg) sugar
3	teaspoons (8.8 g) yeast nutrient
⅓	ounce (9.5 g) bentonite
2	teaspoons (28.8 g) acid blend
1	package (5 g) Red Star Premier Cuvée wine yeast
20	Campden tablets or 2 teaspoons (12.4 g) potassium metabisulfite powder

1. Sanitize all equipment.

2. Put the concentrate, water, sugar, yeast nutrient, bentonite, and acid blend into a clean 6- or 7-gallon (23–27 L) fermentation container. Stir well, making sure that all ingredients are dissolved.

3. Dissolve the wine yeast in 1 cup (240 mL) of warm water, add a teaspoon (6.2 g) of sugar, and let it start working. Add the yeast to the fermentation vessel and stir. Place in a cool, dry location.

4. Stir the mixture every day.

5. After 3 or 4 days, if there are no bubbles or gas (evidence of fermentation), warm the container to about 75°F (24°C) until surface bubbles appear. Continue stirring the contents once a day. Remove to a cool location as soon as fermentation starts.

6. Fermentation is complete when bubbling stops and sediment forms in the bottom of the container. Specific gravity should read 1.000 or less.

7. Allow the wine to settle for 2 to 3 weeks after fermentation is complete. Do not mix.

8. Add to a sanitized 5-gallon (19 L) glass carboy 5 Campden tablets (crushed to a powder) or ½ teaspoon (3.1 g) potassium metabisulfite powder.

9. Rack. Siphon off the top clear wine into the 5-gallon (19 L) carboy, being careful not to disturb the sediment. Discard sediment.

10. Rack the wine three or four more times over the next 5 to 6 months, or until the wine is crystal clear. When the wine clears, it is ready for bottling.

11. Sanitize 26 750-mL (25.4 oz) or 13 1.5-L (50.8 oz) bottles, fill them, and insert closures. Leave about ½ inch (1.3 cm) of space between cork and wine. Wait 6 months, then taste your wine.

RED WINE FROM PETITE SIRAH WINE CONCENTRATE

This is one of the most full-bodied, tannic wines. It is rich and extremely dark, with a tarry plum flavor. Now considered a cult wine by many, Petite Sirah can act as a great blending wine to assist lighter-colored reds and reds with less complexity. On its own, the Petite Sirah stands up to most hearty foods and the wine has a long life span due to its high acid count. It's a great wine to serve with pasta. It requires aerating before drinking: Let it breathe for 30 minutes. The extra effort is worth it.

Yield: 5 gallons (19 L)

- 1 can (96 oz; 2.8 L) Petite Sirah wine concentrate
- 5¾ cans (16.3 L) cold water
- 8 cups (1.8 kg) sugar
- 3 teaspoons (8.8 g) yeast nutrient
- ⅓ ounce (9.5 g) bentonite
- 2 teaspoons (28.8 g) acid blend
- 1 package (5 g) Wyeast Bordeaux wine yeast
- 20 Campden tablets or 2 teaspoons (12.4 g) potassium metabisulfite powder

1. Sanitize all equipment.

2. Put the concentrate, water, sugar, yeast nutrient, bentonite, and acid blend into a clean 6- or 7-gallon (23–27 L) fermentation container. Stir well, making sure that all ingredients are dissolved.

3. Dissolve the wine yeast in 1 cup (240 mL) of the above mixture, and let stand for 30 minutes, then add to fermenting vessel and stir well. Place in a cool, dry location.

4. Stir the mixture every day.

5. After 3 or 4 days, if there is no evidence of fermentation, warm the container to about 75°F (24°C) until bubbles appear. Stir the contents daily, and remove to a cool location when fermentation starts.

6. Fermentation is complete when bubbling stops and sediment forms in the bottom.

7. Allow the wine to settle for 2 to 3 weeks after fermentation is complete. Do not mix.

8. Sanitize a 5-gallon (19 L) glass carboy and add 5 Campden tablets (crushed to a powder) or ½ teaspoon (3.1 g) potassium metabisulfite powder.

9. Rack. Siphon clear wine off the top into the 5-gallon (19 L) carboy, being careful not to disturb the sediment. Discard sediment.

10. Rack the wine three or four more times over the next 5 to 6 months, or until the wine is crystal clear. When the wine clears, it is ready for bottling.

11. Sanitize 26 750-mL (25.4 oz) or 13 1.5-L (50.8 oz) bottles, fill them, and insert closures. Leave about ½ inch (1.3 cm) of space between cork and wine. Wait 6 months, then taste your wine. 🍇

RED WINE FROM PINOT NOIR WINE CONCENTRATE

This is the great red wine of Burgundy, France, and it's quickly becoming an American favorite. This recipe makes a rich, red wine, hearty in nature, smooth in flavor. The soft texture and dark color complement the flavors of berries, with a subtle raspberry undertone. It ages gracefully, developing a velvety texture. The wine is rich and round with notes of spice paired with a silky feel and a long, lingering finish. It is great with firm cheese, blackened fish, grilled salmon, and spiced pork.

Yield: 5 gallons (19 L)

- 1 can (96 oz; 2.8 L) Pinot Noir wine concentrate
- 5¾ cans (16.3 L) cold water
- 7½ cups (1.7 kg) sugar
- 3 teaspoons (8.8 g) yeast nutrient
- ⅓ ounce (9.5 g) bentonite
- 2 teaspoons (28.8 g) acid blend
- 1 package (5 g) Lalvin L2056 wine yeast
- 20 Campden tablets or 2 teaspoons (12.4 g) potassium metabisulfite powder

1. Sanitize all equipment.

2. Put the concentrate, water, sugar, yeast nutrient, bentonite, and acid blend into a clean 6- or 7-gallon (23–27 L) fermentation container. Stir well, making sure that all ingredients are dissolved.

3. Dissolve the wine yeast in 1 cup (240 mL) of the above mixture and let stand for 30 minutes, then add to fermenting vessel and stir well. Place in a cool, dry location.

4. Stir the mixture every day.

5. After 3 or 4 days, if there is no evidence of fermentation, warm the container to about 75°F (24°C) until bubbles appear. Stir the contents daily, and remove to a cool location when fermentation starts.

6. Fermentation is complete when bubbling stops and sediment forms in the bottom of the container. Specific gravity should read 1.000 or less.

7. Allow the wine to settle for 2 to 3 weeks after fermentation is complete. Do not mix.

8. Sanitize a 5-gallon (19 L) glass carboy and add 5 Campden tablets (crushed to a powder) or ½ teaspoon (3.1 g) potassium metabisulfite powder.

9. Rack. Siphon off the top clear wine into the 5-gallon (19 L) carboy, being careful not to disturb the sediment. Discard sediment.

10. Rack the wine three or four more times over the next 5 to 6 months, or until the wine is crystal clear. When the wine clears, it is ready for bottling.

11. Sanitize 26 750-mL (25.4 oz) or 13 1.5-L (50.8 oz) bottles, then fill them and insert closures. Leave about ½ inch (1.3 cm) of space between cork and wine. Wait 6 months, then taste your wine. 🍇

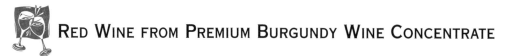

Red Wine from Premium Burgundy Wine Concentrate

This pleasant wine has a bouquet of sweet cherries accompanied by dusty tannins, which produces a lingering flavor. Medium in color, dry and crisp in the mouth, this is an early-drinking red wine with the rich flavors to complement a wide variety of foods, including cheese dishes, red meats, ham, and smoked salmon.

Yield: 5 gallons (19 L)

- 1 can (96 oz; 2.8 L) Premium Burgundy wine concentrate
- 5¾ cans (16.3 L) cold water
- 7½ cups (1.7 kg) sugar
- 3 teaspoons (8.8 g) yeast nutrient
- ⅓ ounce (9.5 g) bentonite
- 3 tablespoons (11.1 g) Oak-Mor
- 2 teaspoons (28.8 g) acid blend
- 1 package (5 g) Lallamand K1-V116 wine yeast
- 15 Campden tablets or 1½ teaspoons (9.3 g) potassium metabisulfite powder

1. Sanitize all equipment.

2. Put the concentrate, water, sugar, yeast nutrient, bentonite, acid blend, and Oak-Mor into a clean 6- or 7-gallon (23–27 L) fermentation container. Stir well, making sure that all ingredients are dissolved.

3. Dissolve the wine yeast in 1 cup (240 mL) of the above mixture and let stand for 30 minutes; then add to fermenting vessel and stir well. Move to a cool, dry location.

4. Stir the mixture every day.

5. After 3 or 4 days, if there is no evidence of fermentation, warm the container to about 75°F (24°C) until bubbles appear. Stir the contents daily, and remove to a cool location when fermentation starts.

6. Fermentation is complete when bubbling stops and sediment forms in the bottom of the container. Specific gravity should read 1.000 or less.

7. Allow the wine to settle for 2 to 3 weeks after fermentation is complete. Do not mix.

8. Sanitize a 5-gallon (19 L) glass carboy and add 5 Campden tablets (crushed to a powder) or ½ teaspoon (3.1 g) potassium metabisulfite powder to the container before racking.

9. Rack. Siphon off the top clear wine into the 5-gallon (19 L) glass carboy, being careful not to disturb the sediment. Discard sediment.

10. Rack the wine at least two more times in the next four months, using the above procedure. When the wine clears, it's ready for bottling.

11. Sanitize 26 750-mL (25.4 oz) or 13 1.5-L (50.8 oz) bottles, fill them, and insert closures. Leave about ½ inch (1.3 cm) of space between cork and wine. Wait 4 months, then taste your wine. 🍇

RED WINE FROM SPANISH RIOJA WINE CONCENTRATE

Rioja wines are unique and inviting. Dense purple in color, the wine shows flavors of cloves and anise. Different styles are created with light or heavy oaking. Vanilla and toast are evident in the finish. When consumed young, the wine seems somewhat closed, but patience will yield a beautiful wine. This is a substantial, earthy wine worth savoring. It's best with hearty dishes like paella, meat stews, most cheeses, tapas, and tomato pasta dishes.

Yield: 5 gallons (19 L)

- 1 can (96 oz; 2.8 L) Rioja wine concentrate
- 5¾ cans (16.3 L) cold water
- 8 cups (1.8 kg) sugar
- 3 teaspoons (8.8 g) yeast nutrient
- ⅓ ounce (9.5 g) bentonite
- 2 teaspoons (28.8 g) acid blend
- 1 package (5 g) Red Star Pasteur Red wine yeast
- 20 Campden tablets or 2 teaspoons (12.4 g) potassium metabisulfite powder

1. Sanitize all equipment.

2. Put the concentrate, water, sugar, yeast nutrient, bentonite, and acid blend into a clean 6- or 7-gallon (23–27 L) fermentation container. Stir well, making sure that all ingredients are dissolved.

3. Dissolve the wine yeast in 1 cup (240 mL) of the above mixture and let stand for 30 minutes, then add to fermenting vessel and stir well. Move to a cool, dry location.

4. Stir the mixture every day.

5. Fermentation should start in a day or two. If not, move the fermentation container to a warmer environment and shake vigorously.

6. Fermentation is complete when bubbling stops and sediment forms in the bottom of the container. Specific gravity should read 1.000 or less.

7. After the fermentation is completed, let wine sit for several weeks to settle. After fermentation, stop mixing.

8. Sanitize a 5-gallon (19 L) glass carboy and add 5 Campden tablets (crushed to a powder) or ½ teaspoon (3.1 g) potassium metabisulfite powder.

9. Rack. Siphon off top clear wine into the 5-gallon (19 L) carboy, being careful not to disturb the sediment. Discard sediment.

10. During the next 4 months, rack the wine at least three times, using the above racking procedure. When the wine clears, it is ready for bottling.

11. Sanitize 26 750-mL (25.4 oz) or 13 1.5-L (50.8 oz) bottles, fill them, and insert closures. Leave about ½ inch (1.3 cm) of space between cork and wine. Wait 4 months, then taste your wine. 🍇

RED WINE FROM RUBY CABERNET WINE CONCENTRATE

With many of the qualities of its cousin, the Cabernet Sauvignon, the Ruby Cabernet is a well-balanced wine showing colors of medium red in the glass. A selection of berry flavors, violets, and green pepper is also evident. Enjoyed young or with some age, the wine is an excellent choice for prime rib, steak, lamb, and hard cheeses. This variety has the potential to become a cult wine favorite.

Yield: 5 gallons (19 L)

- 1 can (96 oz; 2.8 L) Ruby Cabernet wine concentrate
- 5¾ cans (16.3 L) cold water
- 8 cups (1.8 kg) sugar
- 3 teaspoons (8.8 g) yeast nutrient
- ⅓ ounce (9.5 g) bentonite
- 2 teaspoons (28.8 g) acid blend
- 3 tablespoons (11.1 g) Oak-Mor
- 1 package (5 g) Red Star Pasteur Red wine yeast
- 20 Campden tablets or 2 teaspoons (12.4 g) potassium metabisulfite powder

1. Sanitize all equipment.

2. Put the concentrate, water, sugar, yeast nutrient, bentonite, acid blend, and Oak-Mor into a clean 6- or 7-gallon (23–27 L) fermentation container. Stir well, making sure that all ingredients are dissolved.

3. Dissolve the wine yeast in 1 cup (240 mL) of the above mixture and let stand for 30 minutes, then add to the fermentation vessel and stir well. Move to a cool, dry location.

4. Stir the mixture every day.

5. After 3 or 4 days, if there is no evidence of fermentation, warm the container to about 75°F (24°C) until bubbles appear. Stir the contents daily, and remove to a cool location when fermentation starts.

6. Fermentation is complete when bubbling stops and sediment forms in the bottom of the container.

7. After fermentation is completed, stop mixing the wine and let it settle for a few weeks.

8. Sanitize a 5-gallon (19 L) glass carboy and add 5 Campden tablets (crushed to a powder) or ½ teaspoon (3.1 g) potassium metabisulfite powder.

9. Rack. Siphon off the top clear wine into the 5-gallon (19 L) carboy, being careful not to disturb the sediment. Discard sediment.

10. Rack the wine twice more, using the above procedure, over the next 5 or 6 months until wine is crystal clear.

11. Sanitize 26 750-mL (25.4 oz) or 13 1.5-L (50.8 oz) bottles, then fill them and insert closures. Leave about ½ inch (1.3 cm) of space between cork and wine. Wait 4 months, then taste your wine. 🍇

RED WINE FROM ZINFANDEL WINE CONCENTRATE

This is America's great red wine grape. It is highly flavorful, and rich in color, aromas, and taste. Overtones of blackberry and pepper come to the front, and the wine finishes full in the mouth. Aging traditionally brings out the best with Zinfandel, but the varietal is well suited to a wide variety of styles. This wine goes well with spicy pastas, all garlic dishes, and stews.

Yield: 5 gallons (19 L)

- 1 can (96 oz; 2.8 L) Zinfandel wine concentrate
- 5¾ cans (16.3 L) cold water
- 7½ cups (1.7 kg) sugar
- 3 teaspoons (8.8 g) yeast nutrient
- ⅓ ounce (9.5 g) bentonite
- 2 teaspoons (28.8 g) acid blend
- 1 package (5 g) Gist-fermirouge wine yeast
- 20 Campden tablets or 2 teaspoons (12.4 g) potassium metabisulfite powder

1. Sanitize all equipment.

2. Put the concentrate, water, sugar, yeast nutrient, bentonite, and acid blend into a clean 6- or 7-gallon (23–27 L) fermentation container. Stir well, making sure that all ingredients are dissolved.

3. Dissolve the wine yeast in 1 cup (240 mL) of the above mixture, and let stand for 30 minutes, then add to fermentation vessel and stir well. Move to a cool, dry location.

4. Stir the mixture every day.

5. After 3 or 4 days, if there is no evidence of fermentation, warm the container to about 75°F (24°C) until bubbles appear. Stir the contents daily, and remove to a cool location when fermentation starts.

6. Fermentation is complete when bubbling stops and sediment forms in the bottom of the container. Specific gravity should read 1.000 or less.

7. After fermentation is completed, let wine sit for several weeks to settle. After fermentation, stop mixing.

8. Sanitize a 5-gallon (19 L) glass carboy and add 5 Campden tablets (crushed to a powder) or ½ teaspoon (3.1 g) potassium metabisulfite powder.

9. Rack. Siphon off the top clear wine into the 5-gallon (19 L) carboy, being careful not to disturb the sediment. Discard sediment.

10. Rack the wine three or four more times, using the above procedure, over the next 4 months until wine is crystal clear.

11. Sanitize 26 750-mL (25.4 oz) or 13 1.5-L (50.8 oz) bottles, fill them, and insert closures. Leave about ½ inch (1.3 cm) of space between cork and wine. Wait 4 months, then taste your wine. 🍇

RED WINE FROM ZINFANDEL BLUSH WINE CONCENTRATE

With a hint of rosé, this light Zinfandel is fruity and refreshingly reminiscent of candied raspberries as it rolls across the palate. It is an easy-drinking wine due to the ideal acid balance. This is a wine for immediate use, as it requires little aging. It has been the most popular wine in America for many years. Zinfandel blush is strictly a social wine, best served with finger foods.

Yield: 5 gallons (19 L)

1	can (96 oz; 2.8 L) Zinfandel Blush concentrate
5¾	cans (16.3 L) cold water
7	cups (1.7 kg) sugar
3	teaspoons (8.8 g) yeast nutrient
⅓	ounce (9.5 g) bentonite
2	teaspoons (28.8 g) acid blend
1	package (5 g) Red Star Côtes des Blancs wine yeast
15	Campden tablets or 1½ teasopons (9.3 g) potassium metabisulfite powder

1. Sanitize all equipment.

2. Put the concentrate, water, sugar, yeast nutrient, bentonite, and acid blend into a clean 6- or 7-gallon (23–27 L) fermentation container. Stir well, making sure that all ingredients are dissolved.

3. Dissolve the wine yeast in 1 cup (240 mL) of the above mixture and let stand for 30 minutes; then add to the fermentation vessel and stir well. Move to a cool, dry location.

4. Stir the mixture every day.

5. If after several days no bubbles are evident, move the fermentation vessel to a warmer environment and shake vigorously.

6. Fermentation is complete when bubbling stops and sediment forms in the bottom of the container. Specific gravity should read 1.000 or less.

7. After fermentation is completed, let wine sit for several weeks to settle. After fermentation, stop mixing.

8. Sanitize a 5-gallon (19 L) glass carboy and add 5 Campden tablets (crushed to a powder) or ½ teaspoon (3.1 g) potassium metabisulfite powder to the container. Repeat at each racking.

10. Rack. Siphon off the top clear wine into the 5-gallon (19 L) carboy, being careful not to disturb the sediment. Discard sediment.

10. Rack the wine at least two more times in the next 4 months, using the above procedure. When the wine is crystal clear, it is ready for bottling.

11. Sanitize 26 750-mL (25.4 oz) or 13 1.5-L (50.8 oz) bottles, then fill them and insert closures. Leave about ½ inch (1.3 cm) of space between cork and wine. Wait 3 months, then taste your wine. 🍇

Red Wine from Concord Grape Concentrate

This popular eastern and northern United States native variety, also a favorite in Canada, is known for its heartiness and productivity. It is used for making sweet kosher wine. Concord has also been made as a dry red table wine with some success. It makes a fruity, quaffing-type wine.

Yield: 5 gallons (19 L)

- 1 can (64 oz; 1.9 L) Concord Grape concentrate
- 9 cans (4.5 gal; 17 L) water
- 8 cups (1.8 kg) sugar
- 6 ounces (170 g) dried elderberries
- 3 teaspoons (8.8 g) yeast nutrient
- 2 teaspoons (28.8 g) acid blend
- 1 package (5 g) Gist-brocades Fermiblanc yeast
- 20 Campden tablets or 2 teaspoons (12.4 g) potassium metabisulfite powder

1. Sanitize all equipment.

2. Put the concentrate, water, sugar, berries, yeast nutrient, and acid blend into a clean 6- or 7-gallon (23–27 L) fermentation container. Stir well, making sure all ingredients are dissolved.

3. Dissolve the yeast in 1 cup (240 mL) of the above mixture, then add to fermentation vessel and mix well. Move to a cool, dry location.

4. Stir vessel once a day until fermentation starts, then stop.

5. After 3 or 4 days, if there are no bubbles or gas (evidence of fermentation), warm the container to about 75°F (24°C) until surface bubbles appear. Continue stirring the contents once a day. Remove to a cool location as soon as fermentation starts.

6. Fermentation is complete when bubbling stops and sediment forms in the bottom of the container. Specific gravity should read 1.000 or less.

7. When fermentation is complete, press out the elderberries, stop mixing, and let the wine settle for 2 weeks.

8. Sanitize a 5-gallon (19 L) glass carboy and add 5 Campden tablets (crushed to a powder) or ½ teaspoon (3.1 g) potassium metabisulfate powder before racking.

9. Rack. Siphon off the top clear wine into the 5-gallon (19 L) carboy, being careful not to disturb the sediment. Discard sediment.

10. Rack again in 3 months. When the wine is clear and stable, it is ready for bottling.

11. Sanitize 26 750-mL (25.4 oz) bottles, fill them, and insert closures. Wait 3 months, then drink your wine. For sweeter wines, it is recommended that you add an instant wine conditioner (see page 259) before bottling.

WINE FROM JUICES 5

Let us drink the juice divine,
the gift of Bacchus, god of wine.

—Anacreon, Greek poet (c. 570–c. 480 B.C.)

TIME AND SPACE CONSTRAINTS make purchasing, crushing, and pressing fresh grapes an impractical option for many home winemakers. Happily, as with kits and concentrates, juices provide a wonderful alternative, and top-quality varieties are available from all of the world's great grape regions.

Thanks to recent technological advances, juice producers now can stabilize their products, so that the juices will retain their quality for 2 or more years. Consequently, you're able to purchase juices whenever it's convenient for you to make wine.

WAYS PRODUCERS PRESERVE JUICES

Grape producers can preserve the quality of the juices they sell in a number of different ways. Some methods are better than others, and this knowledge will help you as you shop for wine juice for the various recipes.

FREEZING

This method is particularly popular in the United States. The grapes are processed as soon as they're picked. Grapes for white wines are crushed and pressed and the juice is poured into containers — the 5-gallon (19 L) size seems to be the most popular — and blast-frozen. The process is a little different with grapes for red wines. For these grapes, skins and pulp are frozen along with the juice (see the section on red wines in chapter 1).

In either case, the juice is analyzed for sugar and acid counts and the results are listed on the container. These figures tend to be accurate, and, for the most part, no adjustments are necessary prior to inoculating the juice with yeast in order to start the fermentation process. Frozen juices retain their quality indefinitely, provided they remain frozen!

PASTEURIZATION

This method is used throughout Europe. Likewise, Chilean, Australian, and South African grape growers pasteurize. A number of Canadian companies have also had great success with it. Pasteurized juices have a multiyear shelf life, and the acid-sugar balances are such that the numbers on the container can be trusted, so you can inoculate the juice with yeast whenever you're ready to begin making wine.

SULFITED JUICES

This approach to stabilization tends to be less effective than freezing or pasteurizing juices. In fact, the juice often begins to ferment on its own, resulting in a poor-quality product.

It all starts out in a logical fashion. The producers add large amount of sulfites to fresh juice, and then either keep the containers chilled or at least store them in a cool area. So far, so good. The problems begin when the juice is shipped in nonrefrigerated vehicles and stored at room temperature in wine supply stores. Once the heat rises, fermentation begins. A hissing container clearly indicates that this has happened. Simply put: Don't purchase sulfited juice if you can hear it! You should also double-check the sugar/acid numbers on the containers of "quiet" juices, as they're likely to be inaccurate. In order to extract more color, juices for red wines are also subjected to a heating process prior to adding sulfites. This makes a less desirable juice than one that has been either frozen or pasteurized.

CHOOSING A JUICE

We urge you to spend a little more money and purchase frozen or pasteurized juices. They're well worth the expense, and you've already saved money on equipment needed for winemaking from fresh grapes because you won't need to buy a stemmer-crusher and a winepress.

Frozen juices from California, Washington, and Oregon have been used to make many award-winning wines in national competitions. Every home winemaker should consider using frozen juices at some point in his or her career.

Pasteurization enables you to make authentic wines from all of the great grape-growing regions outside of North America. We've had a great deal of success with pasteurized Chilean juices in particular. So if you've tried a foreign wine and really liked it, shop around. Chances are, you'll be able to purchase the juice that will allow you to make it yourself.

EQUIPMENT AND INGREDIENTS NEEDED FOR JUICE WINES

You'll need some basic equipment to make wine with your juice. It will not be an expensive investment. For more detailed information on this equipment, see chapter 1.

◆ 1 (5-gallon; 19 L) glass or plastic carboy
◆ 2 (1-gallon; 3.8 L) jugs
◆ Siphon tube
◆ Stirring spoon or paddle
◆ Fermentation locks (air locks)
◆ Carboy bungs (rubber stoppers)
◆ Screened funnel
◆ Measuring cup
◆ Hydrometer (saccharometer)
◆ Hydrometer jar
◆ Bottles
◆ Corks
◆ Potassium metabisulfite powder or Campden tablets
◆ Fining agents for white wines
◆ Commercial wine yeast
◆ Yeast nutrient
◆ Oak-Mor or another oak flavoring (optional, depending on style)
◆ Acid titration kit
◆ Acid blend
◆ Sugar

SANITIZING EQUIPMENT

The need to sanitize all equipment that comes in contact with your wine cannot be overstated. Here is a method we use with success.

Potassium metabisulfite powder
Hot water
Jug

1. Put 3 tablespoons (56 g) of potassium metabisulfite into a 1-liter (33.8 oz) jug of hot water — 85°F (29°C) — to make a reusable sanitizing solution. It will last up to 6 months if kept tightly sealed. (Store at room temperature.)
2. Rinse all equipment thoroughly in the solution.
3. After sanitizing, rinse with cold water.

MAKING WINE FROM JUICES

Because juices are fresh and in a natural state, they are much more preferable to using chemically altered concentrates and kits for winemaking. And what you gain in freshness, you don't lose in ease. The procedure for making wine from juice is pretty straightforward, and similar to making wine from a kit or a concentrate.

DEFROSTING FROZEN JUICE

If you are using frozen juices for your wine-making, you'll need to thaw them first. It is ideal to defrost frozen juice at room temperature — 60° to 70°F (16°–21°C). Thaw only the amount of juice you'll need for your recipe, as defrosting and then refreezing leftover juice isn't recommended. (This can result in some bacteria problems.) After your juice is thawed to room temperature, use the same winemaking procedures for pasteurized juice that follow.

PREPARING THE MUST AND YEAST

The following procedure is the basic method of making a 5-gallon (19 L) batch of wine using pasteurized or thawed frozen juices.

1. Pour approximately 4 gallons (15 L) of the must into a sterilized carboy. The "seedlike" sediment (bititrates) need not be poured into the vessel and can be excluded by using a strainer or screened funnel when pouring into your vessel. Divide the remaining juice into two equal parts and pour into two 1-gallon (3.8 L) jugs.

2. Take a specific gravity reading using the hydrometer (see chapter 2 for details on using a hydrometer). The reading should be anywhere from 1.070 to 1.092.

3. In a large bowl, make a yeast starter by mixing approximately 4 ounces (120 mL) of juice and 4 ounces (120 mL) of lukewarm water and sprinkling 1 package (5 g) of commercial wine yeast into this solution. Allow the yeast to proliferate for about 30 minutes at room temperature. Then

KEEP RECORDS!

Keep records of everything you do when you make wine. That way, you'll know what works and you'll be able to go back and replicate past successes. (See pages 239 and 240 for sample forms.)

pour 6 ounces (180 mL) of this mixture into the carboy and 1 ounce (30 mL) into each of the 1 gallon (3.8 L) jugs. Red juices require the addition of pectic enzyme at this point to aid in later clarification.

FERMENTATION

To provide the yeast with the oxygen it needs to multiply, do the following.

1. Place only a paper towel in the neck of the bottles for the first 2 or 3 days, until the must is seen actively "bubbling."

2. Once bubbling occurs, place air locks, filled with fresh water, in the rubber bungs on the bottles for the rest of the fermentation. Fermentation will continue at 71°F (22°C) anywhere from 7 to 12 days.

3. Start to monitor the progress with the hydrometer after 7 days. When the specific gravity is below 1.000, proceed to the next step. If the wine takes longer than a week to 10 days, it is a good idea to gently "swish" the carboy and the jugs to move the viable yeast around the must inside.

STABILIZE AND CLARIFY

Once the specific gravity is below 1.000, siphon the wine from its sediment into sterilized pails or another sterilized carboy. This procedure is called racking. Add 5 crushed Campden tablets or ½ teaspoon (3.1 g) potassium metabisulfite powder to help stabilize the wine by halting oxidation and bacterial infection. Remove and discard any leftover sediment, then sanitize the fermentation containers in preparation for reuse. The wine should now be siphoned back into these containers, this time filling them right up to the top. A smaller container, such as a wine bottle, will probably be necessary in place of the gallon jugs. This smaller bottle must also be filled to the top. Add fresh water to the air locks. Place the wine in a cold spot, like a garage or root cellar, but not lower than 32°F (0°C).

Let the wine sit in the cold place for at least 3 weeks. If it stays longer, it should be racked again every 3 to 4 weeks. Always add the 5 crushed Campden tablets or the ½ teaspoon (3.1 g) of potassium metabisulfite powder with each racking to halt oxidation and bacterial infection. After the fourth racking, the wine should be clear enough to bottle.

Red wine will clarify in about 6 months; white can be more difficult to clarify on its own. If you desire your white wine to clarify faster, use gelatin and kieselsol finings. First, rack the wine, sanitize the containers, and follow the instructions on the package labels for procedure and quantities. With the finings, your white wine, stored in a cold temperature, will clear in an additional 3 weeks.

BOTTLE

When the wine is clear, it is ready to bottle. Taste the wine and sweeten it, if so desired. Remember to add another 5 crushed Campden tablets or ½ teaspoon (3.1 g) potassium metabisulfite powder to stabilize the wine just prior to bottling. Push-top corks are the easiest and most cost-effective option for beginners. With traditional corks, a hand-corking device will give you quite a workout. If you are committed to the hobby, you might want to invest in the more expensive table-style corking machine, which allows you to use traditional corks without any great strain. Age the wine according to desired varietal characteristics.

WHITE WINE FROM CHARDONNAY JUICE

Chardonnay is the great white Burgundy and the most popular white wine in North America. It can be made in a wide variety of styles, and they are all enjoyed with great enthusiasm. The finished Chardonnay goes well with an assortment of foods, including chicken, fish, and some pasta dishes. A little oak flavoring seems to bring out the complex characteristics of the wine.

Yield: 5 gallons (19 L)

- 5 gallons (19 L) Chardonnay grape juice
- 1 package (5 g) Red Star Montrachet yeast
- 3 tablespoons (11.1 g) Oak-Mor
- 3 teaspoons (8.8 g) yeast nutrient
- 20 Campden tablets or 2 teaspoons (12.4 g) potassium metabisulfite powder

1. Sanitize all equipment.

2. Through a screened funnel, pour approximately 4 gallons (15 L) of juice into a 5-gallon (19 L) carboy and the remaining gallon (3.8 L) of juice into two 1-gallon (3.8 L) jugs.

3. Test for acid and sugar and make adjustments, if necessary. When the specific gravity is 1.070–1.092, make a yeast starter by pouring approximately 4 ounces (120 mL) of juice and 4 ounces (120 mL) of lukewarm water into a bowl. Sprinkle the yeast, Oak-Mor, and yeast nutrient into the solution, allowing it to proliferate for about 30 minutes. Add 6 ounces (180 mL) of the yeast starter to the carboy and 1 ounce (30 mL) of the starter to each of the 1-gallon (3.8 L) containers. Swish the containers to aid in the mixing.

4. Place a sheet of paper toweling, a wad of cotton, or a paper napkin into the necks of the containers. Fermentation will start in 2 or 3 days. When the must is seen actively "bubbling," replace the paper or cotton stoppers with air locks, filled with clean water, for the rest of the fermentation.

5. Fermentation will continue for 7 to 12 days. Start to monitor the progress with the hydrometer after 7 days. When the specific gravity is below 1.000 (that is, 0.995 or lower), proceed to the next step. If it's above 1.000, allow the wine to ferment longer until it reaches a specific gravity below 1.000.

6. Once the specific gravity is below 1.000, siphon the wine from the three containers into a sanitized carboy. This procedure is called racking. Stabilize the wine by adding 5 Campden

tablets (crushed to a powder) or ½ teaspoon (3.1 g) potassium metabisulfite powder. Then fill the container up to the top. Place the wine in a cool spot (such as a garage or root cellar).

7. Let the wine sit in this cool location for 3 to 4 weeks. If it stays longer, rack again every 3 to 4 weeks. Always add the crushed Campden tablets or the potassium metabisulfite powder with each racking to halt oxidation and bacterial infection. After the fourth racking, the wine should be clear enough to bottle.

8. If the wine does not clear, use gelatin or kieselsol finings. (If using gelatin or kieselsol, follow directions for procedure and quantities.) When fining, the wine will need an additional 3 to 4 weeks to clear.

9. When the wine is clear, it is ready to bottle. Taste the wine and adjust its sweetness, if desired, then bottle. Age for at least 6 months. White wines from juices are at their best between 6 months and 1 year in the bottle. 🍇

White Wine from Chenin Blanc Juice

This is one of the most versatile varieties available to the home winemaker. It can be made in a dry, off-dry, or sweet type of wine. Each variety has its advantages. Native to the Loire Valley in France, the Chenin Blanc now flourishes in California and yet it is unappreciated and has lost some popularity. The Chenin Blanc, which features great fruit and acid balance, is lower in cost to the home winemaker and should be considered for its blending possibilities also.

Yield: 5 gallons (19 L)

5 gallons (19 L) Chenin Blanc grape juice
1 package (5 g) Wyeast Chablis yeast
3 teaspoons (8.8 g) yeast nutrient
20 Campden tablets or 2 teaspoons (12.4 g) potasium metabisulfite powder

1. Sanitize all equipment.

2. Through a screened funnel, pour approximately 4 gallons (15 L) of juice into a 5-gallon (19 L) carboy and the remaining gallon (3.8 L) of juice into two 1-gallon (3.8 L) jugs.

3. Test for acid and sugar and make adjustments, if necessary. When the specific gravity is 1.070–1.092, make a yeast starter by pouring approximately 4 ounces (120 mL) of juice and 4 ounces (120 mL) of lukewarm water into a bowl. Sprinkle the yeast and the yeast nutrient into the solution, allowing it to proliferate for about 30 minutes. Add 6 ounces (180 mL) of the yeast starter to the carboy and 1 ounce (30 mL) of the starter to each of the 1-gallon (3.8 L) containers. Swish the containers to aid in the mixing.

4. Place a sheet of paper toweling, a wad of cotton, or a paper napkin into the necks of the containers. Fermentation will start in 2 or 3 days. When the must is seen actively "bubbling," replace the paper or cotton stoppers with air locks, filled with clean water, for the rest of the fermentation.

5. Fermentation will continue for 7 to 12 days. Start to monitor the progress with the hydrometer after 7 days. When the specific gravity is below 1.000 (that is, 0.995 or lower), proceed to the next step. If it's above 1.000, allow the wine to ferment longer until it reaches a specific gravity below 1.000.

6. Once the specific gravity is below 1.000, siphon the wine from the three containers into a sanitized carboy. This procedure is called racking. Stabilize the wine by adding 5 Campden tablets (crushed to a powder) or ½ teaspoon (3.1 g) potassium metabisulfite powder. Then fill the container up to the top. Place the wine in a cool spot (such as a garage or root cellar).

7. Let wine sit in this cool location for 3 to 4 weeks. If it stays longer, rack again every 3 to 4 weeks. Always add the crushed Campden tablets or the potassium metabisulfite powder with each racking to halt oxidation and bacterial infection. After the fourth racking, the wine should be clear enough to bottle.

8. If the wine does not clear, use gelatin or kieselsol finings. (If using gelatin or kieselsol, follow directions for procedure and quantities.) When fining, the wine will need an additional 3 to 4 weeks to clear.

9. When the wine is clear, it is ready to bottle. Taste the wine and adjust its sweetness, if desired, then bottle. Age for at least 6 months. White wines from juices are at their best between 6 months and 1 year in the bottle. 🍇

WHITE WINE FROM FRENCH COLOMBARD GRAPE JUICE

This was traditionally a blending grape, but its flavors are really too pronounced to bury. Crisp, acidic, and extremely fragrant in its youth, it is an enjoyable wine to make and drink. Citrus fruit and melon flavors are dominant, and the aroma is reminiscent of linden and hyacinth. This wine is well suited to many fish and chicken dishes, and goes well with many hard cheeses.

Yield: 5 gallons (19 L)

- 5 gallons (19 L) Colombard grape juice
- 1 package (5 g) Lallamand K1-V116 yeast
- 3 teaspoons (8.8 g) yeast nutrient
- 3 tablespoons (11.1 g) Oak-Mor (optional)
- 20 Campden tablets or 2 teaspoons (12.4 g) potassium metabisulfite powder

1. Sanitize all equipment.

2. Through a screened funnel, pour approximately 4 gallons (15 L) of juice into a 5-gallon (19 L) carboy and the remaining gallon (3.8 L) of juice into two 1-gallon (3.8 L) jugs.

3. Test for acid and sugar and make adjustments, if necessary. When the specific gravity is 1.070–1.092, make a yeast starter by pouring approximately 4 ounces (120 mL) of juice and 4 ounces (120 mL) of lukewarm water into a bowl. Sprinkle the yeast, yeast nutrient, and the optional Oak-Mor into the solution, allowing it to proliferate for about 30 minutes. Add 6 ounces

(180 mL) of the yeast starter to the carboy and 1 ounce (30 mL) of the starter to each of the 1-gallon (3.8 L) containers. Swish the containers to aid in the mixing.

4. Place a paper towel, a wad of cotton, or a paper napkin into the necks of the containers. Fermentation will start in 2 or 3 days. When the must is seen actively "bubbling," replace the paper or cotton stoppers with air locks, filled with clean water, for the rest of the fermentation.

5. Fermentation will continue for 7 to 12 days. Start to monitor the progress with the hydrometer after 7 days. When the specific gravity is below 1.000 (that is, 0.995 or lower), proceed to the next step. If it's above 1.000, allow the wine to ferment longer, until it reaches a specific gravity below 1.000.

6. Once the specific gravity is below 1.000, siphon the wine from the three containers into a sanitized carboy. This procedure is called racking. Stabilize the wine by adding 5 Campden

tablets (crushed to a powder) or ½ teaspoon (3.1 g) potassium metabisulfite powder. Then fill the container up to the top. Place the wine in a cool spot (such as a garage or root cellar).

7. Let wine sit in this cool location for 3 to 4 weeks. If it stays longer, rack again every 3 to 4 weeks. Always add the crushed Campden tablets or the potassium metabisulfite powder with each racking to halt oxidation and bacterial infection. After the fourth racking, the wine should be clear enough to bottle.

8. If the wine does not clear, use gelatin or kieselsol finings. (If using gelatin or kieselsol, follow directions for procedure and quantities.) When fining, the wine will need an additional 3 to 4 weeks to clear.

9. When the wine is clear, it is ready to bottle. Taste the wine and adjust its sweetness, if desired, then bottle. Age for at least 6 months. White wines from juices are at their best between 6 months and 1 year in the bottle. 🍇

 # WHITE WINE FROM GEWÜRZTRAMINER GRAPE JUICE

Gewürz is German for "spicy," and traminer is the name of a white grape variety. When we merge the two words — Gewürztraminer — we have a spicy traminer, or a pleasant, aromatic wine that is easy to drink. The wine peaks with its aromas and flavors exploding on the palate and an off-dry finish. An ideal summer luncheon wine, Gewürztraminer goes well with Thai and Asian foods.

Yield: 5 gallons (19 L)

- 5 gallons (19 L) Gewürztraminer grape juice
- 1 package (5 g) Red Star Côtes des Blancs yeast
- 3 teaspoons (8.8 g) yeast nutrient
- 20 Campden tablets or 2 teaspoons (12.4 g) potassium metabisulfite powder

1. Sanitize all equipment.

2. Through a screened funnel, pour approximately 4 gallons (15 L) of juice into a 5-gallon (19 L) carboy and the remaining gallon (3.8 L) of juice into two 1-gallon (3.8 L) jugs.

3. Test for acid and sugar and make adjustments, if necessary. When the specific gravity is

1.070–1.092, make a yeast starter by pouring approximately 4 ounces (120 mL) of juice and 4 ounces (120 mL) of lukewarm water into a bowl. Sprinkle the yeast and the yeast nutrient into the solution, allowing it to proliferate for about 30 minutes. Add 6 ounces (180 mL) of the yeast starter to the carboy and 1 ounce (30 mL) of the starter to each of the 1-gallon (3.8 L) containers. Swish the containers to aid in the mixing.

4. Place a sheet of paper toweling, a wad of cotton, or a paper napkin into the necks of the containers. Fermentation will start in 2 or 3 days. When the must is seen actively "bubbling," replace the paper or cotton stoppers with air locks, filled with clean water, for the rest of the fermentation.

5. Fermentation will continue for 7 to 12 days. Start to monitor the progress with the hydrometer after 7 days. When the specific gravity is below 1.000 (that is, 0.995 or lower), proceed to the next step. If it's above 1.000, allow the wine to ferment longer, until it reaches a specific gravity below 1.000.

6. Once the specific gravity is below 1.000, siphon the wine from the three containers into a sanitized carboy. This procedure is called racking. Stabilize the wine by adding 5 Campden tablets (crushed to a powder) or ½ teaspoon (3.1 g) potassium metabisulfite powder. Then fill the container up to the top. Place the wine in a cool spot (such as a garage or root cellar).

7. Let wine sit in this cool location for 3 to 4 weeks. If it stays longer, rack again every 3 to 4 weeks. Always add the crushed Campden tablets or the potassium metabisulfite powder with each racking to halt oxidation and bacterial infection. After the fourth racking, the wine should be clear enough to bottle.

8. If the wine does not clear, use gelatin or kieselsol finings. (If using gelatin or kieselsol, follow directions for procedure and quantities.) When fining, the wine will need an additional 3 to 4 weeks to clarify.

9. When the wine is clear, it is ready to bottle. Taste the wine and adjust its sweetness, if desired, then bottle. Age for at least 6 months. White wines from juices are at their best between 6 months and 1 year in the bottle.

WHITE WINE FROM JOHANNISBERG RIESLING GRAPE JUICE

This German-style wine has a clean, tart flavor. Fruity, yet floral, the wine has a full-bodied texture. A little oaking brings out an exciting bouquet and flavor. It can be made in a dry or medium-dry style without losing any quality or complexity. Every wine cellar should stock a few bottles of Johannisberg Riesling. Pair it with Asian and Tex-Mex dishes.

Yield: 5 gallons (19 L)

5 gallons (19 L) Johannisberg Riesling grape juice
1 package (5 g) Red Star Côtes des Blanc yeast
3 teaspoons (8.8 g) yeast nutrient
3 tablespoons (11.1 g) Oak-Mor (optional)
20 Campden tablets or 2 teaspoons (12.4 g) potassium metabisulfite powder

1. Sanitize all equipment.

2. Through a screened funnel, pour approximately 4 gallons (15 L) of juice into a 5-gallon (19 L) carboy and the remaining gallon (3.8 L) of juice into two 1-gallon (3.8 L) jugs.

3. Test for acid and sugar and make adjustments, if necessary. When the specific gravity is 1.070–1.092, make a yeast starter by pouring approximately 4 ounces (120 mL) of juice and 4 ounces (120 mL) of lukewarm water into a bowl. Sprinkle the yeast, yeast nutrient, and the optional Oak-Mor into the solution, allowing it to proliferate for about 30 minutes. Add 6 ounces (180 mL) of the yeast starter to the carboy and 1 ounce (30 mL) of the starter to each of the 1-gallon (3.8 L) containers. Swish the containers to aid in the mixing.

4. Place a sheet of paper toweling, a wad of cotton, or a paper napkin into the necks of the containers. Fermentation will start in 2 or 3 days. When the must is seen actively "bubbling," replace the paper or cotton stoppers with air locks, filled with clean water, for the rest of the fermentation.

5. Fermentation will continue for 7 to 12 days. Start to monitor the progress with the hydrometer after 7 days. When the specific gravity is below 1.000 (that is, 0.995 or lower), proceed to the next step. If it's above 1.000, allow the wine to ferment longer, until it reaches a specific gravity below 1.000.

6. Once the specific gravity is below 1.000, siphon the wine from the three containers into a sanitized carboy. This procedure is called

racking. Stabilize the wine by adding 5 Campden tablets (crushed to a powder) or ½ teaspoon (3.1 g) potassium metabisulfite powder. Then fill the container up to the top. Place the wine in a cool spot (such as a garage or root cellar).

7. Let wine sit in this cool location for 3 to 4 weeks. If it stays loner, rack again every 3 to 4 weeks. Always add the crushed Campden tablets or the potassium metabisulfite powder with each racking to halt oxidation and bacterial infection. After the fourth racking, the wine should be clear enough to bottle.

8. If the wine does not clear, use gelatin or kieselsol finings. (If using gelatin or kieselsol, follow directions for procedure and quantities.) When fining, the wine will need an additional 3 to 4 weeks to clear.

9. When the wine is clear, it is time to bottle. Taste the wine and adjust its sweetness, if desired, then bottle. Age for at least 6 months. White wines from juices are at their best between 6 months and 1 year in the bottle.

WHITE WINE FROM MORIO MUSKAT GRAPE JUICE

The Morio Muskat grape is a cross between Silvaner and Pinot Blanc (Weisser Burgunder) vines. The name is derived from its original cultivator, Peter Morio. The wines from this juice are easily recognized by their pithy bouquet, reminiscent of muscat; their pleasant acidity; and definite taste. This juice comes from Germany and offers an opportunity to make a pleasant, easy-to-drink wine, great for summer quaffing and a good match for most Asian dishes.

Yield: 5 gallons (19 L)

- 5 gallons (19 L) Morio Muskat grape juice
- 1 package (5 g) Red Star Côtes des Blancs yeast
- 3 teaspoons (8.8 g) yeast nutrient
- 20 Campden tablets or 2 teaspoons (12.4 g) potassium metabisulfite powder

1. Sanitize all equipment.

2. Through a screened funnel, pour approximately 4 gallons (15 L) of juice into a 5-gallon (19 L) carboy and the remaining gallon (3.8 L) of juice into two 1-gallon (3.8 L) jugs.

3. Test for acid and sugar balance and make adjustments, if necessary. When the specific gravity is 1.070–1.092, make a yeast starter by pouring approximately 4 ounces (120 mL) of juice and 4 ounces (120 mL) of lukewarm water into a bowl. Sprinkle the yeast and the yeast nutrient into the solution, allowing it to proliferate for about 30 minutes. Add 6 ounces (180 mL) of the yeast starter to the carboy and 1 ounce (30 mL) of the starter to each of the 1-gallon (3.8 L) containers. Swish the containers to aid in the mixing.

4. Place a sheet of paper toweling, a wad of cotton, or a paper napkin into the necks of the containers. Fermentation will start in 2 or 3 days. When the must is seen actively "bubbling," replace the paper or cotton stoppers with air locks, filled with clean water, for the rest of the fermentation.

5. Fermentation will continue for 7 to 12 days. Start to monitor the progress with the hydrometer after 7 days. When the specific gravity is below 1.000 (that is, 0.995 or lower), proceed to the next step. If it's above 1.000, allow the wine to ferment longer, until it reaches a specific gravity below 1.000.

6. Once the specific gravity is below 1.000, siphon the wine from the three containers into a sanitized carboy. This procedure is called racking. Stabilize the wine by adding 5 Campden tablets (crushed to a powder) or ½ teaspoon (3.1 g) potassium metabisulfite powder. Then fill the container up to the top. Place the wine in a cool spot (such as a garage or root cellar).

7. Let wine sit in this cool location for 3 to 4 weeks. If it stays longer, rack again every 3 to 4 weeks. Always add the crushed Campden tablets or the potassium metabisulfite powder with each racking to halt oxidation and bacterial infection. After the fourth racking, the wine should be clear enough to bottle.

8. If the wine does not clear, use gelatin or kieselsol finings. (If using gelatin or kieselsol, follow directions for procedure and quantities.) When fining, the wine will need an additional 3 to 4 weeks to clarify.

9. When the wine is clear, it is time to bottle. Taste the wine and adjust its sweetness, if desired, then bottle. Age for at least 6 months. White wines from juices are at their best between 6 months and 1 year in the bottle. 🍇

White Wine from Pinot Blanc Grape Juice

A cousin, in flavor, to the popular Chardonnay, this grape is often used as a Chardonnay substitute in commercial blends and sparkling wines. Common in the Alsace and other northern regions of France, Pinot Blanc has a pale straw color. The wine is soft, well balanced, with a peachy flavor and overtones of marshmallow. This is an ideal accompaniment to poultry, pasta in cream sauce, and soft cheeses.

Yield: 5 gallons (19 L)

5	gallons (19 L) Pinot Blanc grape juice
1	package (5 g) Red Star Montrachet yeast
3	teaspoons (8.8 g) yeast nutrient
3	tablespoons (11.1 g) Oak-Mor (optional)
20	Campden tablets or 2 teaspoons (12.4 g) potassium metabisulfite powder

1. Sanitize all equipment.

2. Through a screened funnel, pour approximately 4 gallons (15 L) of juice into a 5-gallon (19 L) carboy and the remaining gallon (3.8 L) of juice into two 1-gallon (3.8 L) jugs.

3. Test for acid and sugar and make adjustments, if necessary. When the specific gravity is 1.070–1.092, make a yeast starter by pouring approximately 4 ounces (120 mL) of juice and 4 ounces (120 mL) of lukewarm water into a bowl. Sprinkle the yeast, the yeast nutrient, and the optional Oak-Mor into the solution, allowing it to proliferate for about 30 minutes. Add 6 ounces (180 mL) of the yeast starter to the carboy and 1 ounce (30 mL) of the starter to each of the 1-gallon (3.8 L) containers. Swish the containers to aid in the mixing.

4. Place a sheet of paper toweling, a wad of cotton, or a paper napkin into the necks of the containers. Fermentation will start in 2 or 3 days. When the must is seen actively "bubbling," replace the paper or cotton stoppers with air locks, filled with clean water, for the rest of the fermentation.

5. The fermentation will continue for 7 to 12 days. Start to monitor the progress with the hydrometer after 7 days. When the specific gravity is below 1.000 (that is, 0.995 or lower), proceed to the next step. If it's above 1.000, allow the wine to ferment longer, until it reaches a specific gravity below 1.000.

6. Once the specific gravity is below 1.000, siphon the wine from the three containers into a sanitized carboy. This procedure is called racking. Stabilize the wine by adding 5 Campden tablets (crushed to a powder) or ½ teaspoon (3.1 g) potassium metabisulfite powder. Then fill the container up to the top. Place the wine in a cool spot (such as a garage or root cellar).

7. Let wine sit in this cool location for 3 to 4 weeks. If it stays longer, rack again every 3 to 4 weeks. Always add the crushed Campden tablets or the potassium metabisulfite powder with each racking to halt oxidation and bacterial infection. After the fourth racking, the wine should be clear enough to bottle.

8. If the wine does not clear, use gelatin or kieselsol finings. (If using gelatin or kieselsol, follow directions for procedure and quantities.) When fining, the wine will need an additional 3 to 4 weeks to clear.

9. When the wine is clear, it is ready to bottle. Taste the wine and adjust its sweetness, if desired, then bottle. Age for at least 6 months. White wines from juices are at their best between 6 months and 1 year in the bottle. 🍇

WHITE WINE FROM PINOT GRIS GRAPE JUICE

Also known as Pinot Grigio, this grape is available from several European countries and the United States and Canada. The straw-colored wine is dry with overtones of green melon leading to a crisp, clean finish. A bouquet of honey and herbs completes the complexity. It is ideal with fish, grilled chicken, veal scaloppine, and pasta in cream sauce.

Yield: 5 gallons (19 L)

5 gallons (19 L) Pinot Gris grape juice
1 package (5 g) Red Star Premier Cuvée yeast
3 teaspoons (8.8 g) yeast nutrient
20 Campden tablets or 2 teaspoons (12.4 g) potassium metabisulfite powder

1. Sanitize all equipment.

2. Through a screened funnel, pour approximately 4 gallons (15 L) of juice into a 5-gallon (19 L) carboy and the remaining gallon (3.8 L) of juice into two 1-gallon (3.8 L) jugs.

3. Test for sugar and acid and make adjustments, if necessary. When specific gravity is 1.070–1.092, make a yeast starter by pouring approximately 4 ounces (120 mL) of juice and 4 ounces (120 mL) of lukewarm water into a bowl. Sprinkle the yeast and the yeast nutrient into the solution, allowing it to proliferate for about 30 minutes. Then add this solution directly into the juice. Add 6 ounces (180 mL) of the yeast starter to the carboy and 1 ounce (30 mL) of the starter to each of the 1-gallon (3.8 L) containers. Swish the containers to aid in the mixing.

4. Place a sheet of paper toweling, a wad of cotton, or a paper napkin into the necks of the containers. Fermentation will start in 2 or 3 days. When the must is seen actively "bubbling," replace the paper or cotton stoppers with air locks, filled with clean water, for the rest of the fermentation.

5. Fermentation will continue for 7 to 12 days. Start to monitor the progress with the hydrometer after 7 days. When the specific gravity is below 1.000 (that is, 0.995 or lower), proceed to the next step. If it's above 1.000, allow the wine to ferment longer, until it reaches a specific gravity below 1.000.

6. Once the specific gravity is below 1.000, siphon the wine from the three containers into a sanitized carboy. This procedure is called racking. Stabilize the wine by adding 5 Campden tablets (crushed to a powder) or ½ teaspoon (3.1 g) potassium metabisulfite powder. Then fill the container up to the top. Place the wine in a cool spot (such as a garage or root cellar).

7. Let wine sit in this cool location for 3 to 4 weeks. If it stays longer, rack again every 3 to 4 weeks. Always add the crushed Campden tablets or the potassium metabisulfite powder with each racking to halt oxidation and bacterial infection. After the fourth racking, the wine should be clear enough to bottle.

8. If the wine does not clear, use gelatin or kieselsol finings. (If using gelatin or kieselsol, follow directions for procedure and quantities.) When fining, the wine will need an additional 3 to 4 weeks to clarify.

9. When the wine is clear, it is ready to bottle. Taste the wine and adjust its sweetness, if desired, then bottle. Age for at least 6 months. White wines from juices are at their best between 6 months and 1 year in the bottle.

WHITE WINE FROM SAUVIGNON BLANC GRAPE JUICE

The Sauvignon Blanc produces a wine with a distinctive aroma — herby and sometimes smoke-scented. Clean and refreshing, this popular white variety has green, herbal, and grassy flavors, with just a touch of mint. Sauvignon Blanc, called Fumé Blanc in France, does exhibit smoky characteristics when made in the French style. The second most popular white wine in North America next to Chardonnay, Sauvignon Blanc is an excellent seafood accompaniment.

Yield: 5 gallons (19 L)

- 5 gallons (19 L) Sauvignon Blanc grape juice
- 1 package (5 g) Lalvin EC-1118 yeast
- 3 teaspoons (8.8 g) yeast nutrient
- 3 tablespoons (11.1 g) Oak-Mor (optional)
- 20 Campden tablets or 2 teaspoons (12.4 g) potassium metabisulfite powder

1. Sanitize all equipment.

2. Through a screened funnel, pour approximately 4 gallons (15 L) of juice into a 5-gallon (19 L) carboy and the remaining gallon (3.8 L) of juice into two 1-gallon (3.8 L) jugs.

3. Test for acid and sugar and make adjustments, if necessary. When the specific gravity is 1.070–1.092, make a yeast starter by pouring approximately 4 ounces (120 mL) of juice and 4 ounces (120 mL) of lukewarm water into a bowl. Sprinkle the yeast, the yeast nutrient, and the optional Oak-Mor into the solution, allowing it to proliferate for about 30 minutes. Add 6 ounces (180 mL) of the yeast starter to the carboy and 1 ounce (30 mL) of the starter to each of the 1-gallon (3.8 L) containers. Swish the containers to aid in the mixing.

4. Place a sheet of paper toweling, a wad of cotton, or a paper napkin into the necks of the containers. Fermentation will start in 2 or 3 days. When the must is seen actively "bubbling," replace the paper or cotton stoppers with air locks, filled with clean water, for the rest of the fermentation.

5. Fermentation will continue for 7 to 12 days. Start to monitor the progress with the hydrometer after 7 days. When the specific gravity is below 1.000 (that is, 0.995 or lower), proceed to the next step. If it's above 1.000, allow the wine to ferment longer, until it reaches a specific gravity below 1.000.

6. Once the specific gravity is below 1.000, siphon the wine from the three containers into a sanitized carboy. This procedure is called racking. Stabilize the wine by adding 5 Campden tablets (crushed to a powder) or ½ teaspoon (3.1 g) potassium metabisulfite powder. Then fill the container up to the top. Place the wine in a cool spot (such as a garage or root cellar).

7. Let wine sit in this cool location for 3 to 4 weeks. If it stays longer, rack again every 3 to 4 weeks. Always add the crushed Campden tablets or the potassium metabisulfite powder with each racking to halt oxidation and bacterial infection. After the fourth racking, the wine should be clear enough to bottle.

8. If the wine does not clear, use gelatin or kieselsol finings. (If using gelatin or kieselsol, follow directions for procedure and quantities.) When fining, the wine will need an additional 3 to 4 weeks to clear.

9. When the wine is clear, it is ready to bottle. Taste the wine and adjust its sweetness, if desired, then bottle. Age for at least 6 months. White wines from juices are at their best between 6 months and 1 year in the bottle.

WHITE WINE FROM SCHEUREBE GRAPE JUICE

The Scheurebe is a cross between Silvaner and Riesling and a big producer in Germany and parts of Canada. The wines are characterized by a full, fruity, aromatic taste. They are also spicy, with a pithy aroma and firm, lively acid content. Known as a "softer" Riesling, the Scheurebe offers the home winemaker an opportunity to make a new and different wine, one well suited to Asian and many fish dishes.

Yield: 5 gallons (19 L)

- 5 gallons (19 L) Scheurebe grape juice
- 1 package (5 g) Red Star Côtes des Blancs yeast
- 3 teaspoons (8.8 g) yeast nutrient
- 20 Campden tablets or 2 teaspoons (12.4 g) potassium metabisulfite powder

1. Sanitize all equipment.

2. Through a screened funnel, pour approximately 4 gallons (15 L) of juice into a sterilized 5-gallon (19 L) carboy and the remaining gallon (3.8 L) of juice into two 1-gallon (3.8 L) jugs.

3. Test for acid and sugar and make adjustments if necessary. When the specific gravity is 1.070–1.092, make a yeast starter by pouring approximately 4 ounces (120 mL) of juice and 4 ounces (120 mL) of lukewarm water into a bowl. Sprinkle the yeast and the yeast nutrient into the solution, allowing it to proliferate for about 30 minutes. Add 6 ounces (180 mL) of the yeast starter to the carboy and 1 ounce (30 mL) of the starter to each of the 1-gallon (3.8 L) containers. Swish the containers to aid in the mixing.

4. Place a sheet of paper toweling, a wad of cotton, or a paper napkin into the necks of the containers. Fermentation will start in 2 or 3 days. When the must is seen actively "bubbling," replace the paper or cotton stoppers with air locks, filled with clean water, for the rest of the fermentation.

5. Fermentation will continue for 7 to 12 days. Start to monitor the progress with the hydrometer after 7 days. When the specific gravity is below 1.000 (that is, 0.995 or lower), proceed to the next step. If it's above 1.000, allow the wine to ferment longer until it reaches a specific gravity of below 1.000.

6. Once the specific gravity is below 1.000, siphon the wine off from the three containers into a sanitized carboy. This procedure is called racking. Stabilize the wine by adding 5 crushed Campden tablets or ½ teaspoon (3.1 g) of potassium metabisulfite powder. Then fill up to the top. Place the wine in a cool spot (such as a garage or root cellar).

7. Let wine sit in this cool location for 3 to 4 weeks. If it stays longer, rack again every 3 to 4 weeks. Always add the crushed Campden tablets or the potassium metabisulfite powder with each racking to halt oxidation and bacterial infection. After the fourth racking, the wine should be clear enough to bottle.

8. If the wine does not clear, use gelatin or kieselsol finings. (If using gelatin or kieselsol, follow directions for procedure and quantities.) When fining, your wine will need an additional 3 to 4 weeks to clear.

9. When the wine is clear, it is time to bottle. Taste the wine and adjust its sweetness, if desired, then bottle. Age for at least 6 months. White wines from juices are at their best between 6 months and 1 year in the bottle. 🍇

WHITE WINE FROM SEMILLON GRAPE JUICE

The Semillon is a fine white grape variety that grows in the Bordeaux region of France and in many other parts of the world. As a partner of Sauvignon Blanc, it is used to make Graves and Entre-Deux-Mers in France. Semillon is increasing in acreage in California, Washington, and other northern regions of North America. The wine is fruity, with a crisp and soft spiciness. Aromas of fresh fruit and rose petals add complexity. This is a good match with many fish and chicken dishes.

Yield: 5 gallons (19 L)

- 5 gallons (19 L) Semillon grape juice
- 1 package (5 g) Lalvin EC-1118 yeast
- 3 teaspoons (8.8 g) yeast nutrient
- 20 Campden tablets or 2 teaspoons (12.4 g) potassium metabisulfite powder

1. Sanitize all equipment.

2. Through a screened funnel, pour approximately 4 gallons (15 L) of juice into a 5-gallon (19 L) carboy and the remaining gallon (3.8 L) of juice into two 1-gallon (3.8 L) jugs.

3. Test for acid and sugar and make adjustments, if necessary. When the specific gravity is 1.070–1.092, make a yeast starter by pouring approximately 4 ounces (120 mL) of juice and 4 ounces (120 mL) of lukewarm water into a bowl. Sprinkle the yeast and the yeast nutrient into the solution, allowing it to proliferate for about 30 minutes. Add 6 ounces (180 mL) of the yeast starter to the carboy and 1 ounce (30 mL) of the starter to each of the 1-gallon (3.8 L) containers. Swish the containers to aid in the mixing.

4. Place a sheet of paper toweling, a wad of cotton, or a paper napkin into the necks of the containers. Fermentation will start in 2 or 3 days. When the must is seen actively "bubbling," replace the paper or cotton stoppers with air locks, filled with clean water, for the rest of the fermentation.

5. Fermentation will continue for 7 to 12 days. Start to monitor the progress with the hydrometer after 7 days. When the specific gravity is below 1.000 (that is, 0.995 or lower), proceed to the next step. If it's above 1.000, allow the wine to ferment longer, until it reaches a specific gravity below 1.000.

6. Once the specific gravity is below 1.000, siphon the wine from the three containers into a sanitized carboy. This procedure is called racking. Stabilize the wine by adding 5 Campden

tablets (crushed to a powder) or ½ teaspoon (3.1 g) potassium metabisulfite powder. Then fill the container up to the top. Place the wine in a cool spot (such as a garage or root cellar).

7. Let wine sit in this cool location for 3 to 4 weeks. If it stays longer, rack again every 3 to 4 weeks. Always add the crushed Campden tablets or the potassium metabisulfite powder with each racking to halt oxidation and bacterial infection. After the fourth racking, the wine should be clear enough to bottle.

8. If the wine does not clear, use gelatin or kieselsol finings. (If using gelatin or kieselsol, follow directions for procedure and quantities.) When fining, the wine will need an additional 3 to 4 weeks to clarify.

9. When the wine is clear, it is time to bottle. Taste the wine and adjust its sweetness, if desired, and bottle. Age for at least 6 months. White wines from juices are at their best between 6 months and 1 year in the bottle. 🍇

White Wine from Seyval Blanc Grape Juice

This popular white French hybrid grape variety is grown all over the eastern and midwestern United States and Canada. The grape has a distinctive fruitiness and high acid content. The wine is crisp, with a nice balance of fruit and acid and aromas of pineapple, apple, and melon. A favorite among many home wine-makers, Seyval Blanc is also an excellent blending grape for the acid-shy California white. It's excellent with shellfish, particularly lobster.

Yield: 5 gallons (19 L)

5 gallons (19 L) Seyval Blanc grape juice
1 package (5 g) Red Star Côtes des Blanc yeast
3 tablespoons (11.1 g) Oak-Mor (optional)
3 teaspoons (8.8 g) yeast nutrient
20 Campden tablets or 2 teaspoons (12.4 g) potassium metabisulfite powder

1. Sanitize all equipment.

2. Through a screened funnel, pour approximately 4 gallons (15 L) of juice into a 5-gallon (19 L) carboy and the remaining gallon (3.8 L) of juice into two 1-gallon (3.8 L) jugs.

3. Test for sugar and acid and make adjustments, if necessary. When specific gravity is

1.070–1.092, make a yeast starter by pouring approximately 4 ounces (120 mL) of juice and 4 ounces (120 mL) of lukewarm water into a bowl. Sprinkle the yeast, Oak-Mor (if oak flavor is desired), and yeast nutrient into the solution, allowing it to proliferate for about 30 minutes. Add 6 ounces (180 mL) of the yeast starter to the carboy and 1 ounce (30 mL) of the starter to each of the 1-gallon (3.8 L) containers. Swish the containers to aid in the mixing.

4. Place a sheet of paper toweling, a wad of cotton, or a paper napkin into the necks of the containers. Fermentation will start in 2 or 3 days. When the must is seen actively "bubbling," replace the paper or cotton stoppers with air locks, filled with clean water, for the rest of the fermentation.

5. Fermentation will continue for 7 to 12 days. Start to monitor the progress with the hydrometer after 7 days. When the specific gravity is below 1.000 (that is, 0.995 or lower), proceed to the next step. If it's above 1.000, allow the wine to ferment longer, until it reaches a specific gravity below 1.000.

6. Once the specific gravity is below 1.000, siphon the wine from the three containers into a sanitized carboy. This procedure is called racking. Stabilize the wine by adding 5 Campden tablets (crushed to a powder) or ½ teaspoon (3.1 g) potassium metabisulfite powder. Then fill the container up to the top. Place the wine in a cool spot (such as a garage or root cellar).

7. Let wine sit in this cool location for 3 to 4 weeks. If it stays longer, rack again every 3 to 4 weeks. Always add the crushed Campden tablets or the potassium metabisulfite powder with each racking to halt oxidation and bacterial infection. After the fourth racking, the wine should be clear enough to bottle.

8. If the wine does not clear, use gelatin or kieselsol finings. (If using gelatin or kieselsol, follow directions for procedure and quantities.) When fining, the wine will need an additional 3 to 4 weeks to clear.

9. When the wine is clear, it is ready to bottle. Taste the wine and adjust its sweetness, if desired, then bottle. Age for at least 6 months. White wines from juices are at their best between 6 months and 1 year in the bottle. 🍇

WHITE WINE FROM SOAVE (GARGANEGA) GRAPE JUICE

Garganegas are the principal grapes of Soave, Italy, and make the most popular of all Italian wines. The wine is medium bodied with fresh fruitiness and aromas of citrus and freshly cut flowers. Serve with soft cheeses, fish and chicken dishes, and fresh fruit.

Yield: 5 gallons (19 L)

- 5 gallons (19 L) Soave grape juice
- 1 package (5 g) Lallamand K1-V116 yeast
- 3 teaspoons (8.8 g) yeast nutrient
- 20 Campden tablets or 2 teaspoons (12.4 g) potassium metabisulfite powder

1. Sanitize all equipment.

2. Through a screened funnel, pour approximately 4 gallons (15 L) of juice into a 5-gallon (19 L) carboy and the remaining gallon (3.8 L) of juice into two 1-gallon (3.8 L) jugs.

3. Test for acid and sugar and make adjustments, if necessary. When the specific gravity is 1.070–1.092, make a yeast starter by pouring approximately 4 ounces (120 mL) of juice and 4 ounces (120 mL) of lukewarm water into a bowl. Sprinkle the yeast and yeast nutrient into the solution, allowing it to proliferate for about 30 minutes. Add 6 ounces (180 mL) of the yeast starter to the carboy and 1 ounce (30 mL) of the starter to each of the 1-gallon (3.8 L) containers. Swish the containers to aid in the mixing.

4. Place a sheet of paper toweling, a wad of cotton, or a paper napkin into the necks of the containers. Fermentation will start in 2 or 3 days. When the must is seen actively "bubbling," replace the paper or cotton stoppers with air locks, filled with clean water, for the rest of the fermentation.

5. Fermentation will continue for 7 to 12 days. Start to monitor the progress with the hydrometer after 7 days. When the specific gravity is below 1.000 (that is, 0.995 or lower), proceed to the next step. If it's above 1.000, allow the wine to ferment longer, until it reaches a specific gravity below 1.000.

6. Once the specific gravity is below 1.000, siphon the wine from the three containers into a sanitized carboy. This procedure is called racking. Stabilize the wine by adding 5 Campden tablets (crushed to a powder) or ½ teaspoon (3.1 g) of potassium metabisulfite powder. Then fill the container up to the top. Place the wine in a cool spot (such as a garage or root cellar).

7. Let wine sit in this cool location for 3 to 4 weeks. If it stays longer, rack again every 3 to 4 weeks. Always add the crushed Campden tablets or the potassium metabisulfite powder with each racking to halt oxidation and bacterial infection. After the fourth racking, the wine should be clear enough to bottle.

8. If the wine does not clear, use gelatin or kieselsol finings. (If using gelatin or kieselsol, follow directions for procedure and quantities.) When fining, the wine will need an additional 3 to 4 weeks to clear.

9. When the wine is clear, it is time to bottle. Taste the wine and adjust its sweetness, if desired, then bottle. Age for at least 6 months. White wines from juices are at their best between 6 months and 1 year in the bottle. 🍇

WHITE WINE FROM TREBBIANO GRAPE JUICE

Trebbiano, also known as Ugni Blanc in Italy and Saint-èmilion in France, offers the home winemaker a versatile beverage. It can be either blended or kept as a pure varietal. The wine features good fruitiness and balanced flavors. It is an excellent aperitif and companion for poultry, fish, and cream pasta dishes.

Yield: 5 gallons (19 L)

- 5 gallons (19 L) Trebbiano grape juice
- 1 package (5 g) Red Star Premier Cuvée yeast
- 3 teaspoons (8.8 g) yeast nutrient
- 20 Campden tablets or 2 teaspoons (12.4 g) potassium metabisulfite powder

1. Sanitize all equipment.

2. Through a screened funnel, pour approximately 4 gallons (15 L) of juice into a 5-gallon (19 L) carboy and the remaining gallon (3.8 L) of juice into two 1-gallon (3.8 L) jugs.

3. Test for acid and sugar and make adjustments, if necessary. When the specific gravity is 1.070–1.092, make a yeast starter by pouring approximately 4 ounces (120 mL) of juice and 4 ounces (120 mL) of lukewarm water into a bowl. Sprinkle the yeast and yeast nutrient into the solution, allowing it to proliferate for about 30 minutes. Add 6 ounces (180 mL) of the yeast starter to the carboy and 1 ounce (30 mL) of the starter to each of the 1-gallon (3.8 L) containers. Swish the containers to aid in the mixing.

4. Place a sheet of paper toweling, a wad of cotton, or a paper napkin in the necks of the containers. Fermentation will start in 2 or 3 days. When the must is seen actively "bubbling," replace the paper or cotton stoppers with air locks, filled with clean water, for the rest of the fermentation.

5. Fermentation will continue for 7 to 12 days. Start to monitor the progress with the hydrometer after 7 days. When the specific gravity is below 1.000 (that is, 0.995 or lower), proceed to the next step. If it is above 1.000, allow the wine to ferment longer, until it reaches a specific gravity of below 1.000.

6. Once the specific gravity is below 1.000, siphon the wine from the three containers into a sanitized carboy. This procedure is called racking. Stabilize the wine by adding 5 Campden tablets (crushed to a powder) or ½ teaspoon

(3.1 g) of potassium metabisulfite powder. Then fill the carboy up to the top. Place the wine in a cool spot (such as a garage or root cellar).

7. Let wine sit in this cool location for 3 to 4 weeks. If it stays longer, rack again every 3 to 4 weeks. Always add the crushed Campden tablets or the potassium metabisulfite powder with each racking to halt oxidation and bacterial infection. After the fourth racking, the wine should be clear enough to bottle.

8. If the wine does not clear, use gelatin or kieselsol finings. (If using gelatin or kieselsol, follow directions for procedure and quantities.) When fining, the wine will need an additional 3 to 4 weeks to clear.

9. When the wine is clear, it is time to bottle. Taste the wine and adjust its sweetness, if desired, then bottle. Age for at least 6 months. White wines from juices are at their best between 6 months and 1 year in the bottle.

WHITE WINE FROM VIDAL BLANC GRAPE JUICE

Vidal Blanc is a white French-American hybrid becoming increasingly popular in the eastern United States and Canada. The fine white wines made from this hybrid have considerable character and flavor. This variety, which increases its sugar count as it matures, is featured in many ice wines that have been developed in Canada and the United States. The table wine is spicy, crisp, and pleasant and goes well with Asian dishes.

Yield: 5 gallons (19 L)

- 5 gallons (19 L) Vidal Blanc grape juice
- 1 package (5 g) Lalvin EC-1118 yeast
- 3 tablespoons (11.1 g) Oak-Mor (optional)
- 3 teaspoons (8.8 g) yeast nutrient
- 20 Campden tablets or 2 teaspoons (12.4 g) potassium metabisulfite powder

1. Sanitize all equipment.

2. Through a screened funnel, pour approximately 4 gallons (15 L) of juice into a 5-gallon (19 L) carboy and the remaining gallon (3.8 L) of juice into two 1-gallon (3.8 L) jugs.

3. Test for acid and sugar and make adjustments, if necessary. When the specific gravity is 1.070–1.092, make a yeast starter by pouring approximately 4 ounces (120 mL) of juice and 4 ounces (120 mL) of lukewarm water into a bowl. Sprinkle the yeast, the Oak-Mor (if oak flavor is desired), and the yeast nutrient into the solution, allowing it to proliferate for about 30 min-

utes. Add 6 ounces (180 mL) of the yeast starter to the carboy and 1 ounce (30 mL) of the starter to each of the 1-gallon (3.8 L) containers. Swish the containers to aid in the mixing.

4. Place a sheet of paper toweling, a wad of cotton, or a paper napkin in the necks of the containers. Fermentation will start in 2 or 3 days. When the must is seen actively "bubbling," replace the paper or cotton stoppers with air locks, filled with clean water, for the rest of the fermentation.

5. Fermentation will continue for 7 to 12 days. Start to monitor the progress with the hydrometer after 7 days. When the specific gravity is below 1.000 (that is, 0.995 or lower), proceed to the next step. If it's above 1.000, allow the wine to ferment longer, until it reaches a specific gravity below 1.000.

6. Once the specific gravity is below 1.000, siphon the wine from the three containers into a sanitized carboy. This procedure is called

racking. Stabilize the wine by adding 5 Campden tablets (crushed to a powder) or ½ teaspoon (3.1 g) potassium metabisulfite powder. Then fill the container up to the top. Place the wine in a cool spot (such as a garage or root cellar).

7. Let wine sit in this cool location for 3 to 4 weeks. If it stays loner, rack again every 3 to 4 weeks. Always add the crushed Campden tablets or the potassium metabisulfite powder with each racking to halt oxidation and bacterial infection. After the fourth racking, the wine should be clear enough to bottle.

8. If the wine does not clear, use gelatin or kieselsol finings. (If using gelatin or kieselsol, follow directions for procedure and quantities.) When fining, the wine will need an additional 3 to 4 weeks to clear.

9. When the wine is clear, it is ready to bottle. Taste the wine and adjust its sweetness, if desired, then bottle. Age for at least 6 months. White wines from juices are at their best between 6 months and 1 year in the bottle. 🍇

RED WINE FROM BARBERA GRAPE JUICE

Barbera is a good-quality red wine grape, planted exclusively in northern Italy and in California. Hearty, robust, medium-bodied red wines are usually made from the Barbera juice. Barbera is a long-aging variety requiring time to soften and balance. The wine is usually dark in color and possesses flavors of fresh cherries, raspberries, and vanilla. Meat roasts, tomato pastas, and game dishes go well with the Barbera wine.

Yield: 5 gallons (19 L)

5 gallons (19 L) Barbera grape juice
1 package (5 g) Wyeast Chianti yeast
3 tablespoons (11.1 g) Oak-Mor
3 teaspoons (8.8 g) yeast nutrient
20 drops (1 mL) pectic enzyme liquid
20 Campden tablets or 2 teaspoons (12.4 g) potassium metabisulfite powder

1. Sanitize all equipment.

2. Through a screened funnel, pour approximately 4 gallons (15 L) of juice into a 5-gallon (19 L) carboy and the remaining gallon (3.8 L) of juice into two 1-gallon (3.8 L) jugs.

3. Test for sugar and acid and make adjustments, if necessary. When the specific gravity is 1.070–1.092, make a yeast starter by pouring approximately 4 ounces (120 mL) of juice and 4 ounces (120 mL) of lukewarm water into a bowl. Sprinkle the yeast, the Oak-Mor, and the yeast nutrient into the solution, allowing it to proliferate for about 30 minutes. Add the 20 drops (1 mL) of pectic enzyme liquid to this mixture. Add 6 ounces (180 mL) of the yeast starter to the carboy and 1 ounce (30 mL) of the starter to each of the 1-gallon (3.8 L) containers. Swish the containers to aid in the mixing.

4. Place a sheet of paper toweling, a wad of cotton, or a paper napkin into the necks of the containers. Fermentation will start in 2 or 3 days. When the must is seen actively "bubbling," replace the paper or cotton stoppers with air locks, filled with clean water, for the rest of the fermentation.

5. Fermentation will continue for 7 to 12 days. Start to monitor the progress with the hydrometer after 7 days. When the specific gravity is below 1.000 (that is, 0.995 or lower), proceed to the next step. If it's above 1.000, allow the wine to ferment longer, until it reaches a specific gravity of below 1.000.

6. Once the specific gravity is below 1.000, siphon the wine from the three containers into a sanitized carboy. This procedure is called racking. Stabilize the wine by adding 5 Campden tablets (crushed to a powder) or ½ teaspoon (3.1 g) of potassium metabisulfite powder, then fill the carboy up to the top. Place the wine in a cool spot (such as a garage or root cellar).

7. Let the wine sit in this cool location, for 3 to 4 weeks, then rack again into a sanitized carboy. Three or four more rackings, spaced 3 to 4 weeks apart, should pace the wine to its finish. After the second racking, use just 3 crushed Campden tablets (or ¼ tsp [1.4 g] potassium metabisulfite).

8. If the wine does not clear, let it sit for another 3 to 4 weeks and rack again. It should clear itself naturally.

9. When the wine is clear, it is time to bottle. Taste the wine and adjust its sweetness, if desired, then bottle. Age for at least 1 year before tasting. Most red wines will improve from the second year on, depending on the variety. Periodic tasting will determine when the wine is at its peak. 🍇

RED WINE FROM BLAUFRANKISCH GRAPE JUICE

This grape, whose name means "blue French," is the most important red wine grape from Austria. It is related to the French Gamay, but it gives a darker and rather characteristically different taste to Austrian red wine. Dry, fruity, with a nose of plums and cherries, the wine is best drunk young and made in a Beaujolais style. Slight chilling will enhance the flavors. This wine is a fine complement to soft cheeses, pink meats, and light salads.

Yield: 5 gallons (19 L)

- 5 gallons (19 L) Blaufrankisch grape juice
- 20 drops (1 mL) pectic enzyme liquid
- 3 teaspoons (8.8 g) yeast nutrient
- 1 package (5 g) Red Star Premier Cuvée yeast
- 20 Campden tablets or 2 teaspoons (12.4 g) potassium metabisulfite powder

1. Sanitize all equipment.

2. Through a screened funnel, pour approximately 4 gallons (15 L) of juice into a 5-gallon (19 L) carboy and the remaining gallon (3.8 L) of juice into two 1-gallon (3.8 L) jugs.

3. Test for sugar and acid and make adjustments, if necessary. When the specific gravity is 1.070–1.092, make a yeast starter by pouring approximately 4 ounces (120 mL) of juice and 4 ounces (120 mL) of lukewarm water into a bowl. Sprinkle the yeast and the yeast nutrient into the solution, allowing it to proliferate for about 30 minutes. Add the 20 drops (1 mL) of pectic enzyme liquid to this mixture. Add 6 ounces (180 mL) of the yeast starter to the carboy and 1 ounce (30 mL) of the starter to each of the 1-gallon (3.8 L) containers. Swish the containers to aid in the mixing.

4. Place a sheet of paper toweling, a wad of cotton, or a paper napkin into the necks of the containers. Fermentation will start in 2 or 3 days. When the must is seen actively "bubbling," replace the paper or cotton stoppers with air locks, filled with clean water, for the rest of the fermentation.

5. Fermentation will continue for 7 to 12 days. Start to monitor the progress with the hydrometer after 7 days. When the specific gravity is below 1.000 (that is, 0.995 or lower), proceed to the next step. If it's above 1.000, allow the wine to ferment longer, until it reaches a specific gravity of below 1.000.

6. Once the specific gravity is below 1.000, siphon the wine from the three containers into a sanitized carboy. This procedure is called racking. Stabilize the wine by adding 5 Campden tablets (crushed to a powder) or ½ teaspoon (3.1 g) of potassium metabisulfite powder, then fill the carboy up to the top. Place the wine in a cool spot (such as a garage or root cellar).

7. Let wine sit in this cool location for 3 to 4 weeks, then rack again into a sanitized carboy. Three or four more rackings, spaced 3 to 4 weeks apart, should pace the wine to its finish. After the second racking, use just 3 crushed Campden tablets (or ¼ tsp [1.4 g] potassium metabusulfite).

8. If the wine does not clear, let it sit for another 3 to 4 weeks and rack again. It should clear itself naturally.

9. When the wine is clear, it is time to bottle. Taste the wine and adjust its sweetness, if desired, then bottle. Age at least 1 year before tasting. Most red wines will improve from the second year on, depending on the variety. Periodic tasting will determine when the wine is at its peak. 🍇

RED WINE FROM CABERNET FRANC GRAPE JUICE

Cabernet Franc, a close relative of the Cabernet Sauvignon, shares many of the same qualities but makes a softer, more aromatic wine. Widely grown in California and the Bordeaux region of France, Cabernet Franc is enjoying wide success in the eastern and northeastern United States. An excellent blending wine, Cabernet Franc can also stand on its own; it's best served with red meat or pasta.

Yield: 5 gallons (19 L)

 5 gallons (19 L) Cabernet Franc grape juice
 1 package (5 g) Red Star Pasteur Red yeast
 3 tablespoons (11.1 g) Oak-Mor
 3 teaspoons (8.8 g) yeast nutrient
20 Campden tablets or 2 teaspoons (12.4 g) potassium metabisulfite powder
20 drops (1 mL) pectic enzyme liquid

1. Sanitize all equipment.

2. Through a screened funnel, pour approximately 4 gallons (15 L) of juice into a 5-gallon (19 L) carboy and the remaining gallon (3.8 L) of juice into two 1-gallon (3.8 L) jugs.

3. Test for sugar and acid and make adjustments, if necessary. When the specific gravity is 1.070–1.092, make a yeast starter by pouring approximately 4 ounces (120 mL) of juice and 4 ounces (120 mL) of lukewarm water into a bowl. Sprinkle the yeast, the Oak-Mor, and the yeast nutrient into the solution, allowing it to proliferate for about 30 minutes. Add the 20 drops (1 mL) of pectic enzyme liquid to this mixture. Add 6 ounces (180 mL) of the yeast starter to the carboy and 1 ounce (30 mL) of the starter to each of the 1-gallon (3.8 L) containers. Swish the containers to aid in the mixing.

4. Place a sheet of paper toweling, a wad of cotton, or a paper napkin into the necks of the containers. Fermentation will start in 2 or 3 days. When the must is seen actively "bubbling," replace the paper or cotton stoppers with air locks, filled with clean water, for the rest of the fermentation.

5. Fermentation will continue for 7 to 12 days. Start to monitor the progress with the hydrometer after 7 days. When the specific gravity is below 1.000 (that is, 0.995 or lower), proceed to the next step. If it's above 1.000, allow the wine to ferment longer, until it reaches a specific gravity of below 1.000.

6. Once the specific gravity is below 1.000, siphon the wine from the three containers into a sanitized carboy. This procedure is called racking. Stabilize the wine by adding 5 Campden tablets (crushed to a powder) or ½ teaspoon (3.1 g) of potassium metabisulfite powder and fill the carboy up to the top. Place the wine in a cool spot (such as a garage or root cellar).

7. Let the wine sit in this cool location for 3 to 4 weeks, then rack again into a sanitized carboy. Three or four more rackings, spaced 3 to 4 weeks apart, should pace the wine to its finish. After the second racking, use just 3 crushed Campden tablets (or ¼ tsp [1.4 g] potassium metabisulfite).

8. If the wine does not clear, let it sit for another 3 to 4 weeks and rack again. It should clear itself naturally.

9. When the wine is clear, it is time to bottle. Taste the wine and adjust its sweetness, if desired, then bottle. Age at least 1 year before tasting. Most red wines will improve from the second year on, depending on the variety. Periodic tasting will determine when the wine is at its peak.

RED WINE FROM CABERNET SAUVIGNON GRAPE JUICE

This full-flavored, medium-dark red wine offers a light bell pepper nose and a clean, well-balanced taste, with a hint of violet in the bouquet. This is the most popular red wine in the United States. It ages well and improves with oaking. Cabernet Sauvignon is a good accompaniment to barbecue, steak, and roast beef.

Yield: 5 gallons (19 L)

- 5 gallons (19 L) Cabernet Sauvignon grape juice
- 1 package (5 g) Red Star Pasteur Red yeast
- 3 tablespoons (11.1 g) Oak-Mor
- 3 teaspoons (8.8 g) yeast nutrient
- 20 drops (1 mL) pectic enzyme iquid
- 20 Campden tablets or 2 teaspoons (12.4 g) potassium metabisulfite powder

1. Sanitize all equipment.

2. Through a screened funnel, pour approximately 4 gallons (15 L) of juice into a 5-gallon (19 L) carboy and the remaining gallon (3.8 L) of juice into two 1-gallon (3.8 L) jugs.

3. Test for sugar and acid and make adjustments, if necessary. When the specific gravity is 1.070–1.092, make a yeast starter by pouring approximately 4 ounces (120 mL) of juice and 4 ounces (120 mL) of lukewarm water into a bowl. Sprinkle the yeast, the Oak-Mor, and the yeast nutrient into the solution, allowing it to proliferate for about 30 minutes. Add the 20 drops

(1 mL) of pectic enzyme liquid to this mixture. Add 6 ounces (180 mL) of the yeast starter to the carboy and 1 ounce (30 mL) of the starter to each of the 1-gallon (3.8 L) containers. Swish the containers to aid in the mixing.

4. Place a sheet of paper toweling, a wad of cotton, or a paper napkin into the necks of the containers. The fermentation will start in 2 or 3 days. When the must is seen actively "bubbling," replace the paper or cotton stoppers with air locks, filled with clean water, for the rest of the fermentation.

5. Fermentation will continue for 7 to 12 days. Start to monitor the progress with the hydrometer after 7 days. When the specific gravity is below 1.000 (that is, 0.995 or lower), proceed to the next step. If it is above 1.000, allow the wine to ferment longer until it reaches a specific gravity of below 1.000.

6. Once the specific gravity is below 1.000, siphon the wine from the three containers into a sanitized carboy. This procedure is called

racking. Stabilize the wine by adding 5 Campden tablets (crushed to a powder) or ½ teaspoon (3.1 g) of potassium metabisulfite powder and fill the carboy up to the top. Place the wine in a cool spot (such as a garage or root cellar).

7. Let the wine sit in this cool location for 3 to 4 weeks, then rack again into a sanitized carboy. Three or four more rackings, spaced 3 to 4 weeks apart, should pace the wine to its finish. After the second racking, use just 3 crushed Campden tablets (or ¼ tsp [1.4 g] potassium metabisulfite).

8. If the wine does not clear, let it sit for another 3 to 4 weeks and rack again. It should clear itself naturally.

9. When the wine is clear, it is time to bottle. Taste the wine and adjust its sweetness, if desired, then bottle. Age at least 1 year before tasting. Most red wines will improve from the second year on, depending on the variety. Periodic tasting will determine when the wine is at its peak. 🍇

RED WINE FROM CARIGNANE GRAPE JUICE

This productive red wine is planted extensively in France, Spain, Algeria, and California. It's an excellent blending wine, which also produces sound, inky-red, medium-bodied wine. Carignane is peppery with high tannins and a firm structure. It is great for aging. Match it with robust foods like stews, roasts, and pasta dishes.

Yield: 5 gallons (19 L)

- 5 gallons (19 L) Carignane grape juice
- 1 package (5 g) Wyeast Bordeaux yeast
- 3 tablespoons (11.1 g) Oak-Mor
- 3 teaspoons (8.8 g) yeast nutrient
- 20 drops (1 mL) pectic enzyme liquid
- 20 Campden tablets or 2 teaspoons (12.4 g) potassium metabisulfite powder

1. Sanitize all equipment.

2. Through a screened funnel, pour approximately 4 gallons (15 L) of juice into a 5-gallon (19 L) carboy and the remaining gallon (3.8 L) of juice into two 1-gallon (3.8 L) jugs.

3. Test for sugar and acid and make adjustments, if necessary. When the specific gravity is 1.070–1.092, make a yeast starter by pouring approximately 4 ounces (120 mL) of juice and 4 ounces (120 mL) of lukewarm water into a bowl. Sprinkle the yeast, the Oak-Mor, and the yeast nutrient into the solution, allowing it to proliferate for about 30 minutes. Add the 20 drops (1 mL) of pectic enzyme liquid to this mixture. Now add 6 ounces (180 mL) of the yeast starter to the carboy and 1 ounce (30 mL) of the starter to each of the 1-gallon (3.8 L) containers. Swish the containers to aid in the mixing.

4. Place a sheet of paper toweling, a wad of cotton, or a paper napkin into the necks of the containers. The fermentation will start in 2 or 3 days. When the must is seen actively "bubbling," replace the paper or cotton stoppers with air locks, filled with clean water, for the rest of the fermentation.

5. Fermentation will continue for 7 to 12 days. Start to monitor the progress with the hydrometer after 7 days. When the specific gravity is below 1.000 (that is, 0.995 or lower), proceed to the next step. If it's above 1.000, allow the wine to ferment longer, until it reaches a specific gravity of below 1.000.

6. Once the specific gravity is below 1.000, siphon the wine from the three containers into a sanitized carboy. This procedure is called racking. Stabilize the wine by adding 5 Campden tablets (crushed to a powder) or ½ teaspoon (3.1 g) of potassium metabisulfite powder and fill the carboy up to the top. Place the wine in a cool spot (such as a garage or root cellar).

7. Let the wine sit in this cool location for 3 to 4 weeks, then rack again into a sanitized carboy. Three or four more rackings, spaced 3 to 4 weeks apart, should pace the wine to its finish. After the second racking, use just 3 crushed Campden tablets (or ¼ tsp [1.4 g] potassium metabisulfite).

8. If the wine does not clear, let it sit for another 3 to 4 weeks and rack again. It should clear itself naturally.

9. When the wine is clear, it is time to bottle. Taste the wine and adjust its sweetness, if desired, then bottle. Age at least 1 year before tasting. Most red wines will improve from the second year on, depending upon the variety. Periodic tasting will determine when the wine is at its peak. 🍇

RED WINE FROM GAMAY GRAPE JUICE

The Gamay is grown in many countries and is usually made in a fruity, easy-drinking style. The variety produces low-acid wines with a flowery aroma and flavor. Slightly chilled, the wine develops a crisp, quaffing element. The Gamay should be made in the Beaujolais manner and not aged long.

Yield: 5 gallons (19 L)

- 5 gallons (19 L) Gamay grape juice
- 1 package (5 g) Red Star Côtes des Blancs yeast
- 3 teaspoons (8.8 g) yeast nutrient
- 20 drops (1 mL) pectic enzyme liquid
- 20 Campden tablets or 2 teaspoons (12.4 g) potassium metabisulfite powder

1. Sanitize all equipment.

2. Through a screened funnel, pour approximately 4 gallons (15 L) of juice into a 5-gallon (19 L) carboy and the remaining gallon (3.8 L) of juice into two 1-gallon (3.8 L) jugs.

3. Test for sugar and acid and make adjustments, if necessary. When the specific gravity is 1.070–1.092, make a yeast starter by pouring approximately 4 ounces (120 mL) of juice and 4 ounces (120 mL) of lukewarm water into a bowl. Sprinkle the yeast and the yeast nutrient into the solution, allowing it to proliferate for about 30 minutes. Add the 20 drops (1 mL) of pectic enzyme liquid to this mixture. Add 6 ounces

(180 mL) of the yeast starter to the carboy and 1 ounce (30 mL) of the starter to each of the 1-gallon (3.8 L) containers. Swish the containers to aid in the mixing.

4. Place a sheet of paper toweling, a wad of cotton, or a paper napkin into the necks of the containers. Fermentation will start in 2 or 3 days. When the must is seen actively "bubbling," replace the paper or cotton stoppers with air locks, filled with clean water, for the rest of the fermentation.

5. Fermentation will continue for 7 to 12 days. Start to monitor the progress with the hydrometer after 7 days. When the specific gravity is below 1.000 (that is, 0.995 or lower), proceed to the next step. If it's above 1.000, allow the wine to ferment longer, until it reaches a specific gravity of below 1.000.

6. Once the specific gravity is below 1.000, siphon the wine from the three containers into a sanitized carboy. This procedure is called racking. Stabilize the wine by adding 5 Campden

tablets (crushed to a powder) or ½ teaspoon (3.1 g) of potassium metabisulfite powder and fill the carboy up to the top. Place the wine in a cool spot (such as a garage or root cellar).

7. Let the wine sit in this cool location for 3 to 4 weeks, then rack again into a sanitized carboy. Three or four more rackings, spaced 3 to 4 weeks apart, should pace the wine to its finish. After the second racking, use just 3 crushed Campden tablets (or ¼ tsp [1.4 g] potassium metabisulfite).

8. If the wine does not clear, let it sit for another 3 to 4 weeks and rack again. It should clear itself naturally.

9. When the wine is clear, it is time to bottle. Taste the wine and adjust its sweetness, if desired, then bottle. Age at least 6 months before tasting. This "fruity"-style wine should be enjoyed younger, rather than letting it age too long. 🍇

RED WINE FROM GRENACHE GRAPE JUICE

This is a pink grape variety used in France to add character to the Châteauneuf-du-Papes, and, on its own, to make the popular rosés of Tavel and Lirac. California Grenaches are used for blending and for fine rosé wines. This young-drinking, fruity red is popular with home winemakers because of lower initial costs, availability, and freshness of the wine. Serve with finger and picnic foods.

Yield: 5 gallons (19 L)

5 gallons (19 L) Grenache grape juice
1 package (5 g) Gist-brocades Fermiblanc yeast
3 teaspoons (8.8 g) yeast nutrient
20 drops (1 mL) pectic enzyme liquid
20 Campden tablets or 2 teaspoons (12.4 g) potassium metabisulfite powder

1. Sanitize all equipment.

2. Through a screened funnel, pour approximately 4 gallons (15 L) of juice into a 5-gallon (19 L) carboy and the remaining gallon (3.8 L) of juice into two 1-gallon (3.8 L) jugs.

3. Test for sugar and acid and make adjustments, if necessary. When the specific gravity is

1.070–1.092, make a yeast starter by pouring approximately 4 ounces (120 mL) of juice and 4 ounces (120 mL) of lukewarm water into a bowl. Sprinkle the yeast and the yeast nutrient into the solution, allowing it to proliferate for about 30 minutes. Add the 20 drops (1 mL) of pectic enzyme liquid to this mixture. Add 6 ounces (180 mL) of the yeast starter to the carboy and 1 ounce (30 mL) of the starter to each of the 1-gallon (3.8 L) containers. Swish the containers to aid in the mixing.

4. Place a sheet of paper toweling, a wad of cotton, or a paper napkin into the necks of the containers. Fermentation will start in 2 or 3 days. When the must is seen actively "bubbling," replace the paper or cotton stoppers with air locks, filled with clean water, for the rest of the fermentation.

5. Fermentation will continue for 7 to 12 days. Start to monitor the progress with the hydrometer after 7 days. When the specific gravity is below 1.000 (that is, 0.995 or lower), proceed to the next step. If it's above 1.000, allow the wine to ferment longer, until it reaches a specific gravity of below 1.000.

6. Once the specific gravity is below 1.000, siphon the wine from the three containers into a sanitized carboy. This procedure is called racking. Stabilize the wine by adding 5 Campden tablets (crushed to a powder) or ½ teaspoon (3.1 g) of potassium metabisulfite powder and fill the carboy up to the top. Place the wine in a cool spot (such as a garage or root cellar).

7. Let the wine sit in this cool location for 3 to 4 weeks, then rack again into a sanitized carboy. Three or four more rackings, spaced 3 to 4 weeks apart, should pace the wine to its finish. After the second racking, use just 3 crushed Campden tablets (or ¼ tsp [1.4 g] potassium metabisulfite).

8. If the wine does not clear, let it sit for another 3 to 4 weeks and rack again. It should clear itself naturally.

9. When the wine is clear, it is time to bottle. Taste the wine and adjust its sweetness, if desired, then bottle. Age at least 6 months before tasting. This "fruity"-style wine should be enjoyed younger, rather than letting it age too long.

RED WINE FROM MERLOT GRAPE JUICE

Merlot is a smooth, rich wine with a medium-dark red color. The wine's taste has hints of blackberry, currant, and green olive. A great blending wine, it also can stand alone as a pure varietal. Long aging enhances the wine, but early drinking can prove beneficial and appropriate. Merlot stars when paired with steak, lamb, and veal dishes.

Yield: 5 gallons (19 L)

5 gallons (19 L) Merlot grape juice
1 package (5 g) Wyeast Bordeaux yeast
3 tablespoons (11.1 g) Oak-Mor
3 teaspoons (8.8 g) yeast nutrient
20 drops (1 mL) pectic enzyme liquid
20 Campden tablets or 2 teaspoons (12.4 g) potassium metabisulfite powder

1. Sanitize all equipment.

2. Through a screened funnel, pour approximately 4 gallons (15 L) of juice into a 5-gallon (19 L) carboy and the remaining gallon (3.8 L) of juice into two 1-gallon (3.8 L) jugs.

3. Test for sugar and acid and make adjustments, if necessary. When the specific gravity is 1.070–1.092, make a yeast starter by pouring approximately 4 ounces (120 mL) of juice and 4 ounces (120 mL) of lukewarm water into a bowl. Sprinkle the yeast, the Oak-Mor, and the yeast nutrient into the solution, allowing it to proliferate for about 30 minutes. Add the 20 drops

(1 mL) of pectic enzyme liquid to this mixture. Add 6 ounces (180 mL) of the yeast starter to the carboy and 1 ounce (30 mL) of the starter to each of the 1-gallon (3.8 L) containers. Swish the containers to aid in the mixing.

4. Place a sheet of paper toweling, a wad of cotton, or a paper napkin into the necks of the containers. Fermentation will start in 2 or 3 days. When the must is seen actively "bubbling," replace the paper or cotton stoppers with air locks, filled with clean water, for the rest of the fermentation.

5. Fermentation will continue for 7 to 12 days. Start to monitor the progress with the hydrometer after 7 days. When the specific gravity is below 1.000 (that is, 0.995 or lower), proceed to the next step. If it's above 1.000, allow the wine to ferment longer until it reaches a specific gravity of below 1.000.

6. Once the specific gravity is below 1.000, siphon the wine from the three containers into a sanitized carboy. This procedure is called racking. Stabilize the wine by adding 5 Campden tablets (crushed to a powder) or ½ teaspoon (3.1 g) of potassium metabisulfite powder and fill the carboy up to the top. Place the wine in a cool spot (such as a garage or root cellar).

7. Let the wine sit in this cool location for 3 to 4 weeks, then rack again into a sanitized carboy. Three or four more rackings, spaced 3 to 4 weeks apart, should pace the wine to its finish. After the second racking, use just 3 crushed Campden tablets (or ¼ tsp [1.4 g] potassium metabisulfite).

8. If the wine does not clear, let it sit for another 3 to 4 weeks and rack again. It should clear itself naturally.

9. When the wine is clear, it is time to bottle. Taste the wine and adjust its sweetness, if desired, then bottle. Age at least 1 year before tasting. Most red wines will improve from the second year on, depending on the variety. Periodic tasting will determine when the wine is at its peak. 🍇

RED WINE FROM PINOT NOIR GRAPE JUICE

Pinot Noir is a hearty red wine with a smooth flavor. The soft texture and dark color complement the berry flavors. It is rich and round with notes of spice and a long, lingering finish. Serve with firm cheese, blackened fish, grilled salmon, and spiced pork.

Yield: 5 gallons (19 L)

5 gallons (19 L) Pinot Noir grape juice
1 package (5 g) Wyeast Bordeaux yeast
3 tablespoons (11.1 g) Oak-Mor
3 teaspoons (8.8 g) yeast nutrient
20 drops (1 mL) pectic enzyme liquid
20 Campden tablets or 2 teaspoons (12.4 g) potassium metabisulfite powder

1. Sanitize all equipment.

2. Through a screened funnel, pour approximately 4 gallons (15 L) of juice into a 5-gallon (19 L) carboy and the remaining gallon (3.8 L) of juice into two 1-gallon (3.8 L) jugs.

3. Test for sugar and acid and make adjustments, if necessary. When the specific gravity is 1.070–1.092, make a yeast starter by pouring approximately 4 ounces (120 mL) of juice and 4 ounces (120 mL) of lukewarm water into a bowl. Sprinkle the yeast, the Oak-Mor, and the yeast nutrient into the solution, allowing it to proliferate for about 30 minutes. Add the 20 drops (1 mL) of pectic enzyme liquid to this mixture. Add 6 ounces (180 mL) of the yeast starter to the carboy and 1 ounce (30 mL) of the starter to each of the 1-gallon (3.8 L) containers. Swish containers to aid in the mixing.

4. Place a sheet of paper toweling, a wad of cotton, or a paper napkin into the necks of the containers. Fermentation will start in 2 or 3 days. When the must is seen actively "bubbling," replace the paper or cotton stoppers with air locks, filled with clean water, for the rest of the fermentation.

5. Fermentation will continue for 7 to 12 days. Start to monitor the progress with the hydrometer after 7 days. When the specific gravity is below 1.000 (that is, 0.995 or lower), proceed to the next step. If it's above 1.000, allow the wine to ferment longer until it reaches a specific gravity of below 1.000.

6. Once the specific gravity is below 1.000, siphon the wine from the three containers into a sanitized carboy. This procedure is called racking. Stabilize the wine by adding 5 Campden tablets (crushed to a powder) or ½ teaspoon (3.1 g) of potassium metabisulfite powder and fill the carboy up to the top. Place the wine in a cool spot (such as a garage or root cellar).

7. Let the wine sit in this cool location for 3 to 4 weeks, then rack again into a sanitized carboy. Three or four more rackings, spaced 3 to 4 weeks apart, should pace the wine to its finish. After the second racking, use just 3 crushed Campden tablets (or ¼ tsp [1.4 g] potassium metabisulfite).

8. If the wine does not clear, let it sit for another 3 to 4 weeks and rack again. It should clear itself naturally.

9. When the wine is clear, it is time to bottle. Taste the wine and adjust its sweetness, if desired, then bottle. Age at least 1 year before tasting. Most red wines will improve from the second year on, depending on the variety. Periodic tasting will determine when the wine is at its peak. 🍇

RED WINE FROM PETITE SIRAH GRAPE JUICE

A favorite of many old-time home winemakers, the Petite Sirah makes dark, inky wines capable of long aging. It is also an excellent blending wine, adding color, depth, and complexity to many other red varieties. It can produce full-bodied and fruity wines with firm acid structure and a long aftertaste. This wine is well suited to many tomato-pasta dishes, hearty roasts, and game dishes.

Yield: 5 gallons (19 L)

- 5 gallons (19 L) Petite Sirah grape juice
- 1 package (5 g) Wyeast Bordeaux yeast
- 3 tablespoons (11.1 g) Oak-Mor
- 3 teaspoons (8.8 g) yeast nutrient
- 20 drops (1 mL) pectic enzyme liquid
- 20 Campden tablets or 2 teaspoons (12.4 g) potassium metabisulfite powder

1. Sanitize all equipment.

2. Through a screened funnel, pour approximately 4 gallons (15 L) of juice into a 5-gallon (19 L) carboy and the remaining gallon (3.8 L) of juice into two 1-gallon (3.8 L) jugs.

3. Test for sugar and acid and make adjustments, if necessary. When the specific gravity is 1.070–1.092, make a yeast starter by pouring approximately 4 ounces (120 mL) of juice and 4 ounces (120 mL) of lukewarm water into a bowl. Sprinkle the yeast, the Oak-Mor, and the yeast nutrient into the solution, allowing it to proliferate for about 30 minutes. Add the 20 drops (1 mL) of pectic enzyme liquid to this mixture. Add 6 ounces (180 mL) of the yeast starter to the carboy and 1 ounce (30 mL) of the starter to each of the 1-gallon (3.8 L) containers. Swish the containers to aid in the mixing.

4. Place a sheet of paper toweling, a wad of cotton, or a paper napkin into the necks of the containers. Fermentation will start in 2 or 3 days. When the must is seen actively "bubbling," replace the paper or cotton stoppers with air locks, filled with clean water, for the rest of the fermentation.

5. Fermentation will continue for 7 to 12 days. Start to monitor the progress with the hydrometer after 7 days. When the specific gravity is below 1.000 (that is, 0.995 or lower), proceed to the next step. If it's above 1.000, allow the wine to ferment longer, until it reaches a specific gravity of below 1.000.

6. Once the specific gravity is below 1.000, siphon the wine from the three containers into a sanitized carboy. This procedure is called racking. Stabilize the wine by adding 5 Campden tablets (crushed to a powder) or ½ teaspoon (3.1 g) of potassium metabisulfite powder and fill the carboy up to the top. Place the wine in a cool spot (such as a garage or root cellar).

7. Let the wine sit in this cool location for 3 to 4 weeks, then rack again into a sanitized carboy. Three or four more rackings, spaced 3 to 4 weeks apart, should pace the wine to its finish. After the second racking, use just 3 crushed Campden tablets (or ¼ tsp [1.4 g] potassium metabisulfite).

8. If the wine does not clear, let it sit for another 3 to 4 weeks and rack again. It should clear itself naturally.

9. When the wine is clear, it is time to bottle. Taste the wine and adjust its sweetness, if desired, then bottle. Age at least 1 year before tasting. Most red wines will improve from the second year on, depending on the variety. Periodic tasting will determine when the wine is at its peak. 🍇

RED WINE FROM RUBY CABERNET GRAPE JUICE

A cross between Carignane and Cabernet Sauvignon, the Ruby Cabernet was developed to produce quality wines in warmer regions. The result is a medium-bodied red wine with violet and pepper aromas and blackberry and raspberry flavors. The finished wine goes well with many pasta dishes and steak, grilled chicken, and grilled sausage.

Yield: 5 gallons (19 L)

5 gallons (19 L) Ruby Cabernet grape juice
1 package (5 g) Red Star Pasteur Red yeast
3 tablespoons (11.1 g) Oak-Mor
3 teaspoons (8.8 g) yeast nutrient
20 drops (1 mL) pectic enzyme liquid
20 Campden tablets or 2 teaspoons (12.4 g) potassium metabisulfite powder

1. Sanitize all equipment.

2. Through a screened funnel, pour approximately 4 gallons (15 L) of juice into a 5-gallon (19 L) carboy and the remaining gallon (3.8 L) of juice into two 1-gallon (3.8 L) jugs.

3. Test for sugar and acid and make adjustments, if necessary. When the specific gravity is 1.070–1.092, make a yeast starter by pouring approximately 4 ounces (120 mL) of juice and 4 ounces (120 mL) of lukewarm water into a bowl. Sprinkle the yeast, the Oak-Mor, and the yeast nutrient into the solution, allowing it to proliferate for about 30 minutes. Add the 20 drops (1 mL) of pectic enzyme liquid to this mixture. Add 6 ounces (180 mL) of the yeast starter to the carboy and 1 ounce (30 mL) of the starter to each of the 1-gallon (3.8 L) containers. Swish the containers to aid in the mixing.

4. Place a sheet of paper toweling, a wad of cotton, or a paper napkin into the necks of the containers. Fermentation will start in 2 or 3 days. When the must is seen actively "bubbling," replace the paper or cotton stoppers with air locks, filled with clean water, for the rest of the fermentation.

5. Fermentation will continue for 7 to 12 days. Start to monitor the progress with the hydrometer after 7 days. When the specific gravity is below 1.000 (that is, 0.995 or lower), proceed to the next step. If it's above 1.000, allow the wine to ferment longer until it reaches a specific gravity of below 1.000.

6. Once the specific gravity is below 1.000, siphon the wine from the three containers into a sanitized carboy. This procedure is called racking. Stabilize the wine by adding 5 Campden tablets (crushed to a powder) or ½ teaspoon (3.1 g) of potassium metabisulfite powder and fill the carboy up to the top. Place the wine in a cool spot (such as a garage or root cellar).

7. Let the wine sit in this cool location for 3 to 4 weeks, then rack again into a sanitized carboy. Three or four more rackings, spaced 3 to 4 weeks apart, should pace the wine to its finish. After the second racking, use just 3 crushed Campden tablets (or ¼ tsp [1.4 g] potassium metabisulfite).

8. If the wine does not clear, let it sit for another 3 to 4 weeks and rack again. It should clear itself naturally.

9. When the wine is clear, it is time to bottle. Taste the wine and adjust its sweetness, if desired, then bottle. Age at least 1 year before tasting. Most red wines will improve from the second year on, depending on the variety. Periodic tasting will determine when the wine is at its peak. 🍇

RED WINE FROM SANGIOVESE GRAPE JUICE

Sangiovese is one of Italy's great red wines and is now doing well in California. It is the main wine of the famous Chianti, Vino Nobile, and Brunello in Italy. The wine is fruity, with a solid structure, and nicely balanced. Serve with pasta dishes, beef roasts, lamb, grilled kababs, and hard cheeses.

Yield: 5 gallons (19 L)

- 5 gallons (19 L) Sangiovese grape juice
- 1 package (5 g) Red Star Pasteur Red yeast
- 3 tablespoons (11.1 g) Oak-Mor
- 3 teaspoons (8.8 g) yeast nutrient
- 20 drops (1 mL) pectic enzyme liquid
- 20 Campden tablets or 2 teaspoons (12.4 g) potassium metabisulfite powder

1. Sanitize all equipment.

2. Through a screened funnel, pour approximately 4 gallons (15 L) of juice into a 5-gallon (19 L) carboy and the remaining gallon (3.8 L) of juice into two 1-gallon (3.8 L) jugs.

3. Test for sugar and acid and make adjustments, if necessary. When the specific gravity is 1.070–1.092, make a yeast starter by pouring approximately 4 ounces (120 mL) of juice and 4 ounces (120 mL) of lukewarm water into a bowl. Sprinkle the yeast, the Oak-Mor, and the yeast nutrient into the solution, allowing it to proliferate for about 30 minutes. Add the 20 drops (1 mL) of pectic enzyme liquid to this mixture.

Add 6 ounces (180 mL) of the yeast starter to the carboy and 1 ounce (30 mL) of the starter to each of the 1-gallon (3.8 L) containers. Swish the containers to aid in the mixing.

4. Place a sheet of paper toweling, a wad of cotton, or a paper napkin into the necks of the containers. Fermentation will start in 2 or 3 days. When the must is seen actively "bubbling," replace the paper or cotton stoppers with air locks, filled with clean water, for the rest of the fermentation.

5. Fermentation will continue for 7 to 12 days. Start to monitor the progress with the hydrometer after 7 days. When the specific gravity is below 1.000 (that is, 0.995 or lower), proceed to the next step. If it's above 1.000, allow the wine to ferment longer, until it reaches a specific gravity of below 1.000.

6. Once the specific gravity is below 1.000, siphon the wine from the three containers into a sanitized carboy. This procedure is called racking. Stabilize the wine by adding 5 Campden

tablets (crushed to a powder) or ½ teaspoon (3.1 g) of potassium metabisulfite powder and fill the carboy up to the top. Place the wine in a cool spot (such as a garage or root cellar).

7. Let the wine sit in this cool location for 3 to 4 weeks, then rack again into a sanitized carboy. Three or four more rackings, spaced 3 to 4 weeks apart, should pace the wine to its finish. After the second racking, use just 3 crushed Campden tablets (or ¼ tsp [1.4 g] potassium metabisulfite).

8. If the wine does not clear, let it sit for another 3 to 4 weeks and rack again. It should clear itself naturally.

9. When the wine is clear, it is time to bottle. Taste the wine and adjust its sweetness, if desired, then bottle. Age at least 1 year before tasting. Most red wines will improve from the second year on, depending on the variety. Periodic tasting will determine when the wine is at its peak. 🍇

RED WINE FROM SYRAH GRAPE JUICE

A collage of flavors is evident in this medium-dark, rich red wine. Syrah has a soft, spicy bouquet and a peppery taste. It is tannic while young, but a little aging will enhance the development of the wine. Syrah offers the home winemaker a wide range of options as both a blending wine and a varietal. Try it with pepper steak, rack of lamb, and soft cheeses.

Yield: 5 gallons (19 L)

5 gallons (19 L) Syrah grape juice
1 package (5 g) Wyeast Bordeaux yeast
3 tablespoons (11.1 g) Oak-Mor
3 teaspoons (8.8 g) yeast nutrient
20 drops (1 mL) pectic enzyme liquid
20 Campden tablets or 2 teaspoons (12.4 g) potassium metabisulfite powder

1. Sanitize all equipment.

2. Through a screened funnel, pour approximately 4 gallons (15 L) of juice into a 5-gallon (19 L) carboy and the remaining gallon (3.8 L) of juice into two 1-gallon (3.8 L) jugs.

3. Test for sugar and acid and make adjustments, if necessary. When the specific gravity is 1.070–1.092, make a yeast starter by pouring approximately 4 ounces (120 mL) of juice and 4 ounces (120 mL) of lukewarm water into a bowl. Sprinkle the yeast, the Oak-Mor, and the yeast nutrient into the solution, allowing it to proliferate for about 30 minutes. Add the 20 drops (1 mL) of pectic enzyme liquid to this mixture. Add 6 ounces (180 mL) of the yeast starter to the carboy and 1 ounce (30 mL) of the starter to each of the 1-gallon (3.8 L) containers. Swish the containers to aid in the mixing.

4. Place a sheet of paper toweling, a wad of cotton, or a paper napkin into the necks of the containers. Fermentation will start in 2 or 3 days. When the must is seen actively "bubbling," replace the paper or cotton stoppers with air locks, filled with clean water, for the rest of the fermentation.

5. Fermentation will continue for 7 to 12 days. Start to monitor the progress with the hydrometer after 7 days. When the specific gravity is below 1.000 (that is, 0.995 or lower), proceed to the next step. If it's above 1.000, allow the wine to ferment longer, until it reaches a specific gravity of below 1.000.

6. Once the specific gravity is below 1.000, siphon the wine from the three containers into a sanitized carboy. This procedure is called racking. Stabilize the wine by adding 5 Campden tablets (crushed to a powder) or ½ teaspoon (3.1 g) of potassium metabisulfite powder and fill the carboy up to the top. Place the wine in a cool spot (such as a garage or root cellar).

7. Let the wine sit in this cool location for 3 to 4 weeks, then rack again into a sanitized carboy. Three or four more rackings, spaced 3 to 4 weeks apart, should pace the wine to its finish. After the second racking, use just 3 crushed Campden tablets (or ¼ tsp [1.4 g] potassium metabisulfite).

8. If the wine does not clear, let it sit for another 3 to 4 weeks and rack again. It should clear itself naturally.

9. When the wine is clear, it is time to bottle. Taste the wine and adjust its sweetness, if desired, then bottle. Age at least 1 year before tasting. Most red wines will improve from the second year on, depending on the variety. Periodic tasting will determine when the wine is at its peak.

RED WINE FROM VALPOLICELLA GRAPE JUICE

Valpolicella is a delicate, nutty-scented, slightly bitter-tasting wine from the Veneto region of Italy. It is light, fruity, and enjoyable when young. An everyday drinking wine, Valpolicella goes well with luncheon fare, finger foods, light pasta dishes, ham, and veal dishes.

Yield: 5 gallons (19 L)

- 5 gallons (19 L) Valpolicella grape juice
- 1 package (5 g) Wyeast Chianti yeast
- 3 teaspoons (8.8 g) yeast nutrient
- 20 drops (1 mL) pectic enzyme liquid
- 20 Campden tablets or 2 teaspoons (12.4 g) potassium metabisulfite powder

1. Sanitize all equipment.

2. Through a screened funnel, pour approximately 4 gallons (15 L) of juice into a 5-gallon (19 L) carboy and the remaining gallon (3.8 L) of juice into two 1-gallon (3.8 L) jugs.

3. Test for sugar and acid and make adjustments, if necessary. When the specific gravity is 1.070–1.092, make a yeast starter by pouring approximately 4 ounces (120 mL) of juice and 4 ounces (120 mL) of lukewarm water into a bowl. Sprinkle the yeast and the yeast nutrient into the solution, allowing it to proliferate for about 30 minutes. Add the 20 drops (1 mL) of pectic enzyme liquid to this mixture. Add 6 ounces (180 mL) of the yeast starter to the carboy and

1 ounce (30 mL) of the starter to each of the 1-gallon (3.8 L) containers. Swish the containers to aid in the mixing.

4. Place a sheet of paper toweling, a wad of cotton, or a paper napkin into the necks of the containers. Fermentation will start in 2 or 3 days. When the must is seen actively "bubbling," replace the paper or cotton stoppers with air locks, filled with clean water, for the rest of the fermentation.

5. Fermentation will continue for 7 to 12 days. Start to monitor the progress with the hydrometer after 7 days. When the specific gravity is below 1.000 (that is, 0.995 or lower), proceed to the next step. If it's above 1.000, allow the wine to ferment longer, until it reaches a specific gravity of below 1.000.

6. Once the specific gravity is below 1.000, siphon the wine from the three containers into a sanitized carboy. This procedure is called racking. Stabilize the wine by adding 5 Campden tablets (crushed to a powder) or ½ teaspoon

(3.1 g) of potassium metabisulfite powder and fill the carboy up to the top. Place the wine in a cool spot (such as a garage or root cellar).

7. Let the wine sit in this cool location for 3 to 4 weeks, then rack again into a sanitized carboy. Three or four more rackings, spaced 3 to 4 weeks apart, should pace the wine to its finish. After the second racking, use just 3 crushed Campden tablets (or ¼ tsp [1.4 g] potassium metabisulfite).

8. If the wine does not clear, let it sit for another 3 to 4 weeks and rack again. It should clear itself naturally.

9. When the wine is clear, it is time to bottle. Taste the wine and adjust its sweetness, if desired, then bottle. Age at least 1 year before tasting. Most red wines will improve from the second year on, depending on the variety. Periodic tasting will determine when the wine is at its peak. 🍇

RED WINE FROM ZINFANDEL GRAPE JUICE

This is a highly flavorful red with a rich color, aroma, and taste. Overtones of blackberry and pepper come to the front, and the wine finishes full on the palate. Zinfandel has a characteristic "bramble" or "berry" flavor. Considered America's varietal, Zinfandel offers a wine range of types and styles. Serve with roast turkey, spicy pastas, and dishes with garlic.

Yield: 5 gallons (19 L)

5	gallons (19 L) Zinfandel grape juice
1	package (5 g) Red Star Pasteur Red yeast
3	tablespoons (11.1 g) Oak-Mor
3	teaspoons (8.8 g) yeast nutrient
20	drops (1 mL) pectic enzyme liquid
20	Campden tablets or 2 teaspoons (12.4 g) potassium metabisulfite powder

1. Sanitize all equipment.

2. Through a screened funnel, pour approximately 4 gallons (15 L) of juice into a 5-gallon (19 L) carboy and the remaining gallon (3.8 L) of juice into two 1-gallon (3.8 L) jugs.

3. Test for sugar and acid and make adjustments, if necessary. When the specific gravity is

1.070–1.092, make a yeast starter by pouring approximately 4 ounces (120 mL) of juice and 4 ounces (120 mL) of lukewarm water into a bowl. Sprinkle the yeast, the Oak-Mor, and the yeast nutrient into the solution, allowing it to proliferate for about 30 minutes. Add the 20 drops (1 mL) of pectic enzyme liquid to this mixture. Add 6 ounces (180 mL) of the yeast starter to the carboy and 1 ounce (30 mL) of the starter to each of the 1-gallon (3.8 L) containers. Swish the containers to aid in the mixing.

4. Place a sheet of paper toweling, a wad of cotton, or a paper napkin into the necks of the containers. Fermentation will start in 2 or 3 days. When the must is seen actively "bubbling," replace the paper or cotton stoppers with air locks, filled with clean water, for the rest of the fermentation.

5. Fermentation will continue for 7 to 12 days. Start to monitor the progress with the hydrometer after 7 days. When the specific gravity is below 1.000 (that is, 0.995 or lower), proceed to the next step. If it's above 1.000, allow the wine to ferment longer, until it reaches a specific gravity of below 1.000.

6. Once the specific gravity is below 1.000, siphon the wine from the three containers into a sanitized carboy. This procedure is called racking. Stabilize the wine by adding 5 Campden tablets (crushed to a powder) or ½ teaspoon (3.1 g) of potassium metabisulfite powder and fill the carboy up to the top. Place the wine in a cool spot (such as a garage or root cellar).

7. Let the wine sit in this cool location for 3 to 4 weeks, then rack again into a sanitized carboy. Three or four more rackings, spaced 3 to 4 weeks apart, should pace the wine to its finish. After the second racking, use just 3 crushed Campden tablets (or ¼ tsp [1.4 g] potassium metabisulfite).

8. If the wine does not clear, let it sit for another 3 to 4 weeks and rack again. It should clear itself naturally.

9. When the wine is clear, it is time to bottle. Taste the wine and adjust its sweetness, if desired, then bottle. Age at least 1 year before tasting. Most red wines will improve from the second year on, depending on the variety. Periodic tasting will determine when the wine is at its peak.

BLUSH WINE FROM ZINFANDEL BLUSH GRAPE JUICE

With a hint of rosé, the light Zinfandel Blush is fruity and refreshing. It has a taste reminiscent of candied raspberries and is an easy-drinking wine due to the ideal acid balance. Do not age; drink while it is young and fresh. Strictly a social wine, it is best served with finger foods.

Yield: 5 gallons (19 L)

5 gallons (19 L) Zinfandel Blush grape juice
1 package (5 g) Red Star Côtes des Blancs yeast
3 teaspoons (8.8 g) yeast nutrient
20 drops (1 mL) pectic enzyme liquid
20 Campden tablets or 2 teaspoons (12.4 g) potassium metabisulfite powder

1. Sanitize all equipment.

2. Through a screened funnel, pour approximately 4 gallons (15 L) of juice into a 5-gallon (19 L) carboy and the remaining gallon (3.8 L) of juice into two 1-gallon (3.8 L) jugs.

3. Test for sugar and acid and make adjustments, if necessary. When the specific gravity is 1.070–1.092, make a yeast starter by pouring approximately 4 ounces (120 mL) of juice and 4 ounces (120 mL) of lukewarm water into a bowl. Sprinkle the yeast and the yeast nutrient into the solution, allowing it to proliferate for about 30 minutes. Add the 20 drops (1 mL) of pectic enzyme liquid to this mixture. Now add 6 ounces (180 mL) of the yeast starter to the carboy and 1 ounce (30 mL) of the starter to each of the 1-gallon (3.8 L) containers. Swish the containers to aid in the mixing.

4. Place a sheet of paper toweling, a wad of cotton, or a paper napkin into the necks of the containers. Fermentation will start in 2 or 3 days. When the must is seen actively "bubbling," replace the paper or cotton stoppers with air locks, filled with clean water, for the rest of the fermentation.

5. Fermentation will continue for 7 to 12 days. Start to monitor the progress with the hydrometer after 7 days. When the specific gravity is below 1.000 (that is, 0.995 or lower), proceed to the next step. If it's above 1.000, allow the wine to ferment longer until it reaches a specific gravity of below 1.000.

6. Once the specific gravity is below 1.000, siphon the wine from the three containers into a sanitized carboy. This procedure is called racking. Stabilize the wine by adding 5 Campden tablets (crushed to a powder) or ½ teaspoon (3.1 g) of potassium metabisulfite powder and fill the carboy up to the top. Place the wine in a cool spot (such as a garage or root cellar).

7. Let the wine sit in this cool location for 3 to 4 weeks, then rack again into a sanitized carboy. Three or four more rackings, spaced 3 to 4 weeks apart, should pace the wine to its finish.

After the second racking, use just 3 crushed Campden tablets (or ¼ tsp [1.4 g] potassium metabisulfite).

8. If the wine does not clear, let it sit for another 3 to 4 weeks and rack again. It should clear itself naturally.

9. When the wine is clear, it is time to bottle. Taste the wine and adjust its sweetness, if desired, then bottle. Age at least 6 months before tasting. Drink this wine while it is still young, or it will lose its fruity qualities.

WHITE WINE FROM GRAPES 6

To MANY HOME WINEMAKERS, producing wines from grapes is the ultimate experience. It requires more work than making wines from kits, juices, and concentrates; but starting from scratch provides the opportunity to exercise maximum control and creativity. From grape selection to bottling, you'll be able to claim authorship all the way, so you'll be entitled to full credit for the results.

Traditionally, California has been the source for most of this hemisphere's fresh grapes. That's changing, however, as more and more wineries throughout the United States and Canada are selling grapes to the general public. Buying and using fresh grapes for home winemaking has never been easier, with a wide selection of so many varieties.

GETTING STARTED

You'll need to plan ahead when you're going to make wine from scratch, so that you can purchase your grapes at the peak of freshness. For starters, keep in mind the old rule of thumb: You can't make good wine from bad grapes. For example, Thompson Seedless grapes are readily available and inexpensive. Every year, thousands of cases of this variety are sold to home winemakers. The purchasers then go on to make rather bland wines. The Thompson Seedless should be confined to eating and making raisins only.

We urge you to consider other varieties, which, while a little more costly up front, will yield better results. In this chapter, we present twenty other types of grapes for your consideration. They're among the most popular varieties available on the market, and the descriptive passages at the beginning of each recipe will tell you what you'll get and what foods the wine will complement.

Once you've decided what you want to make, check in with a wholesaler to determine the best time to make your purchase. While you're waiting for that moment, make sure that you have what you need in the way of equipment.

Equipment Needs

If you've made wine from kits, juices, or concentrates, you probably already have a lot of the needed supplies on hand already. Chapter 1 contains a detailed description of the items listed.

Equipment and Supplies

- Stemmer-crusher (for crushing grapes and removing stems)
- Winepress (to squeeze out the juice from the crushed grapes)
- Mesh nylon bag (to line the winepress)
- 2 Fermentation containers, 5 gallons (19 L) or larger (these may be glass carboys or plastic containers)
- Floating thermometer
- Acid titration kit
- Pectic enzyme
- Siphon hose
- Racking tube
- Hydrometer (saccharometer) and cylinder
- Long-handled stirring spoon
- Carboy bung (rubber stopper)
- Funnel with screen
- Measuring cup
- Wine bottles
- Bottle closures (corks, push corks, or screw caps)
- Corking device (for standard wine corks)
- Sal soda and bleach (for cleaning)
- Potassium metabisulfite powder or Campden tablets
- Sugar (for sugar adjustments)

A WORD ABOUT CLEANLINESS

Keep your work areas and equipment squeaky clean. The best ingredients and the finest equipment can't save a wine that's been contaminated by bacteria!

- Commercial wine yeast
- Yeast nutrient
- Fining agent (to clarify wine)
- Acid blend (for acid adjustments)
- Oak-Mor or another oak flavoring (optional, depending on style)

Although a crushing device is not absolutely necessary, most serious winemakers will eventually purchase or at least rent one, as it saves a lot of time. So does a winepress. If you don't want to spend a great deal of money on these devices, consider renting, or perhaps joining a club where the members share in the purchase.

Buying Grapes

We recommend that, if you're a beginner, you seek out local home winemakers for grape-buying assistance. They can help you to avoid common mistakes. Be sure to shop around and compare prices. Check out the reliability and reputation of potential suppliers. After you make a choice, keep a record of your experiences and prices for next year's harvest.

Always go for quality, even if it costs more up front. The end results are well worth it.

There are three sources of fresh grapes:

1. Local grape growers (or regional growers)
2. Local or regional fruit wholesalers
3. Local or regional wine supply stores

BUYING FROM LOCAL GROWERS

If you are lucky enough to live in or near a grape-producing vineyard, you have the option of going directly to the source for your grapes. When buying from local grape growers, talk to the vineyard's owner or manager and see if he or she will sell to you as a home winemaker. Visit in spring or early summer and get the logistical information about buying their grapes. Do I pick my own? What is the cost per pound? What varieties will you sell me? If possible, get the names of previous purchasers for verification of grape growers' credibility. The harvest usually starts in early September and may run through November. If you can strike a deal, you may have to leave a deposit for your order. You buy fresh grapes by the pound. It takes between 12 and 18 pounds (5.4–8.1 kg) of grapes to make 1 gallon (3.8 L) of wine. Compare the vineyard's prices with a local grape wholesaler or wine supply store to see if they are in line with average grape costs.

BUYING FROM WHOLESALERS

Local or regional wholesale fruit dealers are suppliers of wine grapes from other regions (mostly California) in the fall during harvest. Fruit wholesalers are listed in the Yellow Pages of most phone books. If you can get recommendations from fellow winemakers about the ones they use, that is even better than the phone book. Most wholesalers carry a wide variety of grapes and maintain them in refrigerated storage areas, but some do not refrigerate them. Avoid the latter, as grapes rot quickly and will accumulate fungi and bacteria when left in temperate conditions. Fresh grapes usually come in 36-pound (16.3 kg) wooden boxes (some wholesalers may ship with other amounts, but this seems to be the norm now). Call ahead to get the costs of each variety and when they will be available. Try to be there on the day the grapes arrive to confirm freshness.

Look for fresh, clean grapes and inspect each box you buy. Take the time to look at the grapes thoroughly, checking to see that they aren't rotten or moldy. And if the sugar content is too high (your dealer should be able to tell you what it is), don't buy them! Grapes with a sugar content of 26 degrees Brix or higher could cause many problems.

You will need a pickup truck or station wagon to cart home your grapes. If you have a cool location, you can store the grapes for a few days, but don't wait: try to crush them as soon as possible to ensure maximum potential. If the grapes are left too long in a temperate environment, rotting starts and unwanted bacteria invade and ruin the grapes.

BUYING FROM WINEMAKING STORES

Winemaking supply stores usually will carry fresh grapes during fall. They buy them from some of the wholesalers you can buy from, but a few will order directly from the source in California or in other states. Check with the store in the spring and ask when the prices and varieties will be available. Deposits are usually required when the grapes are ordered. Most wine supply stores are reliable sources. They want to keep you as a loyal customer buying all the other supplies necessary for your winemaking. They will, many times, even sell grapes to you at a discounted rate to garner your other business.

GRAPE VARIETIES

The grapes we've prepared recipes for in this chapter tend to be readily available. Every so often, a dealer will offer you a less common variety. It may well be that what's presented is perfectly fine, but we urge you to do some independent research prior to purchasing an unfamiliar variety. If it isn't available in bottled form in a wine shop, you probably don't want to be a pioneer.

Recommended white grape varieties include:

- ◆ Cayuga
- ◆ Chardonnay
- ◆ Chenin Blanc
- ◆ French Colombard

SANITIZING EQUIPMENT

The need to sanitize all equipment that comes in contact with your wine cannot be overstated. Here is a method we use with success.

Potassium metabisulfite powder
Hot water
Jug

1. Put 3 tablespoons (56 g) of potassium metabisulfite into a 1-liter (33.8 oz) jug of hot water — 85°F (29°C) — to make a reusable sanitizing solution. It will last up to 6 months, if kept tightly sealed. (Store at room temperature.)
2. Rinse all equipment thoroughly in the solution.
3. After sanitizing, rinse with cold water.

- ◆ Gewürztraminer
- ◆ Marsanne
- ◆ Pinot Blanc
- ◆ Sauvignon Blanc
- ◆ Semillon
- ◆ Seyval Blanc
- ◆ Vidal Blanc
- ◆ Vignoles
- ◆ White Riesling

Note: Never buy Thompson Seedless grapes for winemaking. They produce very poor wine.

WHITE GRAPE PREPARATION

The first step is to remove all rotten and hard-green (immature) grapes, along with the leaves. Next, sanitize your equipment.

CRUSHING

Now we are ready to crush some grapes. Crushing is exactly what it sounds like — breaking down grapes into a pulpy mixture of skins, seeds, and juice. This prepares the grapes for the step of pressing and allows you to get the most juice possible out of your grapes. Making a few gallons of wine from grapes can be done completely by hand, but larger amounts require more assistance. A standard fruit crusher (one with a handle that is turned when operating) can crush grapes. This type of crusher has a V-shaped basket with metal gears at the lower level that turn and crush the grapes when the handle is turned. It sits on an open container that will catch the crushed grapes and also catch all of the stems. More than one winemaker has acquired his at a garage sale.

REMOVE STEMS

Be careful to remove all stems from the crushed grapes; stems can add bitterness to your wine.

A mechanical (electrical) stemmer-crusher is ideal. It throws away the stems as it crushes the grapes and then drops the crushed grapes and juice into the container it sits on. There are a number of crushers on the market. Our favorite, the flywheel type, usually has a stainless-steel hopper and is about 48 inches (1.2 m) long. Fifty pounds (22.7 kg) of grapes can be crushed and stemmed in 1 or 2 minutes. For the winemaker making a lot of wine, a stemmer-crusher is a time-saving and efficient device. It is relatively expensive, so if you can borrow, rent, or buy one along with some friends, that's even better.

PRESSING

Pressing is nothing more than extracting the juice from the crushed grapes after the stems have been removed. With white wines, pressing is done immediately after crushing the grapes, before any fermentation takes place. This creates a lighter color and more delicate taste. Pressing for red wines occurs after the crushed grapes have been fermented for up to 1 month, encouraging more color and complexity in the wines.

Pressing out juice can be difficult and wasteful. You could press out the grapes by hand, with a pair of paddles, or with whatever device you can think of, but maximizing the potential is difficult this way. A winepress will prove more efficient and productive.

Basket Press. Basket, also called ratchet, presses have been around for many years. They are almost always made of wood, although some stainless-steel models are on the market. These presses usually have a wooden basket, steel base, and steel legs (see illustration on page 9). They work on a hydraulic system of turning and pressing. Sizes of these presses vary: Some hold 20 pounds (9 kg) of grapes; others hold as much as 350 pounds (159 kg).

The process is simple. Fill the basket with crushed grapes. Turn and press down on the top handle to squeeze out the juice from the crushed grapes. The juice runs out the bottom into a container. If you are using a carboy as your container, you will need a funnel to help catch the valuable juice. When the grapes are squeezed out completely, empty the basket and discard the pressed-out grapes, also called pomace.

Fiberglass screening is used by many home winemakers to keep foreign matter from getting into the juice during the pressing process. The screen (an old house screen, properly cut and sanitized, could also do the job) is placed inside the basket cage before the grapes are introduced. It keeps pips, seeds, and other matter from getting into the juice.

Bladder Press. A newer, more efficient press has been developed called the bladder press. It has a rubber bladder attached to the center spike of the press, a wooden or steel basket that holds the grapes, and a steel base and steel legs; some even have rollers. A home garden hose is attached to the bladder. As the bladder fills with water and expands, the grapes are pressed and the juice runs out of the bottom into a container. A valve on the press indicates the pressure in pounds per square inch (psi) as the bladder fills. Pressure up to 60 psi is recommended. This new press has proved to be an efficient method of pressing out juice or wine from skins — albeit a more expensive system.

Buying a Press. Look into purchasing a used press. Most of the time, the only reason it is being replaced is that the winemaker wants to move up to a larger unit. Presses are used for only a few hours a year, so secondhand presses tend to be in excellent condition.

TESTING THE JUICE FOR SUGAR AND ACID

Once you've pressed your grapes, it's time to test the juice to determine sugar and acid counts. (See chapter 2 for specific procedures.) The sugar level should be in the 20 to 22 degrees Brix range. If the numbers are lower than that, you'll have to add sugar per our instructions on

---

FROM POMACE TO COMPOST

Pomace, the pressed-out grape skins and pulp, is sometimes used as the base for making a winelike drink called grappa. We believe that the effort and time required to make "fake" wine and then distill it to make grappa are not worth the results, which are inferior. If you are a gardener, we suggest instead that you just add pomace to your compost pile.

page 37. Make sure that all of the added sugar is dissolved and not simply sitting on the bottom of the container.

Acid readings (see chapter 2) should be no lower than 0.55 percent and no higher than 0.90 percent. It's best to adjust to 0.70 to 0.75 percent. If your initial reading is too high, you will have to ameliorate the juice by adding water to dilute the acid, until you reach the desired level. You're most likely to do this with eastern varieties. If the level is too low — which is frequently the case with California juices — you'll need to add acid. (See page 37) for a chart showing acid blend additions.) Once you've balanced the sugar and acid levels, it's time to stabilize the juice.

STABILIZATION

The juice is laden with all sorts of bacteria that were accumulated in the vineyard. A few of these may be beneficial, but most of them can have a negative impact on your wine. At this point, then, kill off the bacteria by adding sulfur dioxide, either in the form of potassium metabisulfite powder or with Campden tablets. One Campden tablet per gallon (3.8 L) will yield 75 parts per million (ppm), which will do the job, and ½ teaspoon (3.1 mL) of potassium metabisulfite powder per gallon (3.8 L) will generate 80 ppm. Add either of these to the juice and let it sit overnight with a cloth over the container.

YEAST AND FERMENTATION

By the next day, a number of juices will have begun to clarify, and you're likely to see an accumulation of sediment on the bottom of your container. If this is the case, rack off the clear juice into another container and discard the sediment. (See pages 18 and 24 for an explanation of racking.)

Add a yeast culture to the juice at this point. (See pages 40–42 for yeast strain selections.) Add the yeast starter to initiate fermentation. Loosely cover the fermentation container to allow gases to escape and to keep out bugs and debris. If you are fermenting in a glass carboy, an air lock in a rubber bung works fine; or you can put either a wadded-up paper towel or wadded cotton into the neck of the carboy. If you're using an open container, cover it loosely with a towel, cloth, or sheet of plastic.

Fermentation should start within a few days of inoculation with the yeast culture. Monitor the fermenting juice daily by checking the specific gravity with a hydrometer (see chapter 2). When the specific gravity level reaches 1.000 or less, your wine is ready for racking.

GRAPE GUIDE

Generally speaking, grapes from the eastern United States and Canada require additional sugar, but they tend to have elevated acid counts. California and western grapes usually have the opposite characteristics.

FRUITY-STYLE WHITES

Some white wines are best when made in a "fruity" style with a fresh grape taste and aroma. Their chemical makeup offers a better experience when the wine is served at a younger age. Certain yeasts, as outlined in chapter 4, can help make this style of wine. Plus, you can aid the process by storing the wine in an extra-cool place such as a garage, cellar, or refrigerator. The cooler environment helps to stabilize the wine and precipitates the formation of tartrates (the crystal-like formations on the bottom of the container).

Put in additional crushed Campden tablets or potassium metabisulfite powder when racking the wine for the first time. A total of 5 crushed Campden tablets or ½ teaspoon (3.1 g) of potassium metabisulfite powder keeps the wine "fruity" and prevents it from going through a malolactic (secondary) fermentation. Open fruity-style wines after aging them for just a few months and enjoy them while they're still young.

White varieties that should be made in this way include Riesling, Gewürztraminer, Sylvaner, and Muller-Thurgau.

Important Note: Ferment white wines in a cooler environment, such as a garage or basement, for at least 1 month. Ideally the air temperature will be between 55° and 70°F (12.8°–21°C).

RACKING

When the fermentation process has ended, it is important to rack the wine into another sanitized container to prevent the penetration of bacteria. Put 3 crushed Campden tablets or ¼ teaspoon (1.4 g) of potassium metabisulfite powder into the new container before you add the wine.

Try to fill the container right up to the air-lock plug, although ½ inch (1.3 cm) of space is acceptable. If necessary, top off the juice with pre-boiled water or, better yet, a similar wine.

Two or three more rackings into sanitized containers may be necessary to fully clarify the wine. As time goes on, the wine should become progressively clearer, with residues falling to the bottom. If, for some reason, the wine remains murky, you may have to use a fining agent to clear it up. We've had excellent luck clarifying wines with bentonite, kieselsol, and gelatin (see chapter 1).

Finishing

Once the wine clears, it is ready for bottling. This is the point at which you'll do the last of your balancing in order to guarantee that you have the flavor you're looking for. Begin by tasting the wine. If it is too tart, you will need to add sugar. Take a hydrometer reading and, if the Brix scale is below zero, add enough sugar to raise the figure to zero, which will give you a sugar count of 1 to 2 percent (for more on adjusting with sugar, see page 37).

Blending White Wines

Before bottling, consider blending your wine with another one that's either sweeter or more tart. Veteran winemakers do this often. Remember that new wines can be quite harsh and require some aging to mellow. The following white wines blend nicely with each other using a 20:80 or 25:75 mixing ratio.

◆ Sauvignon Blanc and Semillon
◆ Riesling and Gewürztraminer
◆ Pinot Blanc and Riesling or Gewürztraminer
◆ Chenin Blanc and Riesling or Gewürztraminer

Once you've finished balancing, pour the wine into sanitized bottles using a bottle filler or siphon tube and cork them up. If you use tra-

PREVENT REFERMENTATION

When you add sugar, you'll also need to add 2½ teaspoons (7.5 g) potassium sorbate and ½ teaspoon (3.1 g) potassium metabisulfite *or* 2½ crushed Campden tablets in order to prevent refermentation. If you fail to do this, the bottles will ultimately "open" themselves and spew their contents all over the place!

ditional corks, a corking machine is a good investment.

Now comes the hard part: being patient while your wine matures. Each recipe will tell you how long the wine has to age.

Recipes

These recipes are designed to guide you in the production of good, palatable wines. Veteran winemakers frequently experiment by adding to basic recipes and, in time, we hope you will create your own recipes, too. Keep records of everything you do when you make wine. That way, you'll know what works and you'll be able to go back and replicate past successes.

WHITE WINE FROM AURORA FRENCH-AMERICAN HYBRID GRAPES

The Aurora is one of the oldest and most successful French hybrid grape varieties. Located in the eastern, northern, and midwestern sections of the United States and Canada, this variety has proved hardy and cold resistant. Used to make sparkling wines, Aurora also makes a delightful, fruity, crisp white wine. It can also serve as a blending wine. It should be less pricey in most regions where it grows. This wine goes well with finger foods and light, picnic-type dishes.

Yield: 5 gallons (19 L)

60–75 pounds (27–34 kg) fresh grapes
⅛ teaspoon (0.5 g) pectic enzyme
17–20 Campden tablets or 1½–2 teaspoons (9.3–12.4 g) potassium metabisulfite powder
1 package (5 g) Wyeast Chablis or Red Star Côtes des Blancs yeast
3 teaspoons (8.8 g) yeast nutrient

1. Sanitize all equipment.

2. Remove any spoiled grapes from the clusters, then crush the grapes. Add ⅛ teaspoon (0.5 g) pectic enzyme to the crushed grapes. This will maximize the removal of juice from the skins. Let sit for 2 hours.

3. Press out the grapes and put the juice in a fermentation container. Add 5 crushed Campden tablets or ½ teaspoon (3.1 g) potassium metabisulfite powder to the juice and let sit for at least 4 hours or even overnight.

4. Test the acid and sugar and make adjustments, if necessary. Make a yeast starter by pouring 4 ounces (120 mL) of grape juice and 4 ounces (120 mL) of lukewarm water into a bowl, sprinkle in the yeast, and let proliferate for about 30 minutes. Add this yeast starter and the yeast nutrient to the grape juice and swish to help mix.

5. Cover the fermentation container loosely with a sheet of plastic; this allows gases to escape but deters foreign matter from entering. If using a glass carboy, which we recommend, insert a rubber bung and fermentation lock (filled with clean water) into the carboy. Allow some space in the fermentation container — about 20 percent — for foaming and bubbling. Within 3 days, the fermentation will start. It should continue for 7 to 12 days.

6. After several days of fermentation, start to monitor the wine. When the specific gravity gets below 1.000, fermentation is complete and you can proceed to the next step. If the specific

gravity is above 1.000, allow the wine to continue to ferment until it goes below 1.000.

7. Put 5 crushed Campden tablets or ½ teaspoon (3.1 g) of potassium metabisulfite into a sanitized 5-gallon (19 L) carboy. Siphon the wine into the clean carboy and fill up to the bung and fermentation lock. Add water that has been boiled for 15 minutes and cooled to room temperature or a similar wine to fill the new carboy, if necessary. Place the carboy in a cool place like a garage or root cellar. This will clear out the tartrates and stabilize the wine. Two or three more rackings will be necessary to finalize the process. At each subsequent racking, use just 3 crushed Campden tablets or ¼ teaspoon (1.4 g) of potassium metabisulfite powder.

8. If wine does not clear, use gelatin, kieselsol, or bentonite finings following the manufacturer's instructions and allow an additional 3 to 4 weeks for the wine to clear.

9. When the wine is clear, it is time to bottle. If you had to use finings, filter the wine to guarantee complete cleanliness. Taste the wine and adjust for sweetness; then bottle. After bottling, wait 3 months before drinking. 🍇

WHITE WINE FROM CAYUGA FRENCH-AMERICAN HYBRID GRAPES

Cayuga is one of the more popular French-American hybrid varieties. This grape is productive and cold hardy, and wine made from it is fruity and lightly scented. It blends well with other varieties and also makes a pleasant, easy-to-drink quaffing beverage. Serve with broiled fish.

Yield: 5 gallons (19 L)

60–75 pounds (27–34 kg) fresh grapes
⅛ teaspoon (0.5 g) pectic enzyme
17–20 Campden tablets or 1½–2 teaspoons (9.3–12.4 g) potassium metabisulfite powder
1 package (5 g) Red Star Premier Cuvée or Lalvin EC-1118 yeast
3 teaspoons (8.8 g) yeast nutrient

1. Sanitize all equipment.

2. Remove any spoiled grapes from the clusters, then crush the grapes. Add ⅛ teaspoon (0.5 g) pectic enzyme to the crushed grapes. This will maximize the removal of juice from the skins. Let sit for 2 hours.

3. Press out the grapes and put the juice in a fermentation container. Add 5 crushed Campden tablets or ½ teaspoon (3.1 g) potassium metabisulfite powder to the juice and let sit for at least 4 hours or even overnight.

4. Test the acid and sugar and make adjustments, if necessary. Make a yeast starter by pouring 4 ounces (120 mL) of grape juice and 4 ounces (120 mL) of lukewarm water into a bowl, sprinkle in the yeast, and let proliferate for about 30 minutes. Add this yeast starter and the yeast nutrient to the grape juice and swish to help mix.

5. Cover the fermentation container loosely with a sheet of plastic; this allows gases to escape but deters foreign matter from entering. If using a glass carboy, which we recommend, insert a rubber bung and fermentation lock (filled with clean water) into the carboy. Allow some space in the fermentation container — about 20 percent — for foaming and bubbling. Within 3 days, the fermentation will start. It should continue for 7 to 12 days.

6. After several days of fermentation, start to monitor the wine. When the specific gravity gets below 1.000, fermentation is complete and you can proceed to the next step. If the specific gravity is above 1.000, allow the wine to continue to ferment until it goes below 1.000.

7. Put 5 crushed Campden tablets or ½ teaspoon (3.1 g) of potassium metabisulfite into a sanitized 5-gallon (19 L) carboy. Siphon the wine into the clean carboy and fill up to the bung and fermentation lock. Add water that has been boiled for 15 minutes and cooled to room temperature or a similar wine to fill the new carboy, if necessary. Place the carboy in a cool place like a garage or root cellar. This will clear out the tartrates and stabilize the wine. Two or three more rackings will be necessary to finalize the process. At each subsequent racking, use just 3 crushed Campden tablets or ¼ teaspoon (1.4 g) of potassium metabisulfite powder.

8. If wine does not clear, use gelatin, kieselsol, or bentonite finings following the manufacturer's instructions and allow an additional 3 to 4 weeks for the wine to clear.

9. When the wine is clear, it is time to bottle. If you had to use finings, filter the wine to guarantee complete cleanliness. Taste the wine and adjust for sweetness; then bottle. After bottling, wait 3 months before drinking. 🍇

WHITE WINE FROM CHARDONNAY GRAPES

This is the most popular white variety in North America. The Chardonnay can be made in the robust California style, in the French "austere" style, or in the fruity style. Chardonnay seems to do better when it goes through the malolactic fermentation and when it comes in contact with oak. The attractive buttery, vanilla-like flavors are appreciated by connoisseurs. Serve with chicken or lobster dishes.

Yield: 5 gallons (19 L)

60–75 pounds (27–34 kg) fresh grapes
⅛ teaspoon (0.5 g) pectic enzyme
17–20 Campden tablets or 1½–2 teaspoons (9.3–12.4 g) potassium metabisulfite powder
1 package (5 g) Red Star Montrachet or Lallamand K1-V116 yeast
3 teaspoons (8.8 g) yeast nutrient
3 tablespoons (11.1 g) Oak-Mor
1 package malolactic culture

1. Sanitize all equipment.

2. Remove any spoiled grapes from the clusters, then crush the grapes. Add ⅛ teaspoon (0.5 g) pectic enzyme to the crushed grapes. This will maximize the removal of juice from the skins. Let sit for 2 hours.

3. Press out grapes and put juice in a fermentation container. Add 5 crushed Campden tablets or ½ teaspoon (3.1 g) potassium metabisulfite powder to juice; let sit for at least 4 hours or overnight.

4. Test the acid and sugar and make adjustments, if necessary. Make a yeast starter by pouring 4 ounces (120 mL) of grape juice and 4 ounces (120 mL) of lukewarm water into a bowl, sprinkle in the yeast, and let proliferate for about 30 minutes. Add this yeast starter, the yeast nutrient, and the Oak-Mor to the grape juice and swish to help mix.

5. Cover the fermentation container loosely with a sheet of plastic; this allows gases to escape but deters foreign matter from entering. If using a glass carboy, which we recommend, insert a rubber bung and fermentation lock (filled with clean water) into the carboy. Allow some space in the fermentation container — about 20 percent — for foaming and bubbling. Within 3 days, the fermentation will start. It should continue for 7 to 12 days.

6. After several days of fermentation, add the malolactic culture, following instructions on the package. When the specific gravity gets below 1.000, fermentation is complete and you can proceed to the next step. If the specific gravity is above 1.000, allow the wine to continue to ferment until it goes below 1.000.

7. Put 5 crushed Campden tablets or ½ teaspoon (3.1 g) of potassium metabisulfite into a sanitized 5-gallon (19 L) carboy. Siphon the wine into the clean carboy and fill up to the bung and fermentation lock. Add water that has been boiled for 15 minutes and cooled to room temperature or a similar wine to fill the new carboy, if necessary. Place the carboy in a cool place like a garage or root cellar. This will clear out the tartrates and stabilize the wine. Two or three more rackings will be necessary to finalize the process. At each subsequent racking, use just 3 crushed Campden tablets or ¼ teaspoon (1.4 g) of potassium metabisulfite powder.

8. If wine does not clear, use gelatin, kieselsol, or bentonite finings following the manufacturer's instructions and allow an additional 3 to 4 weeks for the wine to clear.

9. When the wine is clear, it is time to bottle. If you had to use finings, filter the wine to guarantee complete cleanliness. Taste the wine and adjust for sweetness; then bottle. After bottling, wait 3 months before drinking. 🍇

White Wine from Chenin Blanc Grapes

Chenin Blanc is an excellent white wine grape grown around the world and usually is reasonably priced. It can be made either dry or semi-dry and excels as a blending variety. Crispness and fruitiness abound, and a hint of sweetness seems to elevate the quality. Serve this wine with cream dishes.

Yield: 5 gallons (19 L)

60–75 pounds (27–34 kg) fresh grapes
⅛ teaspoon (0.5 g) pectic enzyme
17–20 Campden tablets or 1½–2 teaspoons (9.3–12.4 g) potassium metabisulfite powder
1 package (5 g) Wyeast Chablis or Red Star Côtes des Blancs yeast
3 teaspoons (8.8 g) yeast nutrient

1. Sanitize all equipment.

2. Remove any spoiled grapes from the clusters, then crush the grapes. Add ⅛ teaspoon (0.5 g) pectic enzyme to the crushed grapes. This will maximize the removal of juice from the skins. Let sit for 2 hours.

3. Press out the grapes and put the juice in a fermentation container. Add 5 crushed Campden tablets or ½ teaspoon (3.1 g) potassium metabisulfite powder to the juice and let sit for at least 4 hours or even overnight.

4. Test the acid and sugar and make adjustments, if necessary. Make a yeast starter by pouring 4 ounces (120 mL) of grape juice and 4 ounces (120 mL) of lukewarm water into a bowl, sprinkle in the yeast, and let proliferate for about 30 minutes. Add this yeast starter and the yeast nutrient to the grape juice and swish to help mix.

5. Cover the fermentation container loosely with a sheet of plastic; this allows gases to escape but deters foreign matter from entering. If using a glass carboy, which we recommend, insert a rubber bung and fermentation lock (filled with clean water) into the carboy. Allow some space in the fermentation container — about 20 percent — for foaming and bubbling. Within 3 days, the fermentation will start. It should continue for 7 to 12 days.

6. After several days of fermentation, start to monitor the wine. When the specific gravity gets below 1.000, fermentation is complete and you can proceed to the next step. If the specific gravity is above 1.000, allow the wine to continue to ferment until it goes below 1.000.

7. Put 5 crushed Campden tablets or ½ teaspoon (3.1 g) of potassium metabisulfite into a sanitized 5-gallon (19 L) carboy. Siphon the wine into the clean carboy and fill up to the bung and fermentation lock. Add water that has been boiled for 15 minutes and cooled to room temperature or a similar wine to fill the new carboy, if necessary. Place the carboy in a cool place like a garage or root cellar. This will clear out the tartrates and stabilize the wine. Two or three more rackings will be necessary to finalize the process. At each subsequent racking, use just 3 crushed Campden tablets or ¼ teaspoon (1.4 g) of potassium metabisulfite powder.

8. If wine does not clear, use gelatin, kieselsol, or bentonite finings following the manufacturer's instructions and allow an additional 3 to 4 weeks for the wine to clear.

9. When the wine is clear, it is time to bottle. If you had to use finings, filter the wine to guarantee complete cleanliness. Taste the wine and adjust for sweetness; then bottle. After bottling, wait 3 months before drinking. 🍇

WHITE WINE FROM DELAWARE GRAPES

This is a native American grape of the Labrusca variety. It was named after the town of Delaware, Ohio, and is available throughout the eastern and northern regions of the United States and Canada. Although pink, the grape yields white juice and is valuable as both a wine grape and a table grape. It is famous for its high sugar content, and goes well with soft cheeses and fruit.

Yield: 5 gallons (19 L)

60–75	pounds (27–34 kg) fresh grapes
⅛	teaspoon (0.5 g) pectic enzyme
17–20	Campden tablets or 1½–2 teaspoons (9.3–12.4 g) potassium metabisulfite powder
1	package (5 g) Lalvin L2056 or Red Star Côtes des Blancs yeast
3	teaspoons (8.8 g) yeast nutrient

1. Sanitize all equipment.

2. Remove any spoiled grapes from the clusters, then crush the grapes. Add ⅛ teaspoon (0.5 g) pectic enzyme to the crushed grapes. This will maximize the removal of juice from the skins. Let sit for 2 hours.

3. Press out the grapes and put the juice in a fermentation container. Add 5 crushed Campden tablets or ½ teaspoon (3.1 g) potassium metabisulfite powder to the juice and let sit for at least 4 hours or even overnight.

4. Test the acid and sugar and make adjustments, if necessary. Make a yeast starter by pouring 4 ounces (120 mL) of grape juice and 4 ounces (120 mL) of lukewarm water into a bowl, sprinkle in the yeast, and let proliferate for about 30 minutes. Add this yeast starter and the yeast nutrient to the grape juice and swish to help mix.

5. Cover the fermentation container loosely with a sheet of plastic; this allows gases to escape but deters foreign matter from entering. If using a glass carboy, which we recommend, insert a rubber bung and fermentation lock (filled with clean water) into the carboy. Allow some space in the fermentation container — about 20 percent — for foaming and bubbling. Within 3 days, the fermentation will start. It should continue for 7 to 12 days.

6. After several days of fermentation, start to monitor the wine. When the specific gravity gets below 1.000, fermentation is complete and you can proceed to the next step. If the specific

gravity is above 1.000, allow the wine to continue to ferment until it goes below 1.000.

7. Put 5 crushed Campden tablets or ½ teaspoon (3.1 g) of potassium metabisulfite into a sanitized 5-gallon (19 L) carboy. Siphon the wine into the clean carboy and fill up to the bung and fermentation lock. Add water that has been boiled for 15 minutes and cooled to room temperature or a similar wine to fill the new carboy, if necessary. Place the carboy in a cool place like a garage or root cellar. This will clear out the tartrates and stabilize the wine. Two or three more rackings will be necessary to finalize the process. At each subsequent racking, use just 3 crushed Campden tablets or ¼ teaspoon (1.4 g) of potassium metabisulfite powder.

8. If wine does not clear, use gelatin, kieselsol, or bentonite finings following the manufacturer's instructions and allow an additional 3 to 4 weeks for the wine to clear.

9. When the wine is clear, it is time to bottle. If you had to use finings, filter the wine to guarantee complete cleanliness. Taste the wine and adjust for sweetness; then bottle. After bottling, wait 3 months before drinking. 🍇

White Wine from Dutchess Grapes

Dutchess is a native American Labrusca that produces well in northern climates. It is a fragrant wine, with aromas of flowers and fruit, as well as an excellent blending wine. Drink it young, when its fruitiness can be appreciated. It is a fine accompaniment to Asian dishes.

Yield: 5 gallons (19 L)

60–75 pounds (27–34 kg) fresh grapes
⅛ teaspoon (0.5 g) pectic enzyme
17–20 Campden tablets or 1½–2 teaspoons (9.3–12.4 g) potassium metabisulfite powder
1 package (5 g) Wyeast Chablis or Red Star Côtes des Blancs yeast
3 teaspoons (8.8 g) yeast nutrient

1. Sanitize all equipment.

2. Remove any spoiled grapes from the clusters, then crush the grapes. Add ⅛ teaspoon (0.5 g) pectic enzyme to the crushed grapes. This will maximize the removal of juice from the skins. Let sit for 2 hours.

3. Press out the grapes and put the juice in a fermentation container. Add 5 crushed Campden tablets or ½ teaspoon (3.1 g) potassium metabisulfite powder to the juice and let sit for at least 4 hours or even overnight.

4. Test the acid and sugar and make adjustments, if necessary. Make a yeast starter by pouring 4 ounces (120 mL) of grape juice and 4 ounces (120 mL) of lukewarm water into a bowl, sprinkle in the yeast, and let proliferate for about 30 minutes. Add this yeast starter and the yeast nutrient to the grape juice and swish to help mix.

5. Cover the fermentation container loosely with a sheet of plastic; this allows gases to escape but deters foreign matter from entering. If using a glass carboy, which we recommend, insert a rubber bung and fermentation lock (filled with clean water) into the carboy. Allow some space in the fermentation container — about 20 percent — for foaming and bubbling. Within 3 days, the fermentation will start. It should continue for 7 to 12 days.

6. After several days of fermentation, start to monitor the wine. When the specific gravity gets below 1.000, fermentation is complete and you can proceed to the next step. If the specific gravity is above 1.000, allow the wine to continue to ferment until it goes below 1.000.

7. Put 5 crushed Campden tablets or ½ teaspoon (3.1 g) of potassium metabisulfite into a sanitized 5-gallon (19 L) carboy. Siphon the wine into the clean carboy and fill up to the bung and fermentation lock. Add water that has been boiled for 15 minutes and cooled to room temperature or a similar wine to fill the new carboy, if necessary. Place the carboy in a cool place like a garage or root cellar. This will clear out the tartrates and stabilize the wine. Two or three more rackings will be necessary to finalize the process. At each subsequent racking, use just 3 crushed Campden tablets or ¼ teaspoon (1.4 g) of potassium metabisulfite powder.

8. If wine does not clear, use gelatin, kieselsol, or bentonite finings following the manufacturer's instructions and allow an additional 3 to 4 weeks for the wine to clear.

9. When the wine is clear, it is time to bottle. If you had to use finings, filter the wine to guarantee complete cleanliness. Taste the wine and adjust for sweetness; then bottle. After bottling, wait 3 months before drinking. 🍇

WHITE WINE FROM FRENCH COLOMBARD GRAPES

This is a highly productive white grape originally from France. The grape now flourishes in the United States, and produces a light, crisp, fruity wine suitable for fine, light cuisines. A versatile variety, the Colombard can be made in a wide range of styles and is a good blending partner for many wines.

Yield: 5 gallons (19 L)

60–75	pounds (27–34 kg) fresh grapes
⅛	teaspoon (0.5 g) pectic enzyme
17–20	Campden tablets or 1½–2 teaspoons (9.3–12.4 g) potassium metabisulfite powder
1	package (5 g) Red Star Montrachet or Lallamand K1-V116 yeast
3	teaspoons (8.8 g) yeast nutrient
3	tablespoons (11.1 g) Oak-Mor
1	package malolactic culture

1. Sanitize all equipment.

2. Remove any spoiled grapes from the clusters, then crush the grapes. Add ⅛ teaspoon (0.5 g) pectic enzyme to the crushed grapes. This will maximize the removal of juice from the skins. Let sit for 2 hours.

3. Press out the grapes and put the juice in a fermentation container. Add 5 crushed Campden tablets or ½ teaspoon (3.1 g) potassium metabisulfite powder to the juice and let sit for at least 4 hours or even overnight.

4. Test the acid and sugar and make adjustments, if necessary. Make a yeast starter by pouring 4 ounces (120 mL) of grape juice and 4 ounces (120 mL) of lukewarm water into a bowl, sprinkle in the yeast, and let proliferate for about 30 minutes. Add this yeast starter, the yeast nutrient, and the Oak-Mor to the grape juice and swish to help mix.

5. Cover the fermentation container loosely with a sheet of plastic; this allows gases to escape but deters foreign matter from entering. If using a glass carboy, which we recommend, insert a rubber bung and fermentation lock (filled with clean water) into the carboy. Allow some space in the fermentation container — about 20 percent — for foaming and bubbling. Within 3 days, the fermentation will start. It should continue for 7 to 12 days.

6. After several days of fermentation, add the malolactic culture, following instructions on the package. When the specific gravity gets below 1.000, fermentation is complete and you can proceed to the next step. If the specific gravity is above 1.000, allow the wine to continue to ferment until it goes below 1.000.

7. Put 5 crushed Campden tablets or ½ teaspoon (3.1 g) of potassium metabisulfite into a sanitized 5-gallon (19 L) carboy. Siphon the wine into the clean carboy and fill up to the bung and fermentation lock. Add water that has been boiled for 15 minutes and cooled to room temperature or a similar wine to fill the new carboy, if necessary. Place the carboy in a cool place like a garage or root cellar. This will clear out the tartrates and stabilize the wine. Two or three more rackings will be necessary to finalize the process. At each subsequent racking, use just 3 crushed Campden tablets or ¼ teaspoon (1.6 g) of potassium metabisulfite powder.

8. If wine does not clear, use gelatin, kieselsol, or bentonite finings following the manufacturer's instructions and allow an additional 3 to 4 weeks for the wine to clear.

9. When the wine is clear, it is time to bottle. If you had to use finings, filter the wine to guarantee complete cleanliness. Taste the wine and adjust for sweetness; then bottle. After bottling, wait 3 months before drinking. 🍇

WHITE WINE FROM GEWÜRZTRAMINER GRAPES

This is a spicy white wine from France, Germany, Canada, and the United States. Outstanding, unusual wines can be made from these premium grapes. Gewürztraminer is the featured wine in many Asian restaurants, and it matches well with Tex-Mex and Cajun cuisines. The grapes may be difficult to find unless you live near a wine-growing region.

Yield: 5 gallons (19 L)

60–75 pounds (27–34 kg) fresh grapes
⅛ teaspoon (0.5 g) pectic enzyme
17–20 Campden tablets or 1½–2 teaspoons (9.3–12.4 g) potassium metabisulfite powder
1 package (5 g) Wyeast Chablis or Wyeast Steinberg yeast
3 teaspoons (8.8 g) yeast nutrient

1. Sanitize all equipment.

2. Remove any spoiled grapes from the clusters, then crush the grapes. Add ⅛ teaspoon (0.5 g) pectic enzyme to the crushed grapes. This will maximize the removal of juice from the skins. Let sit for 2 hours.

3. Press out the grapes and put the juice in a fermentation container. Add 5 crushed Campden tablets or ½ teaspoon (3.1 g) potassium metabisulfite powder to the juice and let sit for at least 4 hours or even overnight.

4. Test the acid and sugar and make adjustments, if necessary. Make a yeast starter by pouring 4 ounces (120 mL) of grape juice and 4 ounces (120 mL) of lukewarm water into a bowl, sprinkle in the yeast, and let proliferate for about 30 minutes. Add this yeast starter and the yeast nutrient to the grape juice and swish to help mix.

5. Cover the fermentation container loosely with a sheet of plastic; this allows gases to escape but deters foreign matter from entering. If using a glass carboy, which we recommend, insert a rubber bung and fermentation lock (filled with clean water) into the carboy. Allow some space in the fermentation container — about 20 percent — for foaming and bubbling. Within 3 days, the fermentation will start. It should continue for 7 to 12 days.

6. After several days of fermentation, start to monitor the wine. When the specific gravity gets below 1.000, fermentation is complete and you can proceed to the next step. If the specific gravity is above 1.000, allow the wine to continue to ferment until it goes below 1.000.

7. Put 5 crushed Campden tablets or ½ teaspoon (3.1 g) of potassium metabisulfite into a sanitized 5-gallon (19 L) carboy. Siphon the wine into the clean carboy and fill up to the bung and fermentation lock. Add water that has been boiled for 15 minutes and cooled to room temperature or a similar wine to fill the new carboy, if necessary. Place the carboy in a cool place like a garage or root cellar. This will clear out the tartrates and stabilize the wine. Two or three more rackings will be necessary to finalize the process. At each subsequent racking, use just 3 crushed Campden tablets or ¼ teaspoon (1.4 g) of potassium metabisulfite powder.

8. If wine does not clear, use gelatin, kieselsol, or bentonite finings following the manufacturer's instructions and allow an additional 3 to 4 weeks for the wine to clear.

9. When the wine is clear, it is time to bottle. If you had to use finings, filter the wine to guarantee complete cleanliness. Taste the wine and adjust for sweetness; then bottle. After bottling, wait 3 months before drinking. 🍇

WHITE WINE FROM GREY RIESLING GRAPES

Grey Reisling is a white wine variety grown in many sections of California. Its name is deceiving, as it is not actually related to the Riesling family. The grape grows in France, where it is known as the Chauche Gris. The wines are pleasant, rather light, and often crisp. Serve with seafood and broiled chicken.

Yield: 5 gallons (19 L)

60–75	pounds (27–34 kg) fresh grapes
⅛	teaspoon (0.5 g) pectic enzyme
17–20	Campden tablets or 1½–2 teaspoons (9.3–12.4 g) potassium metabisulfite powder
1	package (5 g) Red Star Premier Cuvée or Lalvin EC-1118 yeast
3	teaspoons (8.8 g) yeast nutrient

1. Sanitize all equipment.

2. Remove any spoiled grapes from the clusters, then crush the grapes. Add ⅛ teaspoon (0.5 g) pectic enzyme to the crushed grapes. This will maximize the removal of juice from the skins. Let sit for 2 hours.

3. Press out the grapes and put the juice in a fermentation container. Add 5 crushed Campden tablets or ½ teaspoon (3.1 g) potassium metabisulfite powder to the juice and let sit for at least 4 hours or even overnight.

4. Test the acid and sugar and make adjustments, if necessary. Make a yeast starter by pouring 4 ounces (120 mL) of grape juice and 4 ounces (120 mL) of lukewarm water into a bowl, sprinkle in the yeast, and let proliferate for about 30 minutes. Add this yeast starter and the yeast nutrient to the grape juice and swish to help mix.

5. Cover the fermentation container loosely with a sheet of plastic; this allows gases to escape but deters foreign matter from entering. If using a glass carboy, which we recommend, insert a rubber bung and fermentation lock (filled with clean water) into the carboy. Allow some space in the fermentation container — about 20 percent — for foaming and bubbling. Within 3 days, the fermentation will start. It should continue for 7 to 12 days.

6. After several days of fermentation, start to monitor the wine. When the specific gravity gets below 1.000, fermentation is complete and you can proceed to the next step. If the specific gravity is above 1.000, allow the wine to continue to ferment until it goes below 1.000.

7. Put 5 crushed Campden tablets or ½ teaspoon (3.1 g) of potassium metabisulfite into a sanitized 5-gallon (19 L) carboy. Siphon the wine into the clean carboy and fill up to the bung and fermentation lock. Add water that has been boiled for 15 minutes and cooled to room temperature or a similar wine to fill the new carboy, if necessary. Place the carboy in a cool place like a garage or root cellar. This will clear out the tartrates and stabilize the wine. Two or three more rackings will be needed. At each subsequent racking, use just 3 crushed Campden tablets or ¼ teaspoon (1.4 g) of potassium metabisulfite powder.

8. If wine does not clear, use gelatin, kieselsol, or bentonite finings following the manufacturer's instructions and allow an additional 3 to 4 weeks for the wine to clear.

9. When the wine is clear, it is time to bottle. If you had to use finings, filter the wine to guarantee complete cleanliness. Taste the wine and adjust for sweetness; then bottle. After bottling, wait 3 months before drinking. 🍇

 ## White Wine from Johannisberg Riesling Grapes

This great white grape of Germany is now planted in many areas of the United States. Sometimes known as White Riesling, the Johannisberg produces spicy wines that enhance many foods. Late-harvest Rieslings feature sweet, luscious flavors. In Germany, they are known as Auslesen. This table wine is a rewarding one to home winemakers.

Yield: 5 gallons (19 L)

60–75	pounds (27–34 kg) fresh grapes
⅛	teaspoon (0.5 g) pectic enzyme
17–20	Campden tablets or 1½–2 teaspoons (9.3–12.4 g) potassium metabisulfite powder
1	package (5 g) Wyeast Steinberg or Wyeast Assmannhausen yeast
3	teaspoons (8.8 g) yeast nutrient

1. Sanitize all equipment.

2. Remove any spoiled grapes from the clusters, then crush the grapes. Add ⅛ teaspoon (0.5 g) pectic enzyme to the crushed grapes. This will maximize the removal of juice from the skins. Let sit for 2 hours.

3. Press out the grapes and put the juice in a fermentation container. Add 5 crushed Campden tablets or ½ teaspoon (3.1 g) potassium metabisulfite powder to the juice and let sit for at least 4 hours or even overnight.

4. Test the acid and sugar and make adjustments, if necessary. Make a yeast starter by pouring 4 ounces (120 mL) of grape juice and 4 ounces (120 mL) of lukewarm water into a bowl, sprinkle in the yeast, and let proliferate for about 30 minutes. Add this yeast starter and the yeast nutrient to the grape juice and swish to help mix.

5. Cover the fermentation container loosely with a sheet of plastic; this allows gases to escape but deters foreign matter from entering. If using a glass carboy, which we recommend, insert a rubber bung and fermentation lock (filled with clean water) into the carboy. Allow some space in the fermentation container — about 20 percent — for foaming and bubbling. Within 3 days, the fermentation will start. It should continue for 7 to 12 days.

6. After several days of fermentation, start to monitor the wine. When the specific gravity gets below 1.000, fermentation is complete and you can proceed to the next step. If the specific gravity is above 1.000, allow the wine to continue to ferment until it goes below 1.000.

7. Put 5 crushed Campden tablets or ½ teaspoon (3.1 g) of potassium metabisulfite into a sanitized 5-gallon (19 L) carboy. Siphon the wine into the clean carboy and fill up to the bung and fermentation lock. Add water that has been boiled for 15 minutes and cooled to room temperature or a similar wine to fill the new carboy, if necessary. Place the carboy in a cool place like a garage or root cellar. This will clear out the tartrates and stabilize the wine. Two or three more rackings will be necessary to finalize the process. At each subsequent racking, use just 3 crushed Campden tablets or ¼ teaspoon (1.4 g) of potassium metabisulfite powder.

8. If wine does not clear, use gelatin, kieselsol, or bentonite finings following the manufacturer's instructions and allow an additional 3 to 4 weeks for the wine to clear.

9. When the wine is clear, it is time to bottle. If you had to use finings, filter the wine to guarantee complete cleanliness. Taste the wine and adjust for sweetness; then bottle. After bottling, wait 3 months before drinking. 🍇

WHITE WINE FROM MUSCAT GRAPES

Muscat is one of the world's oldest grapes, featuring a powerful bouquet, low acid, and a grapey taste. Its rich flavor and scent make it a good blending variety. A tinge of sweetness usually improves the wine. Serve with dessert.

Yield: 5 gallons (19 L)

60–75	pounds (27–34 kg) fresh grapes
⅛	teaspoon (0.5 g) pectic enzyme
17–20	Campden tablets or 1½–2 teaspoons (9.3–12.4 g) potassium metabisulfite powder
1	package (5 g) Red Star Premier Cuvée or Lallamand K1-V116 yeast
3	teaspoons (8.8 g) yeast nutrient

1. Sanitize all equipment.

2. Remove any spoiled grapes from the clusters, then crush the grapes. Add ⅛ teaspoon (0.5 g) pectic enzyme to the crushed grapes. This will maximize the removal of juice from the skins. Let sit for 2 hours.

3. Press out the grapes and put the juice in a fermentation container. Add 5 crushed Campden tablets or ½ teaspoon (3.1 g) potassium metabisulfite powder to the juice and let sit for at least 4 hours or even overnight.

4. Test the acid and sugar and make adjustments, if necessary. Make a yeast starter by pouring 4 ounces (120 mL) of grape juice and 4 ounces (120 mL) of lukewarm water into a bowl, sprinkle in the yeast, and let proliferate for about 30 minutes. Add this yeast starter and the yeast nutrient to the grape juice and swish to help mix.

5. Cover the fermentation container loosely with a sheet of plastic; this allows gases to escape but deters foreign matter from entering. If using a glass carboy, which we recommend, insert a rubber bung and fermentation lock (filled with clean water) into the carboy. Allow some space in the fermentation container — about 20 percent — for foaming and bubbling. Within 3 days, the fermentation will start. It should continue for 7 to 12 days.

6. After several days of fermentation, start to monitor the wine. When the specific gravity gets below 1.000, fermentation is complete and you can proceed to the next step. If the specific gravity is above 1.000, allow the wine to continue to ferment until it goes below 1.000.

7. Put 5 crushed Campden tablets or ½ teaspoon (3.1 g) of potassium metabisulfite into a sanitized 5-gallon (19 L) carboy. Siphon the wine into the clean carboy and fill up to the bung and fermentation lock. Add water that has been boiled for 15 minutes and cooled to room temperature or a similar wine to fill the new carboy, if necessary. Place the carboy in a cool place like a garage or root cellar. This will clear out the tartrates and stabilize the wine. Two or three more rackings will be necessary to finalize the process. At each subsequent racking, use just 3 crushed Campden tablets or ¼ teaspoon (1.4 g) of potassium metabisulfite powder.

8. If wine does not clear, use gelatin, kieselsol, or bentonite finings following the manufacturer's instructions and allow an additional 3 to 4 weeks for the wine to clear.

9. When the wine is clear, it is time to bottle. If you had to use finings, filter the wine to guarantee complete cleanliness. Taste the wine and adjust for sweetness; then bottle. After bottling, wait 3 months before drinking. 🍇

WHITE WINE FROM NIAGARA GRAPES

Niagara is one of the native American species of the Labrusca grape, grown in the northern regions of the United States and in Canada. It is a fruity variety that makes a pleasant, sweeter wine. Niagara grape wines are enjoyed by new wine drinkers and those who prefer the easy, quaffing-style wines. Serve with apple pie or soft cheese.

Yield: 5 gallons (19 L)

60–75	pounds (27–34 kg) fresh grapes
⅛	teaspoon (0.5 g) pectic enzyme
17–20	Campden tablets or 1½–2 teaspoons (9.3–12.4 g) potassium metabisulfite powder
1	package (5 g) Red Star Côtes des Blancs or Wyeast Chablis yeast
3	teaspoons (8.8 g) yeast nutrient

1. Sanitize all equipment.

2. Remove any spoiled grapes from the clusters, then crush the grapes. Add ⅛ teaspoon (0.5 g) pectic enzyme to the crushed grapes. This will maximize the removal of juice from the skins. Let sit for 2 hours.

3. Press out the grapes and put the juice in a fermentation container. Add 5 crushed Campden tablets or ½ teaspoon (3.1 g) potassium metabisulfite powder to the juice and let sit for at least 4 hours or even overnight.

4. Test the acid and sugar and make adjustments, if necessary. Make a yeast starter by pouring 4 ounces (120 mL) of grape juice and 4 ounces (120 mL) of lukewarm water into a bowl, sprinkle in the yeast, and let proliferate for about 30 minutes. Add this yeast starter and the yeast nutrient to the grape juice and swish to help mix.

5. Cover the fermentation container loosely with a sheet of plastic; this allows gases to escape but deters foreign matter from entering. If using a glass carboy, which we recommend, insert a rubber bung and fermentation lock (filled with clean water) into the carboy. Allow some space in the fermentation container — about 20 percent — for foaming and bubbling. Within 3 days, the fermentation will start. It should continue for 7 to 12 days.

6. After several days of fermentation, start to monitor the wine. When the specific gravity gets below 1.000, fermentation is complete and you can proceed to the next step. If the specific gravity is above 1.000, allow the wine to continue to ferment until it goes below 1.000.

7. Put 5 crushed Campden tablets or ½ teaspoon (3.1 g) of potassium metabisulfite into a sanitized 5-gallon (19 L) carboy. Siphon the wine into the clean carboy and fill up to the bung and fermentation lock. Add water that has been boiled for 15 minutes and cooled to room temperature or a similar wine to fill the new carboy, if necessary. Place the carboy in a cool place like a garage or root cellar. This will clear out the tartrates and stabilize the wine. Two or three more rackings will be necessary to finalize the process. At each subsequent racking, use just 3 crushed Campden tablets or ¼ teaspoon (1.4 g) of potassium metabisulfite powder.

8. If wine does not clear, use gelatin, kieselsol, or bentonite finings following the manufacturer's instructions and allow an additional 3 to 4 weeks for the wine to clear.

9. When the wine is clear, it is time to bottle. If you had to use finings, filter the wine to guarantee complete cleanliness. Taste the wine and adjust for sweetness; then bottle. After bottling, wait 3 months before drinking. 🍇

WHITE WINE FROM PINOT BLANC GRAPES

Popular in France, northern Italy, and Germany, Pinot Blanc has also found a home in the United States. Often mistaken for the Chardonnay, the Pinot Blanc offers outstanding, well-balanced, crisp, fruity white wines. Less expensive than many other varieties, the Pinot Blanc is the choice of many home winemakers. You'll enjoy it with seafood and poultry.

Yield: 5 gallons (19 L)

60–75 pounds (27–34 kg) fresh grapes

⅛ teaspoon (0.5 g) pectic enzyme

17–20 Campden tablets or 1½–2 teaspoons (9.3–12.4 g) potassium metabisulfite powder

1 package (5 g) Red Star Montrachet or Lallamand K1-V116 yeast

3 teaspoons (8.8 g) yeast nutrient

3 tablespoons (11.1 g) Oak-Mor

1 package malolactic culture

1. Sanitize all equipment.

2. Remove any spoiled grapes from the clusters, then crush the grapes. Add ⅛ teaspoon (0.5 g) pectic enzyme to the crushed grapes. This will maximize the removal of juice from the skins. Let sit for 2 hours.

3. Press out grapes and put juice in a fermentation container. Add 5 crushed Campden tablets or ½ teaspoon (3.1 g) potassium metabisulfite powder to juice; let sit for at least 4 hours or overnight.

4. Test the acid and sugar and make adjustments, if necessary. Make a yeast starter by pouring 4 ounces (120 mL) of grape juice and 4 ounces (120 mL) of lukewarm water into a bowl, sprinkle in the yeast, and let proliferate for about 30 minutes. Add this yeast starter, the yeast nutrient, and the Oak-Mor to the grape juice and swish to help mix.

5. Cover the fermentation container loosely with a sheet of plastic; this allows gases to escape but deters foreign matter from entering. If using a glass carboy, which we recommend, insert a rubber bung and fermentation lock (filled with clean water) into the carboy. Allow some space in the fermentation container — about 20 percent — for foaming and bubbling. Within 3 days, the fermentation will start. It should continue for 7 to 12 days.

6. After several days of fermentation, add the malolactic culture, following instructions on the package. When the specific gravity gets below 1.000, fermentation is complete and you can proceed to the next step. If the specific gravity is above 1.000, allow the wine to continue to ferment until it goes below 1.000.

7. Put 5 crushed Campden tablets or ½ teaspoon (3.1 g) of potassium metabisulfite into a sanitized 5-gallon (19 L) carboy. Siphon the wine into the clean carboy and fill up to the bung and fermentation lock. Add water that has been boiled for 15 minutes and cooled to room temperature or a similar wine to fill the new carboy, if necessary. Place the carboy in a cool place like a garage or root cellar. This will clear out the tartrates and stabilize the wine. Two or three more rackings will be necessary to finalize the process. At each subsequent racking, use just 3 crushed Campden tablets or ¼ teaspoon (1.4 g) of potassium metabisulfite powder.

8. If wine does not clear, use gelatin, kieselsol, or bentonite finings following the manufacturer's instructions and allow an additional 3 to 4 weeks for the wine to clear.

9. When the wine is clear, it is time to bottle. If you had to use finings, filter the wine to guarantee complete cleanliness. Taste the wine and adjust for sweetness; then bottle. After bottling, wait 3 months before drinking.

White Wine from Pinot Gris Grapes

Known as Pinot Grigio in Italy, Rulander in Germany, and Malvoisie in Switzerland, Pinot Gris makes fruity, full wines of great complexity and character. It is finally gaining favor in the United States, particularly in the Northwest. Serve as an aperitif or with cream dishes.

Yield: 5 gallons (19 L)

60–75	pounds (27–34 kg) fresh grapes
⅛	teaspoon (0.5 g) pectic enzyme
17–20	Campden tablets or 1½–2 teaspoons (9.3–12.4 g) potassium metabisulfite powder
1	package (5 g) Red Star Premier Cuvée or Lalvin EC-1118 yeast
3	teaspoons (8.8 g) yeast nutrient

1. Sanitize all equipment.

2. Remove any spoiled grapes from the clusters, then crush the grapes. Add ⅛ teaspoon (0.5 g) pectic enzyme to the crushed grapes. This will maximize the removal of juice from the skins. Let sit for 2 hours.

3. Press out the grapes and put the juice in a fermentation container. Add 5 crushed Campden tablets or ½ teaspoon (3.1 g) potassium metabisulfite powder to the juice and let sit for at least 4 hours or even overnight.

4. Test the acid and sugar and make adjustments, if necessary. Make a yeast starter by pouring 4 ounces (120 mL) of grape juice and 4 ounces (120 mL) of lukewarm water into a bowl, sprinkle in the yeast, and let proliferate for about 30 minutes. Add this yeast starter and the yeast nutrient to the grape juice and swish to help mix.

5. Cover the fermentation container loosely with a sheet of plastic; this allows gases to escape but deters foreign matter from entering. If using a glass carboy, which we recommend, insert a rubber bung and fermentation lock (filled with clean water) into the carboy. Allow some space in the fermentation container — about 20 percent — for foaming and bubbling. Within 3 days, the fermentation will start. It should continue for 7 to 12 days.

6. After several days of fermentation, start to monitor the wine. When the specific gravity gets below 1.000, fermentation is complete and you can proceed to the next step. If the specific gravity is above 1.000, allow the wine to continue to ferment until it goes below 1.000.

7. Put 5 crushed Campden tablets or ½ teaspoon (3.1 g) of potassium metabisulfite into a sanitized 5-gallon (19 L) carboy. Siphon the wine into the clean carboy and fill up to the bung and fermentation lock. Add water that has been boiled for 15 minutes and cooled to room temperature or a similar wine to fill the new carboy, if necessary. Place the carboy in a cool place like a garage or root cellar. This will clear out the tartrates and stabilize the wine. Two or three more rackings will be necessary to finalize the process. At each subsequent racking, use just 3 crushed Campden tablets or ¼ teaspoon (1.4 g) of potassium metabisulfite powder.

8. If wine does not clear, use gelatin, kieselsol, or bentonite finings following the manufacturer's instructions and allow an additional 3 to 4 weeks for the wine to clear.

9. When the wine is clear, it is time to bottle. If you had to use finings, filter the wine to guarantee complete cleanliness. Taste the wine and adjust for sweetness; then bottle. After bottling, wait 3 months before drinking. 🍇

WHITE WINE FROM RAVAT 51 GRAPES

Also known as Vignoles, this French-American hybrid grows in cooler climates and is distinguished by its distinctive bouquet and fullness. Pleasant, fruity, and aromatic wines come from this grape variety. Ravats are usually less expensive than many other premium varieties. Serve with lobster or stuffed shrimp.

Yield: 5 gallons (19 L)

- 60–75 pounds (27–34 kg) fresh grapes
- ⅛ teaspoon (0.5 g) pectic enzyme
- 17–20 Campden tablets or 1½–2 teaspoons (9.3–12.4 g) potassium metabisulfite powder
- 1 package (5 g) Red Star Premier Cuvée or Lalvin EC-1118 yeast
- 3 teaspoons (8.8 g) yeast nutrient

1. Sanitize all equipment.

2. Remove any spoiled grapes from the clusters, then crush the grapes. Add ⅛ teaspoon (0.5 g) pectic enzyme to the crushed grapes. This will maximize the removal of juice from the skins. Let sit for 2 hours.

3. Press out the grapes and put the juice in a fermentation container. Add 5 crushed Campden tablets or ½ teaspoon (3.1 g) potassium metabisulfite powder to the juice and let sit for at least 4 hours or even overnight.

4. Test the acid and sugar and make adjustments, if necessary. Make a yeast starter by pouring 4 ounces (120 mL) of grape juice and 4 ounces (120 mL) of lukewarm water into a bowl, sprinkle in the yeast, and let proliferate for about 30 minutes. Add this yeast starter and the yeast nutrient to the grape juice and swish to help mix.

5. Cover the fermentation container loosely with a sheet of plastic; this allows gases to escape but deters foreign matter from entering. If using a glass carboy, which we recommend, insert a rubber bung and fermentation lock (filled with clean water) into the carboy. Allow some space in the fermentation container — about 20 percent — for foaming and bubbling. Within 3 days, the fermentation will start. It should continue for 7 to 12 days.

6. After several days of fermentation, start to monitor the wine. When the specific gravity gets below 1.000, fermentation is complete and you can proceed to the next step. If the specific

gravity is above 1.000, allow the wine to continue to ferment until it goes below 1.000.

7. Put 5 crushed Campden tablets or ½ teaspoon (3.1 g) of potassium metabisulfite into a sanitized 5-gallon (19 L) carboy. Siphon the wine into the clean carboy and fill up to the bung and fermentation lock. Add water that has been boiled for 15 minutes and cooled to room temperature or a similar wine to fill the new carboy, if necessary. Place the carboy in a cool place like a garage or root cellar. This will clear out the tartrates and stabilize the wine. Two or three more rackings will be necessary to finalize the process. At each subsequent racking, use just 3 crushed Campden tablets or ¼ teaspoon (1.4 g) of potassium metabisulfite powder.

8. If wine does not clear, use gelatin, kieselsol, or bentonite finings following the manufacturer's instructions and allow an additional 3 to 4 weeks for the wine to clear.

9. When the wine is clear, it is time to bottle. If you had to use finings, filter the wine to guarantee complete cleanliness. Taste the wine and adjust for sweetness; then bottle. After bottling, wait 3 months before drinking. 🍇

 ## White Wine from Sauvignon Blanc Grapes

Sauvignon Blanc is an excellent variety grown in many parts of the world. Gravelly soil brings out the grape's smokiness and grassiness, which identify it on the world market. These wines go well with most seafood and poultry dishes. Although wines may be made in a wide variety of styles, the fruity ones are our favorites.

Yield: 5 gallons (19 L)

60–75	pounds (27–34 kg) fresh grapes
⅛	teaspoon (0.5 g) pectic enzyme
17–20	Campden tablets or 1½–2 teaspoons (9.3–12.4 g) potassium metabisulfite powder
1	package (5 g) Wyeast Chablis or Red Star Côtes des Blancs yeast
3	teaspoons (8.8 g) yeast nutrient

1. Sanitize all equipment.

2. Remove any spoiled grapes from the clusters, then crush the grapes. Add ⅛ teaspoon (0.5 g) pectic enzyme to the crushed grapes. This will maximize the removal of juice from the skins. Let sit for 2 hours.

3. Press out the grapes and put the juice in a fermentation container. Add 5 crushed Campden tablets or ½ teaspoon (3.1 g) potassium metabisulfite powder to the juice and let sit for at least 4 hours or even overnight.

4. Test the acid and sugar and make adjustments, if necessary. Make a yeast starter by pouring 4 ounces (120 mL) of grape juice and 4 ounces (120 mL) of lukewarm water into a bowl, sprinkle in the yeast, and let proliferate for about 30 minutes. Add this yeast starter and the yeast nutrient to the grape juice and swish to help mix.

5. Cover the fermentation container loosely with a sheet of plastic; this allows gases to escape but deters foreign matter from entering. If using a glass carboy, which we recommend, insert a rubber bung and fermentation lock (filled with clean water) into the carboy. Allow some space in the fermentation container — about 20 percent — for foaming and bubbling. Within 3 days, the fermentation will start. It should continue for 7 to 12 days.

6. After several days of fermentation, start to monitor the wine. When the specific gravity gets below 1.000, fermentation is complete and you can proceed to the next step. If the specific gravity is above 1.000, allow the wine to continue to ferment until it goes below 1.000.

7. Put 5 crushed Campden tablets or ½ teaspoon (3.1 g) of potassium metabisulfite into a sanitized 5-gallon (19 L) carboy. Siphon the wine into the clean carboy and fill up to the bung and fermentation lock. Add water that has been boiled for 15 minutes and cooled to room temperature or a similar wine to fill the new carboy, if necessary. Place the carboy in a cool place like a garage or root cellar. This will clear out the tartrates and stabilize the wine. Two or three more rackings will be necessary to finalize the process. At each subsequent racking, use just 3 crushed Campden tablets or ¼ teaspoon (1.4 g) of potassium metabisulfite powder.

8. If wine does not clear, use gelatin, kieselsol, or bentonite finings following the manufacturer's instructions and allow an additional 3 to 4 weeks for the wine to clear.

9. When the wine is clear, it is time to bottle. If you had to use finings, filter the wine to guarantee complete cleanliness. Taste the wine and adjust for sweetness; then bottle. After bottling, wait 3 months before drinking. 🍇

WHITE WINE FROM SEMILLON GRAPES

This grape grows in many regions of France, but it has also been successful in the United States, particularly in the Northwest. A citrus flavor, spiciness, and richness are some of the qualities of the Semillon. It blends particularly well with Sauvignon Blanc and is an excellent accompaniment to seafood.

Yield: 5 gallons (19 L)

60–75 pounds (27–34 kg) fresh grapes
⅛ teaspoon (0.5g) pectic enzyme
17–20 Campden tablets or 1½–2 teaspoons (9.3–12.4 g) potassium metabisulfite powder
1 package (5 g) Lalvin EC-1118 or Red Star Premier Cuvée yeast
3 teaspoons (8.8 g) yeast nutrient

1. Sanitize all equipment.

2. Remove any spoiled grapes from the clusters, then crush the grapes. Add ⅛ teaspoon (0.5 g) pectic enzyme to the crushed grapes. This will maximize the removal of juice from the skins. Let sit for 2 hours.

3. Press out the grapes and put the juice in a fermentation container. Add 5 crushed Campden tablets or ½ teaspoon (3.1 g) potassium metabisulfite powder to the juice and let sit for at least 4 hours or even overnight.

4. Test the acid and sugar and make adjustments, if necessary. Make a yeast starter by pouring 4 ounces (120 mL) of grape juice and 4 ounces (120 mL) of lukewarm water into a bowl, sprinkle in the yeast, and let proliferate for about 30 minutes. Add this yeast starter and the yeast nutrient to the grape juice and swish to help mix.

5. Cover the fermentation container loosely with a sheet of plastic; this allows gases to escape but deters foreign matter from entering. If using a glass carboy, which we recommend, insert a rubber bung and fermentation lock (filled with clean water) into the carboy. Allow some space in the fermentation container — about 20 percent — for foaming and bubbling. Within 3 days, the fermentation will start. It should continue for 7 to 12 days.

6. After several days of fermentation, start to monitor the wine. When the specific gravity gets below 1.000, fermentation is complete and you can proceed to the next step. If the specific gravity is above 1.000, allow the wine to continue to ferment until it goes below 1.000.

7. Put 5 crushed Campden tablets or ½ teaspoon (3.1 g) of potassium metabisulfite into a sanitized 5-gallon (19 L) carboy. Siphon the wine into the clean carboy and fill up to the bung and fermentation lock. Add water that has been boiled for 15 minutes and cooled to room temperature or a similar wine to fill the new carboy, if necessary. Place the carboy in a cool place like a garage or root cellar. This will clear out the tartrates and stabilize the wine. Two or three more rackings will be needed. At each subsequent racking, use just 3 crushed Campden tablets or ¼ teaspoon (1.4 g) of potassium metabisulfite powder.

8. If wine does not clear, use gelatin, kieselsol, or bentonite finings following the manufacturer's instructions and allow an additional 3 to 4 weeks for the wine to clear.

9. When the wine is clear, it is time to bottle. If you had to use finings, filter the wine to guarantee complete cleanliness. Taste the wine and adjust for sweetness; then bottle. After bottling, wait 3 months before drinking. 🍇

 ## WHITE WINE FROM SEYVAL BLANC GRAPES

Seyval Blanc is grown all over the eastern and midwestern United States and Canada. This French-American variety is probably the most productive of all hybrids. It produces excellent wines with good fruit flavors and aromas. Well suited to blending, the variety also stands on its own. It usually requires acid and sugar adjustments before fermentation. Serve it with lobster.

Yield: 5 gallons (19 L)

60–75 pounds (27–34 kg) fresh grapes
⅛ teaspoon (0.5 g) pectic enzyme
17–20 Campden tablets or 1½–2 teaspoons (9.3–12.4 g) potassium metabisulfite powder
1 package (5 g) Lalvin EC-1118 or Red Star Côtes des Blancs yeast
3 teaspoons (8.8 g) yeast nutrient

1. Sanitize all equipment.

2. Remove any spoiled grapes from the clusters, then crush the grapes. Add ⅛ teaspoon (0.5 g) pectic enzyme to the crushed grapes. This will maximize the removal of juice from the skins. Let sit for 2 hours.

3. Press out the grapes and put the juice in a fermentation container. Add 5 crushed Campden tablets or ½ teaspoon (3.1 g) potassium metabisulfite powder to the juice and let sit for at least 4 hours or even overnight.

4. Test the acid and sugar and make adjustments, if necessary. Make a yeast starter by pouring 4 ounces (120 mL) of grape juice and 4 ounces (120 mL) of lukewarm water into a bowl, sprinkle in the yeast, and let proliferate for about 30 minutes. Add this yeast starter and the yeast nutrient to the grape juice and swish to help mix.

5. Cover the fermentation container loosely with a sheet of plastic; this allows gases to escape but deters foreign matter from entering. If using a glass carboy, which we recommend, insert a rubber bung and fermentation lock (filled with clean water) into the carboy. Allow some space in the fermentation container — about 20 percent — for foaming and bubbling. Within 3 days, the fermentation will start. It should continue for 7 to 12 days.

6. After several days of fermentation, start to monitor the wine. When the specific gravity gets below 1.000, fermentation is complete and you can proceed to the next step. If the specific gravity is above 1.000, allow the wine to continue to ferment until it goes below 1.000.

7. Put 5 crushed Campden tablets or ½ teaspoon (3.1 g) of potassium metabisulfite into a sanitized 5-gallon (19 L) carboy. Siphon the wine into the clean carboy and fill up to the bung and fermentation lock. Add water that has been boiled for 15 minutes and cooled to room temperature or a similar wine to fill the new carboy, if necessary. Place the carboy in a cool place like a garage or root cellar. This will clear out the tartrates and stabilize the wine. Two or three more rackings will be necessary to finalize the process. At each subsequent racking, use just 3 crushed Campden tablets or ¼ teaspoon (1.4 g) of potassium metabisulfite powder.

8. If wine does not clear, use gelatin, kieselsol, or bentonite finings following the manufacturer's instructions and allow an additional 3 to 4 weeks for the wine to clear.

9. When the wine is clear, it is time to bottle. If you had to use finings, filter the wine to guarantee complete cleanliness. Taste the wine and adjust for sweetness; then bottle. After bottling, wait 3 months before drinking. 🍇

WHITE WINE FROM SYLVANER GRAPES

Similar to the Johannisberg Riesling in character, the Sylvaner (or Silvaner) produces a spicy and pleasant white wine. This noble variety grows well in cooler climates, where it ripens late in the season. It often requires sugar and acid adjustments before fermentation. Serve with Asian cuisine.

Yield: 5 gallons (19 L)

60–75 pounds (27–34 kg) fresh grapes
⅛ teaspoon (0.5 g) pectic enzyme
17–20 Campden tablets or 1½–2 teaspoons (9.3–12.4 g) potassium metabisulfite powder
1 package (5 g) Wyeast Steinberg or Wyeast Assmannhausen yeast
3 teaspoons (8.8 g) yeast nutrient

1. Sanitize all equipment.

2. Remove any spoiled grapes from the clusters, then crush the grapes. Add ⅛ teaspoon (0.5 g) pectic enzyme to the crushed grapes. This will maximize the removal of juice from the skins. Let sit for 2 hours.

3. Press out the grapes and put the juice in a fermentation container. Add 5 crushed Campden tablets or ½ teaspoon (3.1 g) potassium metabisulfite powder to the juice and let sit for at least 4 hours or even overnight.

4. Test the acid and sugar and make adjust-ments, if necessary. Make a yeast starter by pouring 4 ounces (120 mL) of grape juice and 4 ounces (120 mL) of lukewarm water into a bowl, sprinkle in the yeast, and let proliferate for about 30 minutes. Add this yeast starter and the yeast nutrient to the grape juice and swish to help mix.

5. Cover the fermentation container loosely with a sheet of plastic; this allows gases to escape but deters foreign matter from entering. If using a glass carboy, which we recommend, insert a rubber bung and fermentation lock (filled with clean water) into the carboy. Allow some space in the fermentation container — about 20 percent — for foaming and bubbling. Within 3 days, the fermentation will start. It should continue for 7 to 12 days.

6. After several days of fermentation, start to monitor the wine. When the specific gravity gets below 1.000, fermentation is complete and you can proceed to the next step. If the specific gravity is above 1.000, allow the wine to continue to ferment until it goes below 1.000.

7. Put 5 crushed Campden tablets or ½ teaspoon (3.1 g) of potassium metabisulfite into a sanitized 5-gallon (19 L) carboy. Siphon the wine into the clean carboy and fill up to the bung and fermentation lock. Add water that has been boiled for 15 minutes and cooled to room temperature or a similar wine to fill the new carboy, if necessary. Place the carboy in a cool place like a garage or root cellar. This will clear out the tartrates and stabilize the wine. Two or three more rackings will be needed. At each subsequent racking, use just 3 crushed Campden tablets or ¼ teaspoon (1.4 g) of potassium metabisulfite powder.

8. If wine does not clear, use gelatin, kieselsol, or bentonite finings following the manufacturer's instructions and allow an additional 3 to 4 weeks for the wine to clear.

9. When the wine is clear, it is time to bottle. If you had to use finings, filter the wine to guarantee complete cleanliness. Taste the wine and adjust for sweetness; then bottle. After bottling, wait 3 months before drinking.

White Wine from Vidal Blanc Grapes

This popular French-American hybrid produces outstanding wines featuring a spicy taste and pineapple aroma. The variety makes wonderful ice wines, thus helping many Canadian wineries earn international acclaim. The Vidal Blanc is primarily a northern grape with a high degree of sugar that ripens quickly. Serve with cream dishes and soft cheese.

Yield: 5 gallons (19 L)

60–75	pounds (27–34 kg) fresh grapes
⅛	teaspoon (0.5 g) pectic enzyme
17–20	Campden tablets or 1½–2 teaspoons (9.3–12.4 g) potassium metabisulfite powder
1	package (5 g) Red Star Côtes des Blancs or Lalvin EC-1118 yeast
3	teaspoons (8.8 g) yeast nutrient

1. Sanitize all equipment.

2. Remove any spoiled grapes from the clusters, then crush the grapes. Add ⅛ teaspoon (0.5 g) pectic enzyme to the crushed grapes. This will maximize the removal of juice from the skins. Let sit for 2 hours.

3. Press out the grapes and put the juice in a fermentation container. Add 5 crushed Campden tablets or ½ teaspoon (3.1 g) potassium metabisulfite powder to the juice and let sit for at least 4 hours or even overnight.

4. Test the acid and sugar and make adjustments, if necessary. Make a yeast starter by pouring 4 ounces (120 mL) of grape juice and 4 ounces (120 mL) of lukewarm water into a bowl, sprinkle in the yeast, and let proliferate for about 30 minutes. Add this yeast starter and the yeast nutrient to the grape juice and swish to help mix.

5. Cover the fermentation container loosely with a sheet of plastic; this allows gases to escape but deters foreign matter from entering. If using a glass carboy, which we recommend, insert a rubber bung and fermentation lock (filled with clean water) into the carboy. Allow some space in the fermentation container — about 20 percent — for foaming and bubbling. Within 3 days, the fermentation will start. It should continue for 7 to 12 days.

6. After several days of fermentation, start to monitor the wine. When the specific gravity gets below 1.000, fermentation is complete and you can proceed to the next step. If the specific gravity is above 1.000, allow the wine to continue to ferment until it goes below 1.000.

7. Put 5 crushed Campden tablets or ½ teaspoon (3.1 g) of potassium metabisulfite into a sanitized 5-gallon (19 L) carboy. Siphon the wine into the clean carboy and fill up to the bung and fermentation lock. Add water that has been boiled for 15 minutes and cooled to room temperature or a similar wine to fill the new carboy, if necessary. Place the carboy in a cool place like a garage or root cellar. This will clear out the tartrates and stabilize the wine. Two or three more rackings will be necessary to finalize the process. At each subsequent racking, use just 3 crushed Campden tablets or ¼ teaspoon (1.4 g) of potassium metabisulfite powder.

8. If wine does not clear, use gelatin, kieselsol, or bentonite finings following the manufacturer's instructions and allow an additional 3 to 4 weeks for the wine to clear.

9. When the wine is clear, it is time to bottle. If you had to use finings, filter the wine to guarantee complete cleanliness. Taste the wine and adjust for sweetness; then bottle. After bottling, wait 3 months before drinking. 🍇

RED WINE FROM GRAPES 7

*I wonder what the vintners buy
one half so precious as the stuff they sell.*

—Omar Khayyám (1048–1122)

AFTER READING THE PRECEDING CHAPTER, you now have a good idea of the basics of winemaking from grapes. The steps to make red wines are largely the same as for white. The main exception is not pressing out the skins and pulp after crushing: They are key ingredients during the fermentation process.

EQUIPMENT

You'll need the same equipment listed in chapter 6. An experienced home winemaker might also purchase a wooden barrel at this point to further enhance the flavor of his or her red wines. This is expensive in both money and time. You'll have to do a fair amount of work to maintain the barrel in a sanitary state. For most home wine-makers, the results obtained by using either Oak-Mor or oak chips in lieu of a barrel make them a better choice.

BUYING GRAPES

If you live in one of the many areas in the United States or Canada where locally grown red grapes are available, you can purchase them from a nearby vineyard. Going local enables you to follow the grapes through the growing process and purchase them at their peak of maturity. Generally speaking, they'll cost less if you purchase them locally, but cost should not be your only consideration. For example, the Mission grape tends to be quite inexpensive up front; unfortunately, it is a terrible wine grape.

Recommended red grape varieties include:

- Cabernet Franc
- Cabernet Sauvignon
- Chambourcin
- Gamay
- Grenache
- Malbec
- Merlot
- Petite Sirah
- Petit Verdot
- Pinot Noir
- Sangiovese
- Syrah
- Zinfandel

Note: Never buy Mission grapes for winemaking. They produce very poor wine.

Winemaking clubs and wine supply shops can direct you to the best sources for the type of grapes you want to use. If you live on the West Coast, you're in luck; many of the finest vineyards for reds are located in California.

THE BEST REDS

The key to making successful reds is to select the best grapes available, and you determine that by ascertaining their sugar and acid counts. Look for grapes with a sugar count of 20 to 24 degrees Brix. Acid ranges should be from 0.55 to 0.90 percent.

When you determine what wine you want to make, check with potential suppliers to find out when you need to purchase your grapes. Ask experienced home winemakers for help. They can assist you in deciding with whom you should do business. In addition to buying directly from a vineyard, you can purchase grapes through fruit wholesalers and local winemaking supply shops. (See chapter 6 for tips on buying fresh grapes from these various sources.) If you purchase premium grapes, your wines are likely to be a great deal better; in this case, you truly do get what you pay for.

We suggest buying several kinds of grapes, both red and white — this will allow you to blend and create a wider variety of wines. For example, Cabernet Sauvignon and Merlot not only are excellent by themselves, but they also blend quite nicely. We'll give you some specific suggestions on this later in the chapter.

MAKING THE WINE

Making red wine with grapes involves allowing the extra skin and pulp to ferment with the must. This added step gives red wine its deeper color and robust taste.

CRUSHING

Once you've brought home your grapes, go through them carefully. Cull out the leaves and any unripened grapes, as well as any rotten ones. Then review the steps for crushing in chapter 6. Unlike with white wines, we want to keep the skins and pulp after crushing because they are key ingredients during the fermentation process. As a result, pour all the contents from the crushing, minus the stems, into a sanitized container. The pressing will come later, after the fermentation. Prior to covering the container for the night, add either 5 crushed Campden tablets or ½ teaspoon (3.1 g) of potassium metabisulfite powder per 5-gallon (19 L) container. This step kills bacteria and other foreign matter, and prevents natural fermentation from taking place. Cover the container with a cloth or a sheet of plastic, and let it rest until the next day.

Cover the container of juice, pulp, and skins with a cloth or sheet of plastic.

CONTROLLED FERMENTATION

Take acid and sugar readings, and make the necessary adjustments (see chapters 2 and 4, respectively, for instructions). The sugar should be between 20 and 24 degrees Brix, and the acid balance should fall between 0.55 and 0.90 percent.

Preparation of the yeast culture is explained in chapter 6. A standard 5-gram package of com-

SANITIZING EQUIPMENT

The need to sanitize all equipment that comes in contact with your wine cannot be overstated. Here is a method we use with success.

Potassium metabisulfite powder
Hot water
Jug

1. Put 3 tablespoons (56 g) of potassium metabisulfite into a 1-liter (33.8 oz) jug of hot water — 85°F (29°C) — to make a reusable sanitizing solution. It will last up to 6 months, if kept tightly sealed. (Store at room temperature.)
2. Rinse all equipment thoroughly in the solution.
3. After sanitizing, rinse with cold water.

mercial wine yeast is necessary for every 5 gallons (19 L) of juice. You will also need to add 20 drops (1 mL) of liquid pectic enzyme per 5 gallons (19 L) prior to adding the yeast (also called inoculating) for fermentation. Once you've added the yeast, cover the container to keep bugs and foreign matter out of the juice.

Fermentation should begin within a few days of inoculation and continue for up to 2 weeks. If fermentation doesn't get started within 3 days, check our troubleshooting instructions in chapter 10.

Twice a day, what is known as the *cap* (that is, skins and pulp) will need to be pushed back down into the juice, using a sanitized, long-handled spoon.

In some cases, between the fourth and the sixth day, you should inoculate the must with a malolactic culture. This causes a secondary fermentation toward the end of the primary fermentation. The recipes in this chapter indicate which wines benefit from this extra fermentation. Malolactic fermentation converts malic acid into lactic acid and carbon dioxide. This lowers the wine's acidity and generally "softens" the wine, giving it a buttery characteristic. It also helps develop more complex aromas and improves biological stability in the wine. Most red wines benefit from malolactic fermentation; some whites, such as Chardonnay and Pinot Blanc, also are better after this secondary fermentation.

As a rule, once the cap stops rising, fermentation is complete. In any event, check the specific gravity reading daily (see chapter 1 for details on reading a hydrometer). Once it has reached 1.000 or lower, it's time to press out the juice from the grapes and the pulp.

Some winemakers prefer to let the juice have an additional 2 weeks "on the skins"; they don't press until 4 weeks have elapsed from the time of inoculation. They believe that this will give the wine more color and complexity. This option is a stylistic choice only and won't gain any technical advantages.

Push the cap (skins and pulp) down twice daily using a sanitized spoon.

MALOLACTIC CULTURES

There are two malolactic cultures we recommend from experience, Vintner's Choice Malolactic Culture (Logsdon's Wyeast Laboratory, Mt. Hood, OR) and the Vinaflora Oenos Malolactic Culture (Chr. Hansen's Laboratory, Horsholm, Denmark). Both of these are dumped right into the wine either during or at the conclusion of the primary fermentation. Refrigerate these cultures when not in use; if they are to be stored for a long time, freeze them in their packets. Adding this malolactic culture is a simple process, and a productive one.

PRESSING

When fermentation is complete and the wine has sat on the skins and pulp to macerate, it is time to press out the wine juice. The process is the same as pressing white wine juice (see chapter 5), except that the timing is different. With red wines we press *after* fermentation. White wines are pressed *before* fermentation. Whether you choose to use a barrel or bladder press or some other method is a personal choice based on expense versus efficiency. In our opinion, a good winepress is needed if you are going to make homemade wine directly from grapes. Other alternatives are too time-consuming and ultimately too inefficient to get the most wine out of your fermented batch.

A barrel winepress in action.

RACKING

Before you collect the pressed juice in your 5-gallon (19 L) container, sanitize the container. Now you're ready to store the pressed juice.

Put 5 crushed Campden tablets or ½ teaspoon (3.1 g) of potassium metabisulfite powder into the new container before adding the wine. Siphon the pressed juice into container and fill up to the rubber bung stopper. Insert a water-filled air lock to secure the seal. Let the wine sit for 3 to 4 weeks. As time passes, sediment will accumulate at the bottom of the container. Rack the wine again into another sterilized carboy with 5 more crushed Campden tablets or ½ teaspoon (3.1 g) of potassium metabisulfite powder. By racking the wine, you'll gradually remove most of the sediment and help clear the wine. Three or four more rackings, 4 to 6 weeks apart, should pace the wine to its finish. After the second racking, use just 3 crushed Campden tablets or ¼ teaspoon (1.4 g) potassium metabisulfite powder.

During the racking stage, test the wine periodically to see if any adjustments are necessary. If you make adjustments, follow the instructions on page 37. Also add either potassium sorbate, crushed Campden tablets, or potassium metabisulfite to ensure that your bottled wine won't referment and surprise you by opening the bottles by itself, leaving you with a mess to clean up.

The wine should clear itself. If it doesn't, wait longer and rack until it does. When the wine is clear, it's time. Make final adjustments if needed, then bottle the wine and wait at least 6 months before tasting. Most red wines will take a year or more before they are in balance and ready for consumption.

BLENDING

Blending is an easy way to improve many homemade wines. In chapter 3, we suggested considering blending two wines, and we gave the example of using Cabernet Sauvignon and Merlot. Blending often adds complexity to a wine, and it's an easy way to create a more diverse wine cellar. A 20:80 or 25:75 mixing ratio of Merlot to Cabernet Sauvignon will add softness and character; a 20:80 or 25:75 mixing ratio of Cabernet Sauvignon to Merlot will add some body and flavor. The 20:80 or 25:75 mixing ratio works well with many different varieties. (For more blending suggestions, see chapter 3.) Let's say that you now have 5 gallons of each ready for bottling. If you were to do the following, you would have four wines instead of two.

Sample blending of reds. Starting with 5 gallons (19 L) of Cabernet Sauvignon and 5 gallons (19 L) of Merlot:

1. Bottle 2½ gallons (9.5 L) of 100% Cabernet. This will give you a full case.

2. Take ½ gallon (1.9 L) of Cabernet and put it aside.

3. Blend the remaining 2 gallons (7.6 L) with ½ gallon (1.9 L) of Merlot.

4. Do the same with the remaining Merlot that you did with the Cabernet. When you're finished, you'll have one case each of the 100% wines and

RED BLENDING PAIRS

The following red wines blend nicely with each other using a 20:80 or 25:75 mixing ratio.

- ◆ Syrah and Pinot Noir
- ◆ Zinfandel and Syrah
- ◆ Syrah and Cabernet Sauvignon
- ◆ Merlot and Cabernet Sauvignon
- ◆ Cabernet Franc and Merlot
- ◆ Cabernet Sauvignon and Cabernet Franc

two cases of blends. Now you're ready for the next step.

BOTTLING

Your bottles should be thoroughly sanitized (see page 163). Five gallons (19 L) of wine will require about 26 750-mL (25.4 oz) bottles or 12 1.5-liter (50.4 oz) bottles and 1 750-mL (25.4 oz) bottle.

Bottle size. Some home winemakers like to use larger bottles, such as 3-liter (101 oz) or 4-liter (134 oz) jugs. Remember that once the bottles have been opened, it's best to consume the wine within 3 or 4 days, or the flavor will begin to deteriorate.

If you intend to open and drink your wine within a year of bottling, push corks are perfectly acceptable. Otherwise, use regular corks or screw caps.

AGING

Red wines should age for at least 6 months. Most benefit enormously if you allow them to age for a year or more. The process softens the tannins and makes the wine taste even better. Too many homemade reds are consumed earlier than they should be, and they never get to mature. Be patient, and you will be rewarded.

A WORD ABOUT THE RECIPES

We've included twenty basic recipes for some of the most popular reds around. Keep accurate records of the procedures and your results. This is particularly important when you're blending, so you'll be able to determine which wines work best for you.

SERVING TIP

Decant your reds into a pitcher or decanter about 45 minutes before you serve them. This will eliminate any of the harmless sediment that has accumulated at the bottom of the bottle, "cleaning" the wine and removing bottle odors. Allowing the wine to "breathe" in this way makes it even more enjoyable.

RED WINE FROM ALICANTE-BOUSCHET GRAPES

This grape produces inky, robust wines. It is a high-producing variety in California, where it is used as a blending grape for jug wine. Alicante-Bouschet is now available to home winemakers in most of the United States and Canada at reduced prices, thanks to its declining popularity in California winemaking. Serve with red pasta dishes.

Yield: 5 gallons (19 L)

- 60–75 pounds (27–34 kg) fresh grapes
- 20 drops (1 mL) pectic enzyme liquid
- 17–20 Campden tablets or 1½–2 teaspoons (9.3–12.4 g) potassium metabisulfite powder
- 1 package (5 g) Wyeast Bordeaux or Red Star Premier Cuvée yeast
- 3 teaspoons (8.8 g) yeast nutrient
- 3 tablespoons (11.1 g) Oak-Mor
- 1 package malolactic culture

1. Sanitize all equipment.

2. Remove any spoiled grapes from the clusters and then crush the grapes. Place them in a fermentation container. Remove grape stems from the container. Add 20 drops (1 mL) of pectic enzyme liquid to the crushed grapes and juice.

3. Add 5 crushed Campden tablets or ½ teaspoon (3.1 g) of potassium metabisulfite powder. Stir the juice and crushed grapes and let sit overnight.

4. The second day, test for sugar and acid and make appropriate adjustments.

5. Make a yeast starter by pouring 4 ounces (120 mL) of grape juice and 4 ounces (120 mL) of lukewarm water into a bowl, sprinkle in the yeast, and let proliferate for 30 minutes. Add this yeast starter, the yeast nutrient, and the Oak-Mor to the must and stir well. Cover the container loosely with a sheet of plastic.

6. Fermentation will start in 2 or 3 days and continue for 7 to 12 days. The cap (the pulp, skins, and so on) will rise to the top, so twice daily push it down with a sanitized spoon. This allows the color and body to be extracted from the skin and pulp mixture. Between the fourth and sixth day, inoculate the must with malolactic culture (follow the manufacturer's instructions).

7. Monitor the wine each day with a hydrometer. When the specific gravity reaches 1.000 or lower, it's time to press out the wine and store it in another container.

8. Sanitize a 5-gallon (19 L) glass carboy. Put in 5 crushed Campden tablets or ½ teaspoon (3.1 g) of potassium metabisulfite powder. Pour in the must and fill up to the top. Insert a rubber bung and air lock into the jug opening.

9. Let the wine sit 3 to 4 weeks, then rack again into a sanitized carboy. Three or four more rackings, 4 to 6 weeks apart, should pace the wine to its finish. After the second racking, use just 3 crushed Campden tablets or ¼ teaspoon (1.4 g) potassium metabisulfite powder.

10. The wine should clear itself. If it doesn't, wait longer and rack until the wine clears.

11. When the wine is clear, it's time to bottle. Make adjustments if needed, then bottle the wine and wait at least 6 months before tasting. 🍇

RED WINE FROM BACO NOIR GRAPES

This French-American hybrid is widely planted in Canada and the eastern part of the United States. The wine ages well and produces a smoky taste, which is free of the foxy flavors associated with many hybrids. Its inky red color makes it an excellent blending wine. Serve with barbecue dishes and Tex-Mex cuisine.

Yield: 5 gallons (19 L)

60–75 pounds (27–34 kg) fresh grapes
20 drops (1 mL) pectic enzyme liquid
17–20 Campden tablets or 1½–2 teaspoons (9.3–12.4 g) potassium metabisulfite powder
1 package (5 g) Red Star Pasteur Red or Wyeast Chianti yeast
3 teaspoons (8.8 g) yeast nutrient
3 tablespoons (11.1 g) Oak-Mor
1 package malolactic culture

1. Sanitize all equipment.

2. Remove any spoiled grapes from the clusters and then crush the grapes. Place them in a fermentation container. Remove grape stems from the container. Add 20 drops (1 mL) of pectic enzyme liquid to the crushed grapes and juice.

3. Add 5 crushed Campden tablets or ½ teaspoon (3.1 g) of potassium metabisulfite powder. Stir the juice and crushed grapes and let sit overnight.

4. The second day, test for sugar and acid and make appropriate adjustments.

5. Make a yeast starter by pouring 4 ounces (120 mL) of grape juice and 4 ounces (120 mL) of lukewarm water into a bowl, sprinkle in the yeast, and let proliferate for 30 minutes. Add this yeast starter, the yeast nutrient, and the Oak-Mor to the must and stir well. Cover the container loosely with a sheet of plastic.

6. Fermentation will start in 2 or 3 days and continue for 7 to 12 days. The cap (the pulp, skins, and so on) will rise to the top, so twice daily push it down with a sanitized spoon. This allows the color and body to be extracted from the skin and pulp mixture. Between the fourth and sixth day, inoculate the must with malolactic culture (follow the manufacturer's instructions).

7. Monitor the wine each day with a hydrometer. When the specific gravity reaches 1.000 or lower, it's time to press out the wine and store it in another container.

8. Sanitize a 5-gallon (19 L) glass carboy. Put in 5 crushed Campden tablets or ½ teaspoon (3.1 g) of potassium metabisulfite powder. Pour in the must and fill up to the top. Insert a rubber bung and air lock into the jug opening.

9. Let the wine sit 3 to 4 weeks, then rack again into a sanitized carboy. Three or four more rackings, 4 to 6 weeks apart, should pace the wine to its finish. After the second racking, use just 3 crushed Campden tablets or ¼ teaspoon (1.4 g) potassium metabisulfite powder.

10. The wine should clear itself. If it doesn't, wait longer and rack until the wine clears.

11. When the wine is clear, it's time to bottle. Make adjustments if needed, then bottle the wine and wait at least 6 months before tasting. 🍇

 RED WINE FROM BARBERA GRAPES

Barbera is a productive and successful varietal in Italy, but it has had limited success in the United States. It is more suitable for growing in warmer climates. High-quality Barbera grapes from California are rare, but in certain years they are available. Although the wine is highly acidic, it does make a reasonably good accompaniment for hearty fare. The grapes are generally available to home winemakers at a reasonable price. Serve with pasta dishes, beef roasts, and game dishes.

Yield: 5 gallons (19 L)

60–75 pounds (27–34 kg) fresh grapes
20 drops (1 mL) pectic enzyme liquid
17–20 Campden tablets or 1½–2 teaspoons (9.3–12.4 g) potassium metabisulfite powder
1 package (5 g) Wyeast Chianti or Red Star Montrachet yeast
3 teaspoons (8.8 g) yeast nutrient
3 tablespoons (11.1 g) Oak-Mor
1 package malolactic culture

1. Sanitize all equipment.

2. Remove any spoiled grapes from the clusters and then crush the grapes. Place them in a fermentation container. Remove grape stems from the container. Add 20 drops (1 mL) of pectic enzyme liquid to the crushed grapes and juice.

3. Add 5 crushed Campden tablets or ½ teaspoon (3.1 g) of potassium metabisulfite powder.

Stir the juice and crushed grapes and let sit overnight.

4. The second day, test for sugar and acid and make appropriate adjustments.

5. Make a yeast starter by pouring 4 ounces (120 mL) of grape juice and 4 ounces (120 mL) of lukewarm water into a bowl, sprinkle in the yeast, and let proliferate for 30 minutes. Add this yeast starter, the yeast nutrient, and the Oak-Mor to the must and stir well. Cover the container loosely with a sheet of plastic.

6. Fermentation will start in 2 or 3 days and continue for 7 to 12 days. The cap (the pulp, skins, and so on) will rise to the top, so twice daily push it down with a sanitized spoon. This allows the color and body to be extracted from the skin and pulp mixture. Between the fourth and sixth day, inoculate the must with malolactic culture (follow the manufacturer's instructions).

7. Monitor the wine each day with a hydrometer. When the specific gravity reaches 1.000 or lower, it's time to press out the wine and store it in another container.

8. Sanitize a 5-gallon (19 L) glass carboy. Put in 5 crushed Campden tablets or ½ teaspoon (3.1 g) of potassium metabisulfite powder. Pour in the must and fill up to the top. Insert a rubber bung and air lock into the jug opening.

9. Let the wine sit 3 to 4 weeks, then rack again into a sanitized carboy. Three or four more rackings, 4 to 6 weeks apart, should pace the wine to its finish. After the second racking, use just 3 crushed Campden tablets or ¼ teaspoon (1.4 g) potassium metabisulfite powder.

10. The wine should clear itself. If it doesn't, wait longer and rack until the wine clears.

11. When the wine is clear, it's time to bottle. Make adjustments if needed, then bottle the wine and wait at least 6 months before tasting. 🍇

 ## RED WINE FROM CABERNET FRANC GRAPES

The Cabernet Franc is rapidly becoming a favorite throughout the United States and Canada. This early ripening, aromatic red grape makes a pleasant wine. Cabernet Franc is excellent with steak and prime rib.

Yield: 5 gallons (19 L)

60–75	pounds (27–34 kg) fresh grapes
20	drops (1 mL) pectic enzyme liquid
17–20	Campden tablets or 1½–2 teaspoons (9.3–12.4 g) potassium metabisulfite powder
1	package (5 g) Wyeast Bordeaux or Red Star Pasteur Red yeast
3	teaspoons (8.8 g) yeast nutrient
3	tablespoons (11.1 g) Oak-Mor
1	package malolactic culture

1. Sanitize all equipment.

2. Remove any spoiled grapes from the clusters and then crush the grapes. Place them in a fermentation container. Remove grape stems from the container. Add 20 drops (1 mL) of pectic enzyme liquid to the crushed grapes and juice.

3. Add 5 crushed Campden tablets or ½ teaspoon (3.1 g) of potassium metabisulfite powder. Stir the juice and crushed grapes and let sit overnight.

4. The second day, test for sugar and acid and make appropriate adjustments.

5. Make a yeast starter by pouring 4 ounces (120 mL) of grape juice and 4 ounces (120 mL) of lukewarm water into a bowl, sprinkle in the yeast, and let proliferate for 30 minutes. Add this yeast starter, the yeast nutrient, and the Oak-Mor to the must and stir well. Cover the container loosely with a sheet of plastic.

6. Fermentation will start in 2 or 3 days and continue for 7 to 12 days. The cap (the pulp, skins, and so on) will rise to the top, so twice daily push it down with a sanitized spoon. This allows the color and body to be extracted from the skin and pulp mixture. Between the fourth and sixth day, inoculate the must with malolactic culture (follow the manufacturer's instructions).

7. Monitor the wine each day with a hydrometer. When the specific gravity reaches 1.000 or lower, it's time to press out the wine and store it in another container.

8. Sanitize a 5-gallon (19 L) glass carboy. Put in 5 crushed Campden tablets or ½ teaspoon (3.1 g) of potassium metabisulfite powder. Pour in the must and fill up to the top. Insert a rubber bung and air lock into the jug opening.

9. Let the wine sit 3 to 4 weeks, then rack again into a sanitized carboy. Three or four more rackings, 4 to 6 weeks apart, should pace the wine to its finish. After the second racking, use just 3 crushed Campden tablets or ¼ teaspoon (1.4 g) potassium metabisulfite powder.

10. The wine should clear itself. If it doesn't, wait longer and rack until the wine clears.

11. When the wine is clear, it's time to bottle. Make adjustments if needed, then bottle the wine and wait at least 6 months before tasting. 🍇

RED WINE FROM CABERNET SAUVIGNON GRAPES

Cabernet Sauvignon is the premier red variety in the world. Planted on every wine-producing continent, Cabernet Sauvignon, a late-ripening grape, now leads the world in red wine appeal. This medium-bodied wine pairs well with beef, lamb, and poultry dishes.

Yield: 5 gallons (19 L)

60–75	pounds (27–34 kg) fresh grapes
20	drops (1 mL) pectic enzyme liquid
17–20	Campden tablets or 1½–2 teaspoons (9.3–12.4 g) potassium metabisulfite powder
1	package (5 g) Red Star Pasteur Red or Wyeast Bordeaux yeast
3	teaspoons (8.8 g) yeast nutrient
3	tablespoons (11.1 g) Oak-Mor
1	package malolactic culture

1. Sanitize all equipment.

2. Remove any spoiled grapes from the clusters and then crush the grapes. Place them in a fermentation container. Remove grape stems from the container. Add 20 drops (1 mL) of pectic enzyme liquid to the crushed grapes and juice.

3. Add 5 crushed Campden tablets or ½ teaspoon (3.1 g) of potassium metabisulfite powder. Stir the juice and crushed grapes and let sit overnight.

4. The second day, test for sugar and acid and make appropriate adjustments.

5. Make a yeast starter by pouring 4 ounces (120 mL) of grape juice and 4 ounces (120 mL) of lukewarm water into a bowl, sprinkle in the yeast, and let proliferate for 30 minutes. Add this yeast starter, the yeast nutrient, and the Oak-Mor to the must and stir well. Cover the container loosely with a sheet of plastic.

6. Fermentation will start in 2 or 3 days and continue for 7 to 12 days. The cap (the pulp, skins, and so on) will rise to the top, so twice daily push it down with a sanitized spoon. This allows the color and body to be extracted from the skin and pulp mixture. Between the fourth and sixth day, inoculate the must with malolactic culture (follow the manufacturer's instructions).

7. Monitor the wine each day with a hydrometer. When the specific gravity reaches 1.000 or lower, it's time to press out the wine and store it in another container.

8. Sanitize a 5-gallon (19 L) glass carboy. Put in 5 crushed Campden tablets or ½ teaspoon (3.1 g) of potassium metabisulfite powder. Pour in the must and fill up to the top. Insert a rubber bung and air lock into the jug opening.

9. Let the wine sit 3 to 4 weeks, then rack again into a sanitized carboy. Three or four more rackings, 4 to 6 weeks apart, should pace the wine to its finish. After the second racking, use just 3 crushed Campden tablets or ¼ teaspoon (1.4 g) potassium metabisulfite powder.

10. The wine should clear itself. If it doesn't, wait longer and rack until the wine clears.

11. When the wine is clear, it's time to bottle. Make adjustments if needed, then bottle the wine and wait at least 6 months before tasting. 🍇

RED WINE FROM CARIGNANE GRAPES

Carignane is a variety widely planted in France, where it is used as a blending grape. Its wines are high in acidity, color, tannins, and bitterness. They also lack sophistication. The variety is readily available to home winemakers at reasonable prices from many California producers. The finished wine goes well with red pasta dishes and hearty beef roasts.

Yield: 5 gallons (19 L)

60–75	pounds (27–34 kg) fresh grapes
20	drops (1 mL) pectic enzyme liquid
17–20	Campden tablets or 1½–2 teaspoons (9.3–12.4 g) potassium metabisulfite powder
1	package (5 g) Wyeast Chianti or Red Star Premier Cuvée yeast
3	teaspoons (8.8 g) yeast nutrient
3	tablespoons (11.1 g) Oak-Mor
1	package malolactic culture

1. Sanitize all equipment.

2. Remove any spoiled grapes from the clusters and then crush the grapes. Place them in a fermentation container. Remove grape stems from the container. Add 20 drops (1 mL) of pectic enzyme liquid to the crushed grapes and juice.

3. Add 5 crushed Campden tablets or ½ teaspoon (3.1 g) of potassium metabisulfite powder. Stir the juice and crushed grapes and let sit overnight.

4. The second day, test for sugar and acid and make appropriate adjustments.

5. Make a yeast starter by pouring 4 ounces (120 mL) of grape juice and 4 ounces (120 mL) of lukewarm water into a bowl, sprinkle in the yeast, and let proliferate for 30 minutes. Add this yeast starter, the yeast nutrient, and the Oak-Mor to the must and stir well. Cover the container loosely with a sheet of plastic.

6. Fermentation will start in 2 or 3 days and continue for 7 to 12 days. The cap (the pulp, skins, and so on) will rise to the top, so twice daily push it down with a sanitized spoon. This allows the color and body to be extracted from the skin and pulp mixture. Between the fourth and sixth day, inoculate the must with malolactic culture (follow the manufacturer's instructions).

7. Monitor the wine each day with a hydrometer. When the specific gravity reaches 1.000 or lower, it's time to press out the wine and store it in another container.

8. Sanitize a 5-gallon (19 L) glass carboy. Put in 5 crushed Campden tablets or ½ teaspoon (3.1 g) of potassium metabisulfite powder. Pour in the must and fill up to the top. Insert a rubber bung and air lock into the jug opening.

9. Let the wine sit 3 to 4 weeks, then rack again into a sanitized carboy. Three or four more rackings, 4 to 6 weeks apart, should pace the wine to its finish. After the second racking, use just 3 crushed Campden tablets or ¼ teaspoon (1.4 g) potassium metabisulfite powder.

10. The wine should clear itself. If it doesn't, wait longer and rack until the wine clears.

11. When the wine is clear, it's time to bottle. Make adjustments if needed, then bottle the wine and wait at least 6 months before tasting. 🍇

RED WINE FROM CHAMBOURCIN GRAPES

Chambourcin is the best French-American hybrid red grape. It is presently enjoying great success in the eastern United States and France. A hardy and prolific producer, Chambourcin makes pleasant, medium-bodied, fruity red wines. Wood aging adds complexity and depth. Serve with pizza, pasta, and hamburgers.

Yield: 5 gallons (19 L)

60–75	pounds (27–34 kg) fresh grapes
20	drops (1 mL) pectic enzyme liquid
17–20	Campden tablets or 1½–2 teaspoons (9.3–12.4 g) potassium metabisulfite powder
1	package (5 g) Wyeast Assmannhausen or Red Star Premier Cuvée yeast
3	teaspoons (8.8 g) yeast nutrient
3	tablespoons (11.1 g) Oak-Mor
1	package malolactic culture

1. Sanitize all equipment.

2. Remove any spoiled grapes from the clusters and then crush the grapes. Place them in a fermentation container. Remove grape stems from the container. Add 20 drops (1 mL) of pectic enzyme liquid to the crushed grapes and juice.

3. Add 5 crushed Campden tablets or ½ teaspoon (3.1 g) of potassium metabisulfite powder. Stir the juice and crushed grapes and let sit overnight.

4. The second day, test for sugar and acid and make appropriate adjustments.

5. Make a yeast starter by pouring 4 ounces (120 mL) of grape juice and 4 ounces (120 mL) of lukewarm water into a bowl, sprinkle in the yeast, and let proliferate for 30 minutes. Add this yeast starter, the yeast nutrient, and the Oak-Mor to the must and stir well. Cover the container loosely with a sheet of plastic.

6. Fermentation will start in 2 or 3 days and continue for 7 to 12 days. The cap (the pulp, skins, and so on) will rise to the top, so twice daily push it down with a sanitized spoon. This allows the color and body to be extracted from the skin and pulp mixture. Between the fourth and sixth day, inoculate the must with malolactic culture (follow the manufacturer's instructions).

7. Monitor the wine each day with a hydrometer. When the specific gravity reaches 1.000 or lower, it's time to press out the wine and store it in another container.

8. Sanitize a 5-gallon (19 L) glass carboy. Put in 5 crushed Campden tablets or ½ teaspoon (3.1 g) of potassium metabisulfite powder. Pour in the must and fill up to the top. Insert a rubber bung and air lock into the jug opening.

9. Let the wine sit 3 to 4 weeks, then rack again into a sanitized carboy. Three or four more rackings, 4 to 6 weeks apart, should pace the wine to its finish. After the second racking, use just 3 crushed Campden tablets or ¼ teaspoon (1.4 g) potassium metabisulfite powder.

10. The wine should clear itself. If it doesn't, wait longer and rack until the wine clears.

11. When the wine is clear, it's time to bottle. Make adjustments if needed, then bottle the wine and wait at least 6 months before tasting. 🍇

RED WINE FROM CONCORD GRAPES

The Concord grape is best known for jams, jellies, and grape juice. This variety, widely planted in the eastern United States, is popular as a sweet religious wine. It is best made in a fruity, easy-drinking style suitable for early consumption. Costs are usually low and availability is usually high. Drink at poolside with fruit, soft cheeses, and finger foods.

Yield: 5 gallons (19 L)

60–75	pounds (27–34 kg) fresh grapes
20	drops (1 mL) pectic enzyme liquid
17–20	Campden tablets or 1½–2 teapoons (9.3–12.4 g) potassium metabisulfite powder
1	package (5 g) Red Star Côtes des Blancs or Lalvin 71B-1122 yeast
3	teaspoons (8.8 g) yeast nutrient

1. Sanitize all equipment.

2. Remove any spoiled grapes from the clusters and then crush the grapes. Place them in a fermentation container. Remove grape stems from the container. Add 20 drops (1 mL) of pectic enzyme liquid to the crushed grapes and juice.

3. Add 5 crushed Campden tablets or ½ teaspoon (3.1 g) of potassium metabisulfite powder. Stir the juice and crushed grapes and let sit overnight.

4. The second day, test for sugar and acid and make appropriate adjustments.

5. Make a yeast starter by pouring 4 ounces (120 mL) of grape juice and 4 ounces (120 mL) of lukewarm water into a bowl, sprinkle in the yeast, and let proliferate for 30 minutes. Add this yeast starter, the yeast nutrient, and the Oak-Mor to the must and stir well. Cover the container loosely with a sheet of plastic.

6. Fermentation will start in 2 or 3 days and continue for 7 to 12 days. The cap (the pulp, skins, and so on) will rise to the top, so twice daily push it down with a sanitized spoon. This allows the color and body to be extracted from the skin and pulp mixture.

7. Monitor the wine each day with a hydrometer. When the specific gravity reaches 1.000 or lower, it's time to press out the wine and store it in another container.

8. Sanitize a 5-gallon (19 L) glass carboy. Put in 5 crushed Campden tablets or ½ teaspoon (3.1 g) of potassium metabisulfite powder, then transfer the wine into the container, leaving behind the sediment.

9. Let the wine sit 3 to 4 weeks, then rack again into a sanitized carboy. Three or four more rackings, 4 to 6 weeks apart, should pace the wine to its finish. After the second racking, use just 3 crushed Campden tablets or ¼ teaspoon (1.4 g) potassium metabisulfite powder.

10. The wine should clear itself. If it doesn't, wait longer and rack until the wine clears.

11. When the wine is clear, it's time to bottle. Make adjustments if needed, then bottle the wine and wait at least 6 months before tasting. 🍇

RED WINE FROM GAMAY GRAPES

This is the Beaujolais grape variety grown in several regions of France. It is also popular in Switzerland, the former Yugoslavia, Canada, and Croatia. Sometimes called Napa Gamay in California, the variety offers quantity if not always consistent quality. A good blending wine, the Gamay can also stand on its own as a pure varietal. Making wine in the fresh, fruity style seems to be the best strategy. Serve with light dishes, soft cheeses, fruit, and tomato-laced fish dishes.

Yield: 5 gallons (19 L)

60–75	pounds (27–34 kg) fresh grapes
20	drops (1 mL) pectic enzyme liquid
17–20	Campden tablets or 1½–2 teaspoons (9.3–12.4 g) potassium metabisulfite powder
1	package (5 g) Red Star Côtes des Blancs or Lalvin 71B-1122 yeast
3	teaspoons (8.8 g) yeast nutrient
1	package malolactic culture

1. Sanitize all equipment.

2. Remove any spoiled grapes from the clusters and then crush the grapes. Place them in a fermentation container. Remove grape stems from the container. Add 20 drops (1 mL) of pectic enzyme liquid to the crushed grapes and juice.

3. Add 5 crushed Campden tablets or ½ teaspoon (3.1 g) of potassium metabisulfite powder. Stir the juice and crushed grapes and let sit overnight.

4. The second day, test for sugar and acid and make appropriate adjustments.

5. Make a yeast starter by pouring 4 ounces (120 mL) of grape juice and 4 ounces (120 mL) of lukewarm water into a bowl, sprinkle in the yeast, and let proliferate for 30 minutes. Add this yeast starter and the yeast nutrient to the must and stir well. Cover the container loosely with a sheet of plastic.

6. Fermentation will start in 2 or 3 days and continue for 7 to 12 days. The cap (the pulp, skins, and so on) will rise to the top, so twice daily push it down with a sanitized spoon. This allows the color and body to be extracted from the skin and pulp mixture. Between the fourth and sixth day, inoculate the must with malolactic culture (follow the manufacturer's instructions).

7. Monitor the wine each day with a hydrometer. When the specific gravity reaches 1.000 or lower, it's time to press out the wine and store it in another container.

8. Sanitize a 5-gallon (19 L) glass carboy. Put in 5 crushed Campden tablets or ½ teaspoon (3.1 g) of potassium metabisulfite powder. Pour in the must and fill up to the top. Insert a rubber bung and air lock into the jug opening.

9. Let the wine sit 3 to 4 weeks, then rack again into a sanitized carboy. Three or four more rackings, 4 to 6 weeks apart, should pace the wine to its finish. After the second racking, use just 3 crushed Campden tablets or ¼ teaspoon (1.4 g) potassium metabisulfite powder.

10. The wine should clear itself. If it doesn't, wait longer and rack until the wine clears.

11. When the wine is clear, it's time to bottle. Make adjustments if needed, then bottle the wine and wait at least 6 months before tasting. 🍇

 RED WINE FROM GRENACHE GRAPES

Grenache is one of the most widely planted varieties in the world. Southern France and Spain produce the greatest quantities, but it is also grown in the United States, Australia, and South Africa. The variety is readily available to home winemakers. Fruity, fresh, easy-drinking wines are the characteristics of the Grenache. Rosé wines are also attractive when made with Grenache. A quaffing wine, Grenache goes well with soft cheeses, pâtés, finger foods, tapas, and fruit.

Yield: 5 gallons (19 L)

60–75	pounds (27–34 kg) fresh grapes
20	drops (1 mL) pectic enzyme liquid
17–20	Campden tablets or 1½–2 teaspoons (9.3–12.4 g) potassium metabisulfite powder
1	package (5 g) Red Star Côtes des Blancs or Lalvin 71B-1122 yeast
3	teaspoons (8.8 g) yeast nutrient
1	package malolactic culture

1. Sanitize all equipment.

2. Remove any spoiled grapes from the clusters and then crush the grapes. Place them in a fermentation container. Remove grape stems from the container. Add 20 drops (1 mL) of pectic enzyme liquid to the crushed grapes and juice.

3. Add 5 crushed Campden tablets or ½ teaspoon (3.1 g) of potassium metabisulfite powder. Stir the juice and crushed grapes and let sit overnight.

4. The second day, test for sugar and acid and make appropriate adjustments.

5. Make a yeast starter by pouring 4 ounces (120 mL) of grape juice and 4 ounces (120 mL) of lukewarm water into a bowl, sprinkle in the yeast, and let proliferate for 30 minutes. Add this yeast starter and the yeast nutrient to the must and stir well. Cover the container loosely with a sheet of plastic.

6. Fermentation will start in 2 or 3 days and continue for 7 to 12 days. The cap (the pulp, skins, and so on) will rise to the top, so twice daily push it down with a sanitized spoon. This allows the color and body to be extracted from the skin and pulp mixture. Between the fourth and sixth day, inoculate the must with malolactic culture (follow the manufacturer's instructions).

7. Monitor the wine each day with a hydrometer. When the specific gravity reaches 1.000 or lower, it's time to press out the wine and store it in another container.

8. Sanitize a 5-gallon (19 L) glass carboy. Put in 5 crushed Campden tablets or ½ teaspoon (3.1 g) of potassium metabisulfite powder. Pour in the must and fill up to the top. Insert a rubber bung and air lock into the jug opening.

9. Let the wine sit 3 to 4 weeks, then rack again into a sanitized carboy. Three or four more rackings, 4 to 6 weeks apart, should pace the wine to its finish. After the second racking, use just 3 crushed Campden tablets or ¼ teaspoon (1.4 g) potassium metabisulfite powder.

10. The wine should clear itself. If it doesn't, wait longer and rack until the wine clears.

11. When the wine is clear, it's time to bottle. Make adjustments if needed, then bottle the wine and wait at least 6 months before tasting. 🍇

RED WINE FROM LEMBERGER GRAPES

Called Blaufrankisch in Austria and other European countries, Lemberger is gaining acreage in Washington and California as more and more wineries are producing the spicy red wine. Thought to be a relative of the Gamay grape, Lemberger offers a fruity, spicy character. Serve young with veal, lamb, game, and poultry.

Yield: 5 gallons (19 L)

60–75 pounds (27–34 kg) fresh grapes
20 drops (1 mL) pectic enzyme liquid
17–20 Campden tablets or 1½–2 teaspoons (9.3–12.4 g) potassium metabisulfite powder
1 package (5 g) Red Star Côtes des Blancs or Lalvin 71B-1122 yeast
3 teaspoons (8.8 g) yeast nutrient
1 package malolactic culture

1. Sanitize all equipment.

2. Remove any spoiled grapes from the clusters and then crush the grapes. Place them in a fermentation container. Remove grape stems from the container. Add 20 drops (1 mL) of pectic enzyme liquid to the crushed grapes and juice.

3. Add 5 crushed Campden tablets or ½ teaspoon (3.1 g) of potassium metabisulfite powder. Stir the juice and crushed grapes and let sit overnight.

4. The second day, test for sugar and acid and make appropriate adjustments.

5. Make a yeast starter by pouring 4 ounces (120 mL) of grape juice and 4 ounces (120 mL) of lukewarm water into a bowl, sprinkle in the yeast, and let proliferate for 30 minutes. Add this yeast starter and the yeast nutrient to the must and stir well. Cover the container loosely with a sheet of plastic.

6. Fermentation will start in 2 or 3 days and continue for 7 to 12 days. The cap (the pulp, skins, and so on) will rise to the top, so twice daily push it down with a sanitized spoon. This allows the color and body to be extracted from the skin and pulp mixture. Between the fourth and sixth day, inoculate the must with malolactic culture (follow the manufacturer's instructions).

7. Monitor the wine each day with a hydrometer. When the specific gravity reaches 1.000 or lower, it's time to press out the wine and store it in another container.

8. Sanitize a 5-gallon (19 L) glass carboy. Put in 5 crushed Campden tablets or ½ teaspoon (3.1 g) of potassium metabisulfite powder. Pour in the must and fill up to the top. Insert a rubber bung and air lock into the jug opening.

9. Let the wine sit 3 to 4 weeks, then rack again into a sanitized carboy. Three or four more rackings, 4 to 6 weeks apart, should pace the wine to its finish. After the second racking, use just 3 crushed Campden tablets or ¼ teaspoon (1.4 g) potassium metabisulfite powder.

10. The wine should clear itself. If it doesn't, wait longer and rack until the wine clears.

11. When the wine is clear, it's time to bottle. Make adjustments if needed, then bottle the wine and wait at least 6 months before tasting. 🍇

RED WINE FROM MALBEC GRAPES

Originally a blending variety in France, Malbec has found new homes in Chile and the United States. Similar to Merlot in character and flavor, Malbec can stand on its own as a pure varietal. We recommend that you blend Malbec with Cabernet Sauvignon or make it a 100 percent varietal. Serve with beef, lamb, and poultry.

Yield: 5 gallons (19 L)

60–75	pounds (27–34 kg) fresh grapes
20	drops (1 mL) pectic enzyme liquid
17–20	Campden tablets or 1½–2 teaspoons (9.3–12.4 g) potassium metabisulfite powder
1	package (5 g) Red Star Pasteur Red or Wyeast Bordeaux yeast
3	teaspoons (8.8 g) yeast nutrient
3	tablespoons (11.1 g) Oak-Mor
1	package malolactic culture

1. Sanitize all equipment.

2. Remove any spoiled grapes from the clusters and then crush the grapes. Place them in a fermentation container. Remove grape stems from the container. Add 20 drops (1 mL) of pectic enzyme liquid to the crushed grapes and juice.

3. Add 5 crushed Campden tablets or ½ teaspoon (3.1 g) of potassium metabisulfite powder. Stir the juice and crushed grapes and let sit overnight.

4. The second day, test for sugar and acid and make appropriate adjustments.

5. Make a yeast starter by pouring 4 ounces (120 mL) of grape juice and 4 ounces (120 mL) of lukewarm water into a bowl, sprinkle in the yeast, and let proliferate for 30 minutes. Add this yeast starter, the yeast nutrient, and the Oak-Mor to the must and stir well. Cover the container loosely with a sheet of plastic.

6. Fermentation will start in 2 or 3 days and continue for 7 to 12 days. The cap (the pulp, skins, and so on) will rise to the top, so twice daily push it down with a sanitized spoon. This allows the color and body to be extracted from the skin and pulp mixture. Between the fourth and sixth day, inoculate the must with malolactic culture (follow the manufacturer's instructions).

7. Monitor the wine each day with a hydrometer. When the specific gravity reaches 1.000 or lower, it's time to press out the wine and store it in another container.

8. Sanitize a 5-gallon (19 L) glass carboy. Put in 5 crushed Campden tablets or ½ teaspoon (3.1 g) of potassium metabisulfite powder. Pour in the must and fill up to the top. Insert a rubber bung and air lock into the jug opening.

9. Let the wine sit 3 to 4 weeks, then rack again into a sanitized carboy. Three or four more rackings, 4 to 6 weeks apart, should pace the wine to its finish. After the second racking, use just 3 crushed Campden tablets or ¼ teaspoon (1.4 g) potassium metabisulfite powder.

10. The wine should clear itself. If it doesn't, wait longer and rack until the wine clears.

11. When the wine is clear, it's time to bottle. Make adjustments if needed, then bottle the wine and wait at least 6 months before tasting. 🍇

RED WINE FROM MERLOT GRAPES

France's great Bordeaux blending wine, Merlot is also planted in many of the world's premier wine regions. In the United States, Merlot is the fastest-growing red variety in popularity. It is soft and pleasant and easy to drink at an early age. Pair Merlot with lamb, poultry, and soft cheeses.

Yield: 5 gallons (19 L)

60–75 pounds (27–34 kg) fresh grapes
20 drops (1 mL) pectic enzyme liquid
17–20 Campden tablets or 1½–2 teaspoons (9.3–12.4 g) potassium metabisulfite powder
1 package (5 g) Red Star Pasteur Red or Wyeast Bordeaux yeast
3 teaspoons (8.8 g) yeast nutrient
3 tablespoons (11.1 g) Oak-Mor
1 package malolactic culture

1. Sanitize all equipment.

2. Remove any spoiled grapes from the clusters and then crush the grapes. Place them in a fermentation container. Remove grape stems from the container. Add 20 drops (1 mL) of pectic enzyme liquid to the crushed grapes and juice.

3. Add 5 crushed Campden tablets or ½ teaspoon (3.1 g) of potassium metabisulfite powder. Stir the juice and crushed grapes and let sit overnight.

4. The second day, test for sugar and acid and make appropriate adjustments.

5. Make a yeast starter by pouring 4 ounces (120 mL) of grape juice and 4 ounces (120 mL) of lukewarm water into a bowl, sprinkle in the yeast, and let proliferate for 30 minutes. Add this yeast starter, the yeast nutrient, and the Oak-Mor to the must and stir well. Cover the container loosely with a sheet of plastic.

6. Fermentation will start in 2 or 3 days and continue for 7 to 12 days. The cap (the pulp, skins, and so on) will rise to the top, so twice daily push it down with a sanitized spoon. This allows the color and body to be extracted from the skin and pulp mixture. Between the fourth and sixth day, inoculate the must with malolactic culture (follow the manufacturer's instructions).

7. Monitor the wine each day with a hydrometer. When the specific gravity reaches 1.000 or lower, it's time to press out the wine and store it in another container.

8. Sanitize a 5-gallon (19 L) glass carboy. Put in 5 crushed Campden tablets or ½ teaspoon (3.1 g) of potassium metabisulfite powder. Pour in the must and fill up to the top. Insert a rubber bung and air lock into the jug opening.

9. Let the wine sit 3 to 4 weeks, then rack again into a sanitized carboy. Three or four more rackings, 4 to 6 weeks apart, should pace the wine to its finish. After the second racking, use just 3 crushed Campden tablets or ¼ teaspoon (1.4 g) potassium metabisulfite powder.

10. The wine should clear itself. If it doesn't, wait longer and rack until the wine clears.

11. When the wine is clear, it's time to bottle. Make adjustments if needed, then bottle the wine and wait at least 6 months before tasting. 🍇

RED WINE FROM PINOT NOIR GRAPES

This great red grape from Burgundy is now finding a home in the United States and other parts of the world. Once a difficult wine to make well, Pinot Noir challenged winemakers to master its finesse and elegance. Improved technology now enables the home winemaker to make an excellent Pinot Noir. Serve with ham, lamb, and poultry dishes.

Yield: 5 gallons (19 L)

60–75 pounds (27–34 kg) fresh grapes
20 drops (1 mL) pectic enzyme liquid
17–20 Campden tablets or 1½–2 teaspoons (9.3–12.4 g) potassium metabisulfite powder
1 package (5 g) Wyeast Bordeaux or Red Star Premier Cuvée yeast
3 teaspoons (8.8 g) yeast nutrient
3 tablespoons (11.1 g) Oak-Mor
1 package malolactic culture

1. Sanitize all equipment.

2. Remove any spoiled grapes from the clusters and then crush the grapes. Place them in a fermentation container. Remove grape stems from the container. Add 20 drops (1 mL) of pectic enzyme liquid to the crushed grapes and juice.

3. Add 5 crushed Campden tablets or ½ teaspoon (3.1 g) of potassium metabisulfite powder. Stir the juice and crushed grapes and let sit overnight.

4. The second day, test for sugar and acid and make appropriate adjustments.

5. Make a yeast starter by pouring 4 ounces (120 mL) of grape juice and 4 ounces (120 mL) of lukewarm water into a bowl, sprinkle in the yeast, and let proliferate for 30 minutes. Add this yeast starter, the yeast nutrient, and the Oak-Mor to the must and stir well. Cover the container loosely with a sheet of plastic.

6. Fermentation will start in 2 or 3 days and continue for 7 to 12 days. The cap (the pulp, skins, and so on) will rise to the top, so twice daily push it down with a sanitized spoon. This allows the color and body to be extracted from the skin and pulp mixture. Between the fourth and sixth day, inoculate the must with malolactic culture (follow the manufacturer's instructions).

7. Monitor the wine each day with a hydrometer. When the specific gravity reaches 1.000 or lower, it's time to press out the wine and store it in another container.

8. Sanitize a 5-gallon (19 L) glass carboy. Put in 5 crushed Campden tablets or ½ teaspoon (3.1 g) of potassium metabisulfite powder. Pour in the must and fill up to the top. Insert a rubber bung and air lock into the jug opening.

9. Let the wine sit 3 to 4 weeks, then rack again into a sanitized carboy. Three or four more rackings, 4 to 6 weeks apart, should pace the wine to its finish. After the second racking, use just 3 crushed Campden tablets or ¼ teaspoon (1.4 g) potassium metabisulfite powder.

10. The wine should clear itself. If it doesn't, wait longer and rack until the wine clears.

11. When the wine is clear, it's time to bottle. Make adjustments if needed, then bottle the wine and wait at least 6 months before tasting. 🍇

RED WINE FROM PETITE SIRAH GRAPES

This dark, inky, highly acidic red wine is used for blending, but it can also stand on its own. Old-time winemakers often recommended that Petite Sirah be used in all red wines to add color and complexity. Although its acreage is shrinking in California, its grapes are usually available to home winemakers. Hardy dishes like stews, roasts, and Tex-Mex cuisine are enhanced by Petite Sirah.

Yield: 5 gallons (19 L)

60–75	pounds (27–34 kg) fresh grapes
20	drops (1 mL) pectic enzyme liquid
17–20	Campden tablets or 1½–2 teaspoons (9.3–12.4 g) potassium metabisulfite powder
1	package (5 g) Red Star Premier Cuvée or Wyeast Bordeaux yeast
3	teaspoons (8.8 g) yeast nutrient
3	tablespoons (11.1 g) Oak-Mor
1	package malolactic culture

1. Sanitize all equipment.

2. Remove any spoiled grapes from the clusters and then crush the grapes. Place them in a fermentation container. Remove grape stems from the container. Add 20 drops (1 mL) of pectic enzyme liquid to the crushed grapes and juice.

3. Add 5 crushed Campden tablets or ½ teaspoon (3.1 g) of potassium metabisulfite powder. Stir the juice and crushed grapes and let sit overnight.

4. The second day, test for sugar and acid and make appropriate adjustments.

5. Make a yeast starter by pouring 4 ounces (120 mL) of grape juice and 4 ounces (120 mL) of lukewarm water into a bowl, sprinkle in the yeast, and let proliferate for 30 minutes. Add this yeast starter, the yeast nutrient, and the Oak-Mor to the must and stir well. Cover the container loosely with a sheet of plastic.

6. Fermentation will start in 2 or 3 days and continue for 7 to 12 days. The cap (the pulp, skins, and so on) will rise to the top, so twice daily push it down with a sanitized spoon. This allows the color and body to be extracted from the skin and pulp mixture. Between the fourth and sixth day, inoculate the must with malolactic culture (follow the manufacturer's instructions).

7. Monitor the wine each day with a hydrometer. When the specific gravity reaches 1.000 or lower, it's time to press out the wine and store it in another container.

8. Sanitize a 5-gallon (19 L) glass carboy. Put in 5 crushed Campden tablets or ½ teaspoon (3.1 g) of potassium metabisulfite powder. Pour in the must and fill up to the top. Insert a rubber bung and air lock into the jug opening.

9. Let the wine sit 3 to 4 weeks, then rack again into a sanitized carboy. Three or four more rackings, 4 to 6 weeks apart, should pace the wine to its finish. After the second racking, use just 3 crushed Campden tablets or ¼ teaspoon (1.4 g) potassium metabisulfite powder.

10. The wine should clear itself. If it doesn't, wait longer and rack until the wine clears.

11. When the wine is clear, it's time to bottle. Make adjustments if needed, then bottle the wine and wait at least 6 months before tasting. 🍇

RED WINE FROM PETIT VERDOT GRAPES

Petit Verdot, another French Bordeaux red grape used for blending, is now finding new homes in other countries. Acreage is increasing in the United States, and there is greater availability to home winemakers. This varietal is spicy and dark in color. It is an easy grape to work with. It goes well with steak, prime rib, and shish kebab.

Yield: 5 gallons (19 L)

60–75	pounds (27–34 kg) fresh grapes
20	drops (1 mL) pectic enzyme liquid
17–20	Campden tablets or 1½–2 teaspoons (9.3–12.4 g) potassium metabisulfite powder
1	package (5 g) Red Star Pasteur Red or Wyeast Bordeaux yeast
3	teaspoons (8.8 g) yeast nutrient
3	tablespoons (11.1 g) Oak-Mor
1	package malolactic culture

1. Sanitize all equipment.

2. Remove any spoiled grapes from the clusters and then crush the grapes. Place them in a fermentation container. Remove grape stems from the container. Add 20 drops (1 mL) of pectic enzyme liquid to the crushed grapes and juice.

3. Add 5 crushed Campden tablets or ½ teaspoon (3.1 g) of potassium metabisulfite powder. Stir the juice and crushed grapes and let sit overnight.

4. The second day, test for sugar and acid and make appropriate adjustments.

5. Make a yeast starter by pouring 4 ounces (120 mL) of grape juice and 4 ounces (120 mL) of lukewarm water into a bowl, sprinkle in the yeast, and let proliferate for 30 minutes. Add this yeast starter, the yeast nutrient, and the Oak-Mor to the must and stir well. Cover the container loosely with a sheet of plastic.

6. Fermentation will start in 2 or 3 days and continue for 7 to 12 days. The cap (the pulp, skins, and so on) will rise to the top, so twice daily push it down with a sanitized spoon. This allows the color and body to be extracted from the skin and pulp mixture. Between the fourth and sixth day, inoculate the must with malolactic culture (follow the manufacturer's instructions).

7. Monitor the wine each day with a hydrometer. When the specific gravity reaches 1.000 or lower, it's time to press out the wine and store it in another container.

8. Sanitize a 5-gallon (19 L) glass carboy. Put in 5 crushed Campden tablets or ½ teaspoon (3.1 g) of potassium metabisulfite powder. Pour in the must and fill up to the top. Insert a rubber bung and air lock into the jug opening.

9. Let the wine sit 3 to 4 weeks, then rack again into a sanitized carboy. Three or four more rackings, 4 to 6 weeks apart, should pace the wine to its finish. After the second racking, use just 3 crushed Campden tablets or ¼ teaspoon (1.4 g) potassium metabisulfite powder.

10. The wine should clear itself. If it doesn't, wait longer and rack until the wine clears.

11. When the wine is clear, it's time to bottle. Make adjustments if needed, then bottle the wine and wait at least 6 months before tasting. 🍇

RED WINE FROM RUBY CABERNET GRAPES

Ruby Cabernet is a University of California at Davis crossing variety that has enjoyed mixed success through the years. A blend of Carignane and Cabernet Sauvignon, the grape was bred to grow in warmer climates. Available to home winemakers at moderate prices, Ruby Cabernet can be made into a high-quality wine. Serve with soft cheeses, hamburgers, and grilled chicken.

Yield: 5 gallons (19 L)

60–75	pounds (27–34 kg) fresh grapes
20	drops (1 mL) pectic enzyme liquid
17–20	Campden tablets or 1½–2 teaspoons (9.3–12.4 g) potassium metabisulfite powder
1	package (5 g) Red Star Premier Cuvée or Wyeast Bordeaux yeast
3	teaspoons (8.8 g) yeast nutrient
3	tablespoons (11.1 g) Oak-Mor
1	package malolactic culture

1. Sanitize all equipment.

2. Remove any spoiled grapes from the clusters and then crush the grapes. Place them in a fermentation container. Remove grape stems from the container. Add 20 drops (1 mL) of pectic enzyme liquid to the crushed grapes and juice.

3. Add 5 crushed Campden tablets or ½ teaspoon (3.1 g) of potassium metabisulfite powder. Stir the juice and crushed grapes and let sit overnight.

4. The second day, test for sugar and acid and make appropriate adjustments.

5. Make a yeast starter by pouring 4 ounces (120 mL) of grape juice and 4 ounces (120 mL) of lukewarm water into a bowl, sprinkle in the yeast, and let proliferate for 30 minutes. Add this yeast starter, the yeast nutrient, and the Oak-Mor to the must and stir well. Cover the container loosely with a sheet of plastic.

6. Fermentation will start in 2 or 3 days and continue for 7 to 12 days. The cap (the pulp, skins, and so on) will rise to the top, so twice daily push it down with a sanitized spoon. This allows the color and body to be extracted from the skin and pulp mixture. Between the fourth and sixth day, inoculate the must with malolactic culture (follow the manufacturer's instructions).

7. Monitor the wine each day with a hydrometer. When the specific gravity reaches 1.000 or lower, it's time to press out the wine and store it in another container.

8. Sanitize a 5-gallon (19 L) glass carboy. Put in 5 crushed Campden tablets or ½ teaspoon (3.1 g) of potassium metabisulfite powder. Pour in the must and fill up to the top. Insert a rubber bung and air lock into the jug opening.

9. Let the wine sit 3 to 4 weeks, then rack again into a sanitized carboy. Three or four more rackings, 4 to 6 weeks apart, should pace the wine to its finish. After the second racking, use just 3 crushed Campden tablets or ¼ teaspoon (1.4 g) potassium metabisulfite powder.

10. The wine should clear itself. If it doesn't, wait longer and rack until the wine clears.

11. When the wine is clear, it's time to bottle. Make adjustments if needed, then bottle the wine and wait at least 6 months before tasting. 🍇

 RED WINE FROM SANGIOVESE GRAPES

Italy's most planted red grape variety is becoming the new California red "darling." Sangiovese grows well on the West Coast and its acreage there is rapidly increasing. This great red wine of Tuscany and Romagna offers a great deal of versatility to the winemaker. It can also be blended with Cabernet Sauvignon and Merlot with interesting results. It makes a fine accompaniment for lasagna, red pasta, and sausage and pepper dishes.

Yield: 5 gallons (19 L)

60–75 pounds (27–34 kg) fresh grapes
20 drops (1 mL) pectic enzyme liquid
17–20 Campden tablets or 1½–2 teaspoons (9.3–12.4 g) potassium metabisulfite powder
1 package (5 g) Red Star Premier Cuvée or Wyeast Bordeaux yeast
3 teaspoons (8.8 g) yeast nutrient
3 tablespoons (11.1 g) Oak-Mor
1 package malolactic culture

1. Sanitize all equipment.

2. Remove any spoiled grapes from the clusters and then crush the grapes. Place them in a fermentation container. Remove grape stems from the container. Add 20 drops (1 mL) of pectic enzyme liquid to the crushed grapes and juice.

3. Add 5 crushed Campden tablets or ½ teaspoon (3.1 g) of potassium metabisulfite powder. Stir the juice and crushed grapes and let sit overnight.

4. The second day, test for sugar and acid and make appropriate adjustments.

5. Make a yeast starter by pouring 4 ounces (120 mL) of grape juice and 4 ounces (120 mL) of lukewarm water into a bowl, sprinkle in the yeast, and let proliferate for 30 minutes. Add this yeast starter, the yeast nutrient, and the Oak-Mor to the must and stir well. Cover the container loosely with a sheet of plastic.

6. Fermentation will start in 2 or 3 days and continue for 7 to 12 days. The cap (the pulp, skins, and so on) will rise to the top, so twice daily push it down with a sanitized spoon. This allows the color and body to be extracted from the skin and pulp mixture. Between the fourth and sixth day, inoculate the must with malolactic culture (follow the manufacturer's instructions).

7. Monitor the wine each day with a hydrometer. When the specific gravity reaches 1.000 or lower, it's time to press out the wine and store it in another container.

8. Sanitize a 5-gallon (19 L) glass carboy. Put in 5 crushed Campden tablets or ½ teaspoon (3.1 g) of potassium metabisulfite powder. Pour in the must and fill up to the top. Insert a rubber bung and air lock into the jug opening.

9. Let the wine sit 3 to 4 weeks, then rack again into a sanitized carboy. Three or four more rackings, 4 to 6 weeks apart, should pace the wine to its finish. After the second racking, use just 3 crushed Campden tablets or ¼ teaspoon (1.4 g) potassium metabisulfite powder.

10. The wine should clear itself. If it doesn't, wait longer and rack until the wine clears.

11. When the wine is clear, it's time to bottle. Make adjustments if needed, then bottle the wine and wait at least 6 months before tasting. 🍇

RED WINE FROM SYRAH GRAPES

One of the world's oldest varieties, Syrah is productive in the Rhône region of France and now in Australia and South Africa. Syrah is scented with black pepper and leather and offers complexity and structure. It is often blended with other premium varieties, usually with excellent results. Serve with red meat dishes, poultry, and game.

Yield: 5 gallons (19 L)

60–75	pounds (27–34 kg) fresh grapes
20	drops (1 mL) pectic enzyme liquid
17–20	Campden tablets or 1½–2 teaspoons (9.3–12.4 g) potassium metabisulfite powder
1	package (5 g) Lalvin L2056 or Wyeast Bordeaux yeast
3	teaspoons (8.8 g) yeast nutrient
3	tablespoons (11.1 g) Oak-Mor
1	package malolactic culture

1. Sanitize all equipment.

2. Remove any spoiled grapes from the clusters and then crush the grapes. Place them in a fermentation container. Remove grape stems from the container. Add 20 drops (1 mL) of pectic enzyme liquid to the crushed grapes and juice.

3. Add 5 crushed Campden tablets or ½ teaspoon (3.1 g) of potassium metabisulfite powder. Stir the juice and crushed grapes and let sit overnight.

4. The second day, test for sugar and acid and make appropriate adjustments.

5. Make a yeast starter by pouring 4 ounces (120 mL) of grape juice and 4 ounces (120 mL) of lukewarm water into a bowl, sprinkle in the yeast, and let proliferate for 30 minutes. Add this yeast starter, the yeast nutrient, and the Oak-Mor to the must and stir well. Cover the container loosely with a sheet of plastic.

6. Fermentation will start in 2 or 3 days and continue for 7 to 12 days. The cap (the pulp, skins, and so on) will rise to the top, so twice daily push it down with a sanitized spoon. This allows the color and body to be extracted from the skin and pulp mixture. Between the fourth and sixth day, inoculate the must with malolactic culture (follow the manufacturer's instructions).

7. Monitor the wine each day with a hydrometer. When the specific gravity reaches 1.000 or lower, it's time to press out the wine and store it in another container.

8. Sanitize a 5-gallon (19 L) glass carboy. Put in 5 crushed Campden tablets or ½ teaspoon (3.1 g) of potassium metabisulfite powder. Pour in the must and fill up to the top. Insert a rubber bung and air lock into the jug opening.

9. Let the wine sit 3 to 4 weeks, then rack again into a sanitized carboy. Three or four more rackings, 4 to 6 weeks apart, should pace the wine to its finish. After the second racking, use just 3 crushed Campden tablets or ¼ teaspoon (1.4 g) potassium metabisulfite powder.

10. The wine should clear itself. If it doesn't, wait longer and rack until the wine clears.

11. When the wine is clear, it's time to bottle. Make adjustments if needed, then bottle the wine and wait at least 6 months before tasting. 🍇

RED WINE FROM ZINFANDEL GRAPES

Zinfandel is America's own variety. Made in a range of styles, this grape offers the winemaker many options. Use Zinfandel as a blend or make it on its own as a claret style; a lighter, more fruity style; or even as a hardy, robust style. Some like it as a white wine. As a regular red, it goes well with poultry and stuffing, game, and spicy meat dishes.

Yield: 5 gallons (19 L)

60–75 pounds (27–34 kg) fresh grapes
20 drops (1 mL) pectic enzyme liquid
17–20 Campden tablets or 1½–2 teaspoons (9.3–12.4 g) potassium metabisulfite powder
1 package (5 g) Red Star Premier Cuvée or Wyeast Bordeaux yeast
3 teaspoons (8.8 g) yeast nutrient
3 tablespoons (11.1 g) Oak-Mor
1 package malolactic culture

1. Sanitize all equipment.

2. Remove any spoiled grapes from the clusters and then crush the grapes. Place them in a fermentation container. Remove grape stems from the container. Add 20 drops (1 mL) of pectic enzyme liquid to the crushed grapes and juice.

3. Add 5 crushed Campden tablets or ½ teaspoon (3.1 g) of potassium metabisulfite powder. Stir the juice and crushed grapes and let sit overnight.

4. The second day, test for sugar and acid and make appropriate adjustments.

5. Make a yeast starter by pouring 4 ounces (120 mL) of grape juice and 4 ounces (120 mL) of lukewarm water into a bowl, sprinkle in the yeast, and let proliferate for 30 minutes. Add this yeast starter, the yeast nutrient, and the Oak-Mor to the must and stir well. Cover the container loosely with a sheet of plastic.

6. Fermentation will start in 2 or 3 days and continue for 7 to 12 days. The cap (the pulp, skins, and so on) will rise to the top, so twice daily push it down with a sanitized spoon. This allows the color and body to be extracted from the skin and pulp mixture. Between the fourth and sixth day, inoculate the must with malolactic culture (follow the manufacturer's instructions).

7. Monitor the wine each day with a hydrometer. When the specific gravity reaches 1.000 or lower,

it's time to press out the wine and store it in another container.

8. Sanitize a 5-gallon (19 L) glass carboy. Put in 5 crushed Campden tablets or ½ teaspoon (3.1 g) of potassium metabisulfite powder. Pour in the must and fill up to the top. Insert a rubber bung and air lock into the jug opening.

9. Let the wine sit 3 to 4 weeks, then rack again into a sanitized carboy. Three or four more rackings, 4 to 6 weeks apart, should pace the wine to its finish. After the second racking, use just 3 crushed Campden tablets or ¼ teaspoon (1.4 g) potassium metabisulfite powder.

10. The wine should clear itself. If it doesn't, wait longer and rack until the wine clears.

11. When the wine is clear, it's time to bottle. Make adjustments if needed, then bottle the wine and wait at least 6 months before tasting. 🍇

WINE FROM FRUIT 8

*Wine makes daily living easier, less hurried,
with fewer tensions and more tolerance.*

—Benjamin Franklin (1706–1790)

THE UNITED STATES AND CANADA offer the home winemaker an abundant selection of basic ingredients for making fruit wines. Although some winemakers look down on them, these wines are an excellent addition to any cellar and they're fun to make as well.

Fruit wines are great with desserts, at teatime, served with appropriate foods, or as "coolers" (that is, combined with carbonated beverages and fruit) on a hot summer day.

Following our recipes will enable you to produce 5 gallons (19 L) of wine at a time. Traditional fruit wine recipes call for making 1 gallon (3.8 L); however, we believe that with a little more expense and effort, you'll be delighted to have a good supply for home use and still be able to give bottles of your wine as gifts.

EQUIPMENT

The basic equipment for making fruit wines is the same as that needed to produce wine from grapes (see chapter 6).

If you don't have a grape crusher, you can use a potato masher. Otherwise, if you have the basic equipment for winemaking, you're ready to go.

FRUIT SELECTION

Determine which of the fruits listed in our recipe section are grown in your area. Ideally, you'll discover one or more that appeal to you, and we suggest starting with local fruit because you'll be able to buy directly from either the farm or orchard, when the fruit is at its peak.

Failing that, contact a good wholesaler and get there early, so you'll be able to purchase the best fruit available. Choose only fruit that is sound, ripe, and fresh. Be selective! Wash your fruit thoroughly. There is less margin for error with other fruits than there is with grapes, and bacteria from overripe or damaged fruit can destroy your wine.

The amount of fruit you will need varies from one recipe to another. In some cases, you'll need 12 to 15 pounds (5.4–6.8 kg) of fruit to produce 1 gallon (3.8 L) of wine, which is similar to making grape wine. On the other hand, some recipes call for as little as 1½ to 2 pounds (0.7–0.9 kg) of fruit per gallon (raspberry, currant, and blackberry wines).

MAKING THE WINE

Because there are so many variations, we won't attempt to give you a basic recipe at this point. However, we do want to go over a few things before you move on to a specific recipe:

◆ Although most fruits need to be crushed, elderberries and blueberries do not.

◆ Pits and seeds may add bitterness to your wine, so strain them out during the pressing process.

◆ If you are making apple wine with fresh juice, treat it as you would fresh grape juice (see page 126).

◆ You are likely to have to adjust sugar and acid levels (see pages 37–38 for techniques).

◆ Modern technology has made many types of yeast available to the home winemaker. Use a cultured strain that has been designed primarily for fruit wines. A wine supply store or an experienced home winemaker can give you some suggestions.

◆ Once you've adjusted the sugar and acid levels prior to fermentation, stabilize the must by adding either ½ teaspoon (3.1 g) of potassium metabisulfite powder or five crushed Campden tablets per 5-gallon (19 L) container. If the recipe calls for boiled fruit, however, you won't have to add anything; the boiling process kills undesirable bacteria.

HOW MUCH SUGAR?

It's better to "under sugar" fruit wines. Going overboard will result in an excessively sweet wine with too much alcohol. And whenever you add sugar, be sure to put in the correct amount of potassium sorbate to avoid refermentation (see page 18).

◆ Most fruits are low in acids, and many old-time recipes advocated using lemon juice, fresh lemons, or freshly squeezed orange juice to increase the wine's acidity. This has always been a hit-or-miss proposition, and we suggest that you simply purchase an acid blend from a wine supply store. That way, you'll have control over the process.

◆ Add pectic enzyme to every fruit wine in order to break down the pectin (each recipe will tell you how much you'll need and when to add it).

◆ During the fermentation process for some berry-type fruit wines, you'll need to push down the pulp and skin twice a day, just as you would with red wine from grapes.

SANITIZING EQUIPMENT

The need to sanitize all equipment that comes in contact with your wine cannot be overstated. Here is a method we use with success.

Potassium metabisulfite powder
Hot water
Jug

1. Put 3 tablespoons (56 g) of potassium metabisulfite into a 1-liter (33.8 oz) jug of hot water — 85°F (29°C) — to make a reusable sanitizing solution. It will last up to 6 months, if kept tightly sealed. (Store at room temperature.)
2. Rinse all equipment thoroughly in the solution.
3. After sanitizing, rinse with cold water.

SOME LAST THOUGHTS

While it's possible to make good wines from juices and concentrates, our recipes are exclusively for working with whole fruit. They will guide you as you produce perfectly palatable wines, but in time you'll want to add your own personal touches to these basic recipes. By all means, feel free to do so, and when you do, take careful notes. That way, you'll know what works and what doesn't, and you'll be able to repeat your successes.

Patience is not only a virtue, but it is also vital when it comes to fruit wines. They really do improve when you allow them to age in the bottle. Six months is the minimum you should wait before opening your wine, and a year is even better. Frankly, freshly bottled fruit wine won't win any prizes, but properly aged, it can be downright delightful.

APPLE WINE FROM FRESH-SQUEEZED APPLE JUICE

Some of the best fruit wines are apple wines. The raw material is usually easily accessible and the wine can be made in a variety of styles, from very dry to very sweet. Just make sure that no preservatives have been added to your fresh-squeezed apple juice. Dry apple wines go well with Indian cuisine; serve the sweeter apple wines with creamy lobster or fish with Newburg sauce.

Yield: 5 gallons (19 L)

- 5 gallons (19 L) fresh-squeezed apple juice
- 6 pounds (2.7 kg) sugar
- 5 teaspoons (25.5 g) acid blend
- 1¼ teaspoons (5.6 g) yeast nutrient
- 1¼ teaspoons (5.6 g) Epsom salts
- 10 drops (0.5 mL) pectic enzyme liquid
- 1¼ teaspoon (3.4 g) grape tannin
- 1 package (5 g) Wyeast Rudischeimer yeast
- 5 Campden tablets or ½ teaspoon (3.1 g) potassium metabisulfite powder

1. Sanitize all equipment.

2. Remove a quart of apple juice and cold-stabilize it by placing it in the refrigerator.

3. Put the remaining juice in the fermentation container and add the sugar, acid blend, yeast nutrient, Epsom salts, pectic enzyme liquid, and grape tannin and stir well. Make sure that the sugar is dissolved.

4. The juice is now ready for the yeast. Sprinkle it over the juice and stir in well.

5. Fermentation will start in 2 or 3 days and continue for a week to 10 days.

6. Start to check the specific gravity in 3 days. When it goes below 1.000, fermentation is complete.

7. Put 2½ crushed Campden tablets or ¼ teaspoon (1.4 g) of potassium metabisulfite powder into a sanitized 5-gallon (19 L) carboy. Rack the wine into the carboy. Use water to bring up the level to within an inch of the bung. Seal with an air lock.

8. Rack the wine again in 6 weeks, using the same procedure.

9. A few months of aging should clear the wine and prepare it for bottling. Taste the wine, make necessary adjustments, and bottle. (Use the refrigerated apple juice to sweeten wine, if necessary, at this point.)

10. Taste the wine in 6 months.

APPLE WINE FROM FRESH APPLES

Excellent wines are made from apples, and the similarity to many good dry grape wines is noted. Use tart apples like McIntosh or Northern Spy for this wine, or you can even use crab apples. Nice aromas, good fruit flavors, and lingering finishes are features of many apple wines. Serve with cheeses, tapas, finger foods, and ham.

Yield: 5 gallons (19 L)

- 30 pounds (13.6 kg) fresh tart apples (McIntosh, for example)
- 11 pounds (5 kg) sugar (or brown sugar)
- 5 teaspoons (25.5 g) acid blend
- 1¼ teaspoons (5.6 g) yeast nutrient
- 10 drops (0.5 mL) pectic enzyme liquid
- Water enough to make 5 gallons (19 L)
- 1 package (5 g) Wyeast Rudischeimer yeast
- 5 Campden tablets or ½ teaspoon (3.1 g) potassium metabisulfite powder

1. Sanitize all equipment.

2. Wash and cut up the apples into small pieces.

3. Put the apples, sugar, acid blend, yeast nutrient, pectic enzyme, and enough water to make 5 gallons (19 L) into the fermentation container and stir well. Make sure the sugar is dissolved.

4. When the juice is about 70°F (21°C), sprinkle the yeast into the container and stir well to mix.

5. Cover the container and allow the juice to ferment. It will take a week or so to complete. The cap (the pulp and skins) will rise to the top, so twice each day you have to push it down with a sanitized spoon. When the specific gravity reaches 1.040 or lower, it's ready to be racked into another container.

6. Press out the fruit and siphon into a sanitized 5-gallon (19 L) glass carboy in which 2½ crushed Campden tablets or ¼ teaspoon (1.6 g) potassium metabisulfite powder has already been deposited.

7. Rack again in a month, using the same procedure as outlined in step 6.

8. Rack again in 3 months, taste, and make adjustments.

9. When the wine is clear and adjusted, bottle and let sit for 6 months before tasting.

McIntosh, Northern Spy, and crab apples are ideal for this wine due to their tartness.

BANANA WINE FROM FRESH BANANAS

This is a pleasant and interesting wine. The flavors are similar to those of tropical fruit, and the hint of bananas is a nice touch. It makes a nice dessert wine; serve with ice cream, peach Melba, or strawberry à la Ritz.

Yield: 5 gallons (19 L)

- 15 pounds (6.8 kg) bananas (overripe)
- Water enough to make 5 gallons (19 L)
- 1¼ teaspoons (3.4 g) grape tannin
- 12½ pounds (5.7 kg) sugar
- 5 teaspoons (25.5 g) acid blend
- 1¼ pounds (0.6 kg) raisins
- 1¼ teaspoons (5.6 g) yeast nutrient
- 1 yeast package (5 g) Wyeast Mead (Sweet) yeast

1. Sanitize all equipment.

2. Peel and dice the bananas.

3. Put the bananas in a pot with 1 gallon (3.8 L) of water and simmer for 20 minutes.

4. Strain the boiled bananas (cheesecloth is best) into the fermentation container, then add the tannin, sugar, acid blend, and raisins, and enough Water to make 5 gallons (19 L).

5. Stir the contents of the fermentation container and let cool.

6. When the juice is cooled to about 70°F (21°C), add the yeast nutrient and the yeast. Cover the container and let ferment for 5 to 7 days.

7. When the specific gravity reaches 1.000 or lower, rack the wine into a 5-gallon (19 L) carboy. Top up with enough water to fill to the rubber bung and air lock.

8. Rack again when the wine is clear and adjust sweetness.

9. Bottle the wine and let it sit for 6 months, then taste it. It will be ready for consumption between 6 months and a year.

BLACKBERRY WINE FROM FRESH BLACKBERRIES

This is an outstanding dessert wine, well suited to many sweets like Black Forest cake, fruit pies à la mode, cheesecake, and fruit tarts. It is a reasonably easy wine to make, and will earn accolades from friends and relatives.

Yield: 5 gallons (19 L)

30 pounds (13.6 kg) fresh blackberries
2 pounds (0.9 kg) raisins
11 pounds (5 kg) sugar
Water enough to make 5 gallons (19 L)
5 pounds (2.3 kg) bananas (overripe)
1¼ teaspoons (3.4 g) grape tannin
5 teaspoons (25.5 g) acid blend
10 drops (0.5 mL) pectic enzyme
1¼ teaspoons (5.6 g) yeast nutrient
1 package (5 g) Wyeast Mead (Sweet) yeast

1. Sanitize all equipment.

2. Smash the blackberies, mince the raisins, and add the sugar and put into the fermentation container.

3. Boil 1 gallon (3.8 L) of water and pour over the fruit and sugar. Stir well to dissolve the sugar.

4. Dice the bananas and simmer in a quart of water for 20 minutes. Strain the banana mixture and add it to the container with the fruit, sugar, and water.

5. When the juice cools to 70°F (21°C), add the grape tannin, acid blend, pectic enzyme, yeast nutrient, yeast, and enough water to make 5 gallons (19 L).

6. Stir the mixture daily for about 7 days. When the specific gravity reaches 1.000, rack into a sanitized 5-gallon (19 L) glass carboy.

7. Rack again in 90 days and top up with water.

8. Let sit for 8 months to a year. Then taste, sweeten, and bottle.

9. Taste in 6 months.

BLUEBERRY WINE FROM FRESH BLUEBERRIES

One of the most interesting fruit wines is this. Note the option that allows this wine to look and taste like a Cabernet Sauvignon. The basic recipe produces a fruity, easy-drinking, nicely balanced wine. Slightly sweet, it is a match for fruit pies, chocolate cake, ice cream, and soft, creamy cheeses.

Yield: 5 gallons (19 L)

Water enough to make 5 gallons (19 L)
15 pounds (6.8 kg) fresh blueberries
11 pounds (5 kg) sugar
1¼ teaspoons (5.6 g) yeast nutrient
5 teaspoons (25.5 g) acid blend
10 drops (0.5 mL) pectic enzyme liquid
1¼ teaspoons (3.4 g) grape tannin
1 package (5 g) Red Star Côtes des Blancs yeast
5 Campden tablets or ½ teaspoon (3.1 g) potassium metabisulfite powder
3 tablespoons (11.1 g) Oak-Mor (optional)

1. Sanitize all equipment.

2. Pour 1 gallon (3.8 L) of hot water over the berries in a fermentation container and add the sugar.

3. Stir well to dissolve the sugar and let cool to 70°F (21°C).

4. Add the yeast nutrient, acid blend, pectic enzyme, grape tannin, yeast, and enough tepid water to make 5 gallons (19 L) and stir.

5. Stir the juice daily for 5 to 7 days, and then press out the juice. Rack into a sanitized 5-gallon (19 L) carboy. Top up to the rubber bung and air lock with water and let sit for several weeks.

6. When the fermentation has stopped in 4 to 6 weeks, place 5 crushed Campden tablets or ½ teaspoon (3.1 g) potassium metabisulfite powder in a 5-gallon (19 L) glass carboy. Rack the must into the carboy.

7. When the wine is completely clear, rack again.

8. After several weeks, if the wine is clear, adjust sweetness and bottle.

9. Let the wine age for 6 months, then taste it.

Optional: If you wish to make a more grapelike wine, add 3 tablespoons (11.1 g) of Oak-Mor just before fermentation.

CHERRY WINE FROM FRESH SWEET CHERRIES

This wine has a soft blush color and an outstanding aroma. Made slightly sweet, the wine complements poolside finger foods, fresh fruit, and creamy cheeses. Serve on the rocks with a twist and a splash of club soda or ginger ale.

If you have access to a backyard cherry tree, you must try making this wine. If you don't have a tree, buy the cherries and make the wine anyway. You'll love it.

Yield: 5 gallons (19 L)

- 15 pounds (6.8 kg) fresh cherries
- 11 pounds (5 kg) sugar
- 6 teaspoons (30.6 g) acid blend
- 1¼ teaspoons (3.4 g) grape tannin
- 5 teaspoons (23 g) yeast nutrient
- Water enough to make 5 gallons (19 L)
- 10 drops (0.5 mL) pectic enzyme liquid
- 1 package (5 g) Wyeast Mead (Sweet) yeast
- 10 Campden tablets or 1 teaspoon (6.2 g) potassium metabisulfite powder

1. Sanitize all equipment.

2. Crush the cherries and put them, along with the sugar, acid blend, grape tannin, and yeast nutrient, into the fermentation container.

3. Add 1 gallon (3.8 L) of hot water to the mixture and stir to dissolve the sugar.

4. Add enough tepid water to make 5 gallons (19 L) and let cool to 70°F (21°C). Then add 10 drops (0.5 mL) pectic enzyme liquid.

5. When the juice is cooled, add the yeast and stir it into the mix.

6. When the specific gravity gets down to 1.040, strain out the fruit pulp and press out the liquid.

7. Place 5 crushed Campden tablets or ½ teaspoon (3.1 g) potassium metabisulfite powder in a 5-gallon (19 L) glass carboy, then siphon the new wine into the carboy.

8. In a month, put 2½ crushed Campden tablets or ¼ teaspoon (1.4 g) potassium metabisulfite powder into a new carboy and rack the wine again.

9. Let the wine sit 3 more months. It should now be ready for another racking, using the same procedure as in step 8.

10. When the wine is clear and stable, taste it. Adjust for sweetness and bottle. Wait 6 months, then taste.

CRANBERRY WINE FROM FRESH CRANBERRIES

This is a favorite when blended with apple wine and drunk around Thanksgiving. It's fine on its own, but great blended with other fruit wines. A nice pink color, pleasant aromas, and rich fruit flavors make this wine a winner. Serve with turkey and stuffing, other poultry dishes, and game.

Yield: 5 gallons (19 L)

- 15 pounds (6.8 kg) fresh cranberries
- 5 pounds (2.3 kg) raisins
- 15 pounds (6.8 kg) sugar
- 5 teaspoons (23 g) yeast nutrient
- 10 drops (0.5 mL) pectic enzyme liquid
- Water enough to make 5 gallons (19 L)
- 1 package (5 g) Wyeast Mead (Sweet) yeast
- 8 Campden tablets or 1½ teaspoons (9.3 g) potassium metabisulfite powder

1. Sanitize all equipment.

2. Crush the cranberries and chop the raisins.

3. Put the cranberries and raisins into the fermentation container. Add the sugar, yeast nutrient, pectic enzyme, and enough tepid water to make 5 gallons (19 L). Stir well until the sugar is dissolved.

4. When the must has cooled to 70°F (21°C), add the yeast to the container and stir well.

5. In 5 to 7 days, the specific gravity should read 1.040 or lower. Put 2½ crushed Campden tablets or ¼ teaspoon (1.4 g) of potassium metabisulfite powder into a 5-gallon glass carboy. Press out the new wine and rack it into the carboy.

6. Rack again in a month, following the procedure in step 5.

7. Rack again in 3 months and make adjustments as needed, following procedure in step 5.

8. When the wine is clear, it's ready to bottle.

9. Bottle the wine and let sit for 3 months before tasting. 🍇

ORANGE WINE FROM FRESH ORANGES

This is potentially an amazingly good wine. It's easy to make and the results are more than worth cost. This wine is good as a mixer with fruit over ice, with carbonated beverages, or as a punch additive. Drink the wine with finger foods, sorbets, and sweet-and-sour Asian dishes.

Yield: 5 gallons (19 L)

60 juice oranges
  Water enough to make 5 gallons (19 L)
12 pounds (5.4 kg) sugar
 1 pound (0.5 kg) raisins
 5 teaspoons (23 g) yeast nutrient
1¼ teaspoons (3.4 g) grape tannin
10 drops (0.5 mL) pectic enzyme liquid
 1 package (5 g) Wyeast Mead (Sweet) yeast
 5 Campden tablets or ½ teaspoon (3.1 g) potassium metabisulfite powder

1. Sanitize all equipment.

2. Pare the skin from 30 oranges and place the peels in a fermentation container. Pour a gallon of boiling water over the peels and let sit overnight.

3. Strain off the liquid and add the sugar, juice from all of the oranges, and enough tepid water to make 5 gallons (19 L). Stir well to dissolve the sugar.

4. Add the raisins, yeast nutrient, grape tannin, pectic enzyme, and yeast and stir again.

5. Let ferment for 4 days, then strain and pour into a 5-gallon (19 L) glass carboy. Top with water, fit air lock and rubber bung, and complete fermentation.

6. When fermentation is complete, put 2½ crushed Campden tablets or ¼ teaspoon (1.4 g) potassium metabisulfite powder into a sanitized 5-gallon (19 L) glass carboy. Now rack the wine into the carboy.

7. Rack again in a month, following the same procedure as in step 6.

8. Check in 3 months. Adjust the sweetness and bottle.

9. Let sit for 3 months before tasting. 🍇

PEACH WINE FROM FRESH PEACHES

Extremely popular in the southern United States, peach wine can be refreshing and appealing. It's pleasant as a dessert wine or as an aperitif and mixes well with carbonated beverages. You can also serve it on the rocks with a twist. On its own, pair with peach Melba, custards, puddings, and sweet baked goods.

Yield: 5 gallons (19 L)

13 pounds (5.9 kg) fresh peaches
11 pounds (5 kg) sugar
5 teaspoons (23 g) yeast nutrient
20 drops (1 mL) pectic enzyme liquid
1¼ teaspoons (3.4 g) grape tannin
6 teaspoons (30.6 g) acid blend
Water enough to make 5 gallons (19 L)
1 package (5 g) Wyeast Mead (Sweet) yeast
8 Campden tablets or 1½ teaspoons
 (9.3 g) potassium metabisulfite powder

1. Sanitize all equipment.

2. Crush the peaches. Discard the stones and place the peaches in the fermentation container.

3. Put the sugar, yeast nutrient, pectic enzyme liquid, grape tannin, acid blend, and enough warm water to make 5 gallons (19 L) on top of the peaches in the fermentation container. Stir well to dissolve the sugar.

4. When the must cools to 70°F (21°C), add the yeast and cover the container loosely with a sheet of plastic.

5. Allow the must to ferment for 5 or 6 days, or until the specific gravity reaches 1.040, then strain out the fruit pulp and press.

6. Place 2½ crushed Campden tablets or ¼ teaspoon (1.4 g) of potassium metabisulfite powder into a sanitized 5-gallon (19 L) glass carboy and siphon the new wine into it. Top off with water and seal with an air lock.

7. Let the wine settle for a month, then rack again following the same procedure as in step 6.

8. Rack again in 3 months and make adjustments as needed.

9. Let the wine sit another month, then bottle.

10. Wait for 3 months before tasting the wine.

PINK WINE FROM FRESH TOMATOES

By far, tomato wine is the most difficult to identify, fooling even the most confident wine connoisseur. Its crisp, clean taste is appealing, and the wine finishes nicely balanced. Tomato wine can be enjoyed within 3 months of bottling and should be consumed young, as it doesn't have a long life span. It complements a wide variety of foods, including summer salads, cold soups, and tomato-filled quiche dishes.

Yield: 5 gallons (19 L)

17 pounds (7.7 kg) red tomatoes
2½ pounds (1.1 kg) raisins
4 gallons (15 L) lukewarm water
7½ pounds (3.4 kg) sugar
1¼ teaspoons (3.4 g) grape tannin
7 teaspoons (35.7 g) acid blend
5 teaspoons (23 g) yeast nutrient
1 package (5 g) Red Star Premier Cuvée yeast
5 Campden tablets or ½ teaspoon (3.1 g) potassium metabisulfite powder

1. Sanitize all equipment.

2. Wash tomatoes. Cut into small pieces and discard bruised portions.

3. Place tomato pieces into a cheesecloth or nylon straining bag. Mash and squeeze the bag over a 7-gallon (27 L) open-top fermentation container. When all juice has been extracted, tie top of bag — with tomato pulp inside — and place in fermenation container.

4. Put the raisins, water, sugar, grape tannin, acid blend, and yeast nutrient in the fermentation container. Let the ingredients rest for 24 hours, then sprinkle yeast into fermentation container and stir. Cover container loosely with a sheet of plastic.

5. Stir the must and press the bag of pulp daily to assist extraction of ingredients. Take specific gravity reading daily.

6. Allow the must to ferment for 3 to 5 days, or until specific gravity reaches 1.040, then press the fruit pulp into the fermentation container.

7. Place 2½ crushed Campden tablets or ¼ teaspoon (1.4 g) of potassium metabisulfite powder into a sanitized 5-gallon (19 L) glass carboy and siphon the new wine into it. Top off with water, if necessary, and seal with an air lock.

8. Let the wine settle for about 3 weeks (or until the specific gravity reaches 1.000 or lower), then rack again following the same procedure in step 7.

9. Let the wine sit another month until clear, then bottle. Wait for 3 months before tasting the wine.

 PLUM WINE FROM FRESH PLUMS

Crisp fruitiness, a lingering aftertaste, and aromas of fresh berries are all characteristics of this wine. Slightly sweet seems to be the preferred style. This plum wine stands on its own as an aperitif, a punch additive, and a "teatime" wine, as well as an accompaniment to Asian cuisine.

Yield: 5 gallons (19 L)

13 pounds (6 kg) fresh plums
22 pounds (10 kg) sugar
5 teaspoons (23 g) yeast nutrient
10 drops (0.5 mL) pectic enzyme liquid
1¼ teaspoons (3.4 g) grape tannin
6 teaspoons (30.6 g) acid blend
Water enough to make 5 gallons (19 L)
1 package (5 g) Wyeast Mead (Sweet) yeast
8 Campden tablets or 1½ teaspoons (9.3 g) potassium metabisulfite powder

1. Sanitize all equipment.

2. Crush the plums and remove the stones. Place the plums in the fermentation container.

3. Put the sugar, yeast nutrient, pectic enzyme liquid, grape tannin, acid blend, and enough warm water to make 5 gallons (19 L) on top of the plums in the fermentation container. Stir well to dissolve the sugar.

4. When the must cools to 70°F (21°C), add the yeast and cover the container loosely with a sheet of plastic.

5. Allow the must to ferment for 5 or 6 days, or until the specific gravity reaches 1.040, then strain out the fruit pulp and press.

6. Place 2½ crushed Campden tablets or ¼ teaspoon (1.4 g) of potassium metabisulfite powder into a sanitized 5-gallon (19 L) glass carboy and siphon the new wine into it. Top off with water and seal with an air lock.

7. Let the wine settle for a month, then rack again following the same procedure as in step 6.

8. Rack again in 3 months and make adjustments as needed.

9. Let the wine sit another month, then bottle.

10. Wait for 3 months before tasting the wine. 🍇

RASPBERRY WINE FROM FRESH RASPBERRIES

This is a medal winner in competitions. Raspberry wine is also the favorite for blending with cranberry, Muscat grape, and apple wines. Made slightly sweet, the wine goes well with many desserts, finger foods, and pastries. Add an ice cube and a slice of orange, and you have a pleasant summer refresher.

Yield: 5 gallons (19 L)

- 12 pounds (5.4 kg) fresh raspberries
- 10 pounds (4.5 kg) sugar
- 5 teaspoons (23 g) yeast nutrient
- 1¼ teaspoons (3.4 g) grape tannin
- 6 teaspoons (30.6 g) acid blend
- 10 drops (0.5 mL) pectic enzyme liquid
- Water enough to make 5 gallons (19 L)
- 1 package (5 g) Wyeast Mead (Sweet) yeast
- 5 Campden tablets or ½ teaspoon (3.1 g) potassium metabisulfite powder

1. Sanitize all equipment.

2. Crush the fruit and put into the primary fermentation container.

3. Put the sugar, yeast nutrient, grape tannin, acid blend, pectic enzyme liquid, and enough warm water to make 5 gallons (19 L) on top of the raspberries in the fermentation container. Stir well to dissolve the sugar.

4. When the must cools to 70°F (21°C), add the yeast and cover the container loosely with a sheet of plastic.

5. Stir the must daily. In 5 to 7 days, the specific gravity should read 1.040 or lower. When it does, press out the fruit pulp and strain the wine.

6. Place 2½ crushed Campden tablets or ¼ teaspoon (1.4 g) of potassium metabisulfite powder into a carboy and siphon the new wine into the jug. Insert an air lock and top off with water to fill the jug.

7. Rack in a month, using the same procedure as in step 6, and let sit for 3 more months.

8. Your wine should be clear and ready for final preparations. Taste, make adjustments, and let sit for another month.

9. Bottle the wine, then wait 3 months before tasting.

RHUBARB WINE FROM FRESH RHUBARB

Most old-time winemakers make this drink in the "strong" style with high alcohol, but it can be very pleasant with lower alcohol. Rhubarb wine is closer in taste and aroma to a sherry or brandy than to a still wine. Drink it on the rocks or as a spritzer. Serve with tapas or spicy finger foods.

Yield 5 gallons (19 L)

- 15 pounds (6.8 kg) fresh rhubarb
- 11 pounds (5 kg) sugar
- 1 pound (0.5 kg) raisins
- 5 teaspoons (23 g) yeast nutrient
- 10 drops (0.5 mL) pectic enzyme liquid
- 1¼ teaspoons (3.4 g) grape tannin
- 1 pound (0.5 kg) light honey
- 5 Campden tablets or ½ teaspoon (3.1 g) potassium metabisulfite powder
- Water enough to make 5 gallons (19 L)
- 1 package (5 g) Wyeast Mead (Sweet) yeast

1. Sanitize all equipment.

2. Wash the rhubarb stalks and dice into tiny pieces. Put the rhubarb into the primary fermentor.

3. Pour the sugar over the rhubarb, cover the container, and let stand for 1 day.

4. Add the raisins, yeast nutrient, pectic enzyme, grape tannin, honey, the 5 Campden tablets (crushed) or ½ teaspoon (3.1 g) of potassium metabisulfite powder, and enough warm water to make 5 gallons (19 L), then sprinkle the yeast into the container.

5. Let the ingredients ferment for 2 days. Strain out the juice from the pulp, removing as much juice as possible. Let the liquid sit for 3 or 4 days, then siphon the wine into a sanitized 5-gallon (19 L) glass carboy. Attach the fermentation lock.

6. Rack again in a month and top off with water.

7. Rack again in 3 months. When the wine is clear, bottle it.

8. Taste in 6 months. 🍇

STRAWBERRY WINE FROM FRESH STRAWBERRIES

Strawberry maintains the strongest, most delightful aromas of any of the fruit wines. The blush color is appealing and the flavors enhance a wide variety of foods. Strawberry wines go well with fruit, soft cheeses, fruit gelatins, and Italian pastries.

Yield: 5 gallons (19 L)

16 pounds (7.3 kg) fresh strawberries
10 pounds (4.5 kg) sugar
 5 teaspoons (23 g) yeast nutrient
1¼ teaspoons (3.4 g) grape tannin
 6 teaspoons (30.6 g) acid blend
10 drops (0.5 mL) pectic enzyme liquid
   Water enough to make 5 gallons (19 L)
 1 package (5 g) Wyeast Mead (Sweet) yeast
 5 Campden tablets or ½ teaspoon (3.1 g) potassium metabisulfite powder

1. Sanitize all equipment.

2. Crush the fruit and put it into the primary fermentation container.

3. Put the sugar, yeast nutrient, grape tannin, acid blend, pectic enzyme, and enough warm water to make 5 gallons (19 L) on top of the fruit in the fermentation container. Stir well to dissolve sugar.

4. When the must cools to 70°F (21°C), sprinkle the yeast into the container and stir. Cover the container.

5. Stir the must daily. In 5 to 7 days, the specific gravity should read 1.040 or lower. When it does, press out the fruit pulp and strain the wine.

6. Place 2½ crushed Campden tablets or ¼ teaspoon (1.4 g) of potassium metabisulfite powder in the carboy and siphon the new wine into the jug. Add enough water to fill the jug and insert an air lock.

7. Rack in a month, using the same procedure as in step 6, and let sit for 3 more months.

8. Your wine should be clear and ready for final preparations. Taste, make adjustments, and let sit for another month.

9. Bottle the wine, then wait 3 months before tasting. 🍇

Sparkling and Fortified Wines 9

Come quickly, I am tasting stars!

—Dom Perignon (1638–1715)

IT IS TIME TO ADDRESS THE ISSUE of advanced wine-making. If you've successfully produced some of the wines discussed in the earlier chapters, you're ready to make some of the most storied and popular wines in history: champagne, port, sherry, and Madeira. We will give you a recipe for each type.

Planning and patience are crucial when you are producing sparkling and fortified wines. We believe, though, that the results will be worth the extra time and effort involved.

You've already learned the importance of patience when making wine: A great deal of the work is done by Mother Nature, and all the wine-maker has to do is be willing to wait long enough to derive optimum benefit from natural processes.

Because these wines require more time, you'll need to plan well ahead in order to guarantee that your wine is ready for a particular holiday or specific event.

While there are some people who want to take shortcuts, particularly where sparkling wines are concerned, we advocate making them from scratch — and you'll be justifiably proud of the results.

SPARKLING WINES

Technically speaking, you can "make" a sparkler simply by injecting a still wine with carbon dioxide (CO_2); during the days when so-called cold duck wines were the rage, some people did this. We are pleased to see that this method is no longer popular, because what you end up with is something akin to a soft drink with large bubbles. Effervescent, yes, but not for long.

The hallmark of good champagne is tiny, long-lasting bubbles, which are the result of natural fermentation in the bottle itself. It is this quality that led Dom Perignon, a seventeenth-century French Benedictine monk, to utter the words that open this chapter.

When we think of sparkling wine, champagne comes readily to mind, as it has become virtually a generic term throughout the world. Technically speaking, though, champagne is a sparkling wine made in the Champagne region of northern France using three grape varieties: Pinot Noir and Pinot Meunier, which are reds, and Chardonnay, a white.

The process in France is closely regulated by the government, and champagne is still made in the traditional way — the méthode champenoise. Basically, a still wine that has already gone through the fermentation process is blended with other still table wines into a cuvée, a "tubful," and then refermented.

The effervescent bubbles that this secondary fermentation creates are retained in the bottle and give the wine its sparkle.

The wine is aged with the necks of the bottles pointed down at an angle and twisted one-fourth turn each day. This process is called *riddling* and it allows the sediments to settle near the top of the bottle, which is critical to the success of the next step.

Disgorging, or removing the sediment, requires icing or freezing the wine so that the sediment is in a solid form. The ice plug is removed by heating the top of the bottle and taking off its temporary cap. As soon as the ice plug is gone, a chilled mixture of sugar and water is added to top off the bottle. Corking follows. Once corked, the bottle tops are covered with a wire fastener and the champagne undergoes further aging.

Our champagne recipe will follow this traditional method, but there are other systems you should know about, as they are readily available in the commercial marketplace.

TRANSFER PROCESS

Sekt is a sparkling wine from Germany. Most of the time, the steps for producing it are similar to méthode champenoise, although the same types of grapes aren't always used. Otherwise, until disgorgement, the process follows the French method.

Instead of handling disgorgement one bottle at a time, most makers of Sekt pour the contents of all of the bottles, including the sediment, into a large tank. The tank and a filtering system used to remove the fermentation sediment are maintained under counterpressure and nitrogen gas to preserve the effervescence. The sugar/wine dosage is added, then the wine is chilled. After filtering (under isobarometric pressure), the wine is then returned to its original bottles, which have been sanitized and chilled.

This process is not recommended for the home winemaker: It's a very expensive and complex procedure.

The transfer process isn't confined to the makers of Sekt. Any sparkling wine — including those called champagne but not from France — that is labeled as either FERMENTED IN THE BOTTLE or NATURALLY FERMENTED IN THE BOTTLE was made using the transfer process.

If, on the other hand, the label reads FERMENTED IN THIS BOTTLE or NATURALLY FERMENTED IN THIS BOTTLE, the méthode champenoise was used. The key words are *the* and *this* when it comes to determining the method used.

The system of producing a "poor man's champagne" was developed by a Frenchman named Eugene Charmat. The year was 1914, World War I was raging, and the French government was seeking a way to boost the morale of its troops. Charmat, who had been experimenting with making wine in bulk, was given a contract to mass-produce a sparkling wine.

His original process is still in use today. The wine is usually made in large, double-jacketed steel tanks. Every step of the process is rigidly controlled and, to the greatest extent possible, machines do the work. The equipment costs are tremendous, so this method isn't an option for the home winemaker.

In stores, champagne labeled NATURALLY MADE or NATURALLY FERMENTED are usually made using the Charmat Bulk Process. The terms "Bulk Process" and "Charmat Process" indicate this as well.

TYPES OF SPARKLING WINES

There are several varieties of sparklers on the market, but they all employ the same terms that are used when describing champagnes:

- **Brut** is a dry sparkling wine to which no sugar has been added.
- **Extra-dry** or **sec** is a sparkling wine to which a small amount of sugar has been added.
- **Demi-sec** or **doux** is the sweetest type of sparkling wine. It has had more sugar added to it than the extra-dry type.

When sugar is added to wine after disgorgement, it is mixed with either wine or brandy. This mixture is called the *liqueur de tirage,* and the amount of cane sugar plus brandy or water used in it determines how sweet or dry the sparkling wine will be.

The *liqueur de tirage,* or sugar dose, has to be an accurate one. The champagne recipe we'll walk you through has a handy chart that shows exactly how much sugar to add. Too little sugar will preclude a secondary fermentation, and too much can lead to exploding bottles!

As you gain experience, you'll be able to vary the basic recipe somewhat, according to your own taste, but we advocate making a smoother *crémant* (creamy) champagne initially.

During the fermentation process, one molecule of grape juice rapidly explodes into two molecules of carbonic gas and two molecules of wine. The chemical change is highly pressurized, up to 6 atmospheres and 90 pounds of pressure per square inch, and can cause bottles to explode. We advocate trying to produce a less bumptious wine, one that ranges from 2 to 3 atmospheres, and our recipe will allow you to do that.

HOW TO MAKE CHAMPAGNE

1. Sanitize all equipment.

2. Start with a basic white wine that's completely dry, with no residual sugar at all. The alcoholic content should range from 10 to 10½ percent (see page 21 for measuring technique). This content is critical, because wines with a smaller amount of alcohol will not absorb carbon dioxide (hence, no bubbles), and wine with a higher alcohol content may not referment.

3. Check the acid content (see page 22). The wine should have an acidity level of at least 0.8, in order to ensure that the finished wine has crispness and complexity.

4. Add tannin to expedite clearing. We advocate 1 gram (⅟28 oz) per 5 gallons (19 L) of wine.

5. The wine should be sufficiently chilled, 40° to 45°F (4°–7°C), to eliminate the tartrate crystals. It should also be well fined (see page 13) to be absolutely clear. Unlike other recipes, do *not* add potassium metabisulfite (or Campden tablets) now, as it might deter the secondary fermentation.

6. Mix your wine yeast culture according to the directions on the packet. Lay it aside while you mix the sugar dose.

SANITIZING EQUIPMENT

The need to sanitize all equipment that comes in contact with your wine cannot be overstated. Here is a method we use with success.

Potassium metabisulfite powder
Hot water
Jug

1. Put 3 tablespoons (56 g) of potassium metabisulfite into a 1-liter (33.8 oz) jug of hot water — 85°F (29°C) — to make a reusable sanitizing solution. It will last up to 6 months, if kept tightly sealed. (Store at room temperature.)

2. Rinse all equipment thoroughly in the solution.

3. After sanitizing, rinse with cold water.

7. Mix the sugar dose *(liqueur de tirage)* with the yeast and add it to the wine. This mixture is the primary ingredient needed to start the secondary fermentation. Accuracy is critical, and the recipe that follows will give you the correct measurements. The sugar dose consists of brandy or wine mixed with sugar. Stir the wine thoroughly.

8. It's time to bottle the wine in heavy, standard champagne bottles. Fill the bottles to within 1 inch (2.5 cm) of the top and cap them, using a crown capper and crown caps (the kind you see on many beer bottles). When it's time to disgorge the sediment, these caps are easier to remove than standard champagne corks.

9. Shake the filled bottles vigorously; this facilitates the second fermentation.

10. Store the bottles on their sides, using a wine rack, a suitable box, or shelving. The temperature at which the wine is stored determines how long the secondary fermentation will take. Simply put, the higher the temperature, the faster the rate of fermentation. For example, at 75°F (24°C), it will take 3 weeks to a month. At 60°F (16°C), the process may take several months. In any event, leave the wine in storage for at least 6 months. While this is going on, buy or build a riddling rack. This is a wooden frame with holes bored into it at different levels, which allows each bottle to be stored with its neck facing down at an angle.

crown capper

riddling rack

11. Riddling consists of storing the bottles in the rack and turning and shaking them periodically (every other day). The bottles should be marked on the bottom with a small piece of white tape. Envision a clock and put the tape where the 12 would go. Turn the wine "15 minutes" after you've shaken it.

Most commercial wineries in France extend the riddling process for several years prior to disgorgement (cleaning), but 6 months is sufficient for home winemakers.

12. Disgorging is the most difficult step in making champagne. For best results, get someone to help you, or you'll risk losing a lot of wine. Here's what to do.

a. Put the wine in the freezer until the plug (that is, the waste matter at the top) appears to be frozen. Then **take out the bottles and place them, neck down, in a tub filled with shaved ice and coarse salt** (enough to make the water briny). It may take a half hour or so to fully freeze the plug, which will make it easier to remove.

b. This is where having a second pair of hands is vital. One person removes the cap and allows the plug to emerge while the other stands by, ready to add the sugar dosage and recap the bottle. Here's how it works.

◆ **Hold the bottle neck down, in a pot of hot water.** This will loosen the ice plug.

◆ **Hold the bottle at an angle from your face before removing the cap.** Have ready a barrier of some sort (such as a cement cellar wall, an old umbrella, or a box) to buffer the exploding sediment when the bottle is opened.

◆ **As soon as the plug shoots out, cover the top of the bottle with your thumb** and pass the bottle to your assistant.

◆ Now top up the bottle with brandy and **cap the bottle, either with a crown cap or plastic champagne cork,** which you hammer home with a rubber mallet while your assistant holds the bottle. If a cork is used, there's one more step.

◆ The final step is to **wrap the wire-locking device around the top of the cork** and lock it into place.

13. Prior to tasting, store the bottles in an upright position for at least 6 months. A cellar or a cool, shady corner of a garage is a great place to age your wine. Before tasting, make sure that the bottle has been well chilled in the refrigerator.

Don't be concerned that the addition of sugar during the disgorgement phase may cause another fermentation. This will not occur because the yeast cells were in the wine that will have exited as part of the plug during disgorgement, and the addition of alcohol during the topping stage inhibits any further fermentation.

MAKING SPARKLING WINE BY THE CHAMPAGNE METHOD

Being able to make the world's most festive and famous beverage has to be a great thrill for a home winemaker. For that special anniversary, birthday celebration, or dinner party, a well-made sparkling wine with your name on the label can be a rewarding experience. A challenge? Yes! But the accomplishment will earn praise all around.

Yield: 5 gallons (19 L)

Equipment
Wine hydrometer
Sugar testing kit
5-gallon (19 L) carboy
26 750-mL (25.4 oz) champagne bottles
26–52 crown caps
Crown capper
26 plastic champagne corks
Rubber mallet
26 wire champagne hoods

Ingredients
5 gallons (19 L) of a finished wine not
  more than 10% alcohol
1 package (5 g) Red Star champagne
  yeast
Sugar

For refilling bottles after disgorgement
Sugar
1 bottle (750 mL; 25.4 oz) 80 proof
  brandy
1 bottle (750 mL; 25.4 oz) 10% alcohol
  white wine

1. Sanitize all equipment.

2. Test the wine with the sugar testing kit. For best results, the wine should have 0.25 to 1.50 percent sugar.

3. Prepare the yeast culture according to the directions on the packet.

4. Siphon the wine into a sanitized 5-gallon (19 L) carboy.

5. Add the fermenting yeast culture.

6. Add sugar as follows:

Sugar in Wine	Sugar to Be Added Per Gallon
0	2.0 oz (56 g)
0.25%	1.8 oz (50.4 g)
0.50%	1.4 oz (39.2 g)
0.75%	1.2 oz (33.6 g)
1.0%	0.8 oz (22.4 g)
1.25%	0.4 oz (11.2 g)
1.50%	0.2 oz (5.6 g)

7. Stir the sugar into the wine, top up the bottle with brandy, and shake well.

8. Bottle the wine in champagne bottles and cap each with a crown cap.

9. Store the bottles in a warm environment (70°F; 21°C), upside down in a wine carton. Daily for 3 weeks, lift each bottle several inches, twist, and shake, then return to the carton. Use protective gloves and safety eyeglasses to guard against possible bottle explosions.

10. Allow bottles to sit for 6 months.

11. When sediment settles in the neck of the bottles and the wine clears, the wine is ready for disgorgement, or cleaning. Place the bottles in a freezer upside down for about an hour. The sediment will solidify in the neck.

12. Hold a bottle at a 45-degree angle facing away from you and uncap it. The pressure in the bottle will push the ice plug, with the sediment inside, out of the bottle.

13. Top up the bottle with brandy, then insert a plastic cork by banging it into the neck with a rubber mallet. Tie down the cork with the wire champagne hood, or you can use the bottle cap as a closure.

14. Age the bottles upright for 6 months, then taste. 🍇

FORTIFIED WINES

Wines to which alcoholic spirits have been added are called fortified. Ports, sherries, Malagas, and Madeiras all fit into this category. Let's look at port wine first.

PORT: AN OVERVIEW

The original and most famous ports are from the Douro region of Portugal. The process for making them was developed several centuries ago, and the basic approach at the commercial level remains the same today. Ports may be made from white grapes, but reds are preferred.

Once fermentation has begun, Portuguese winemakers continually evaluate the sugar and alcohol levels of the must. When the residual sugar reaches 5 to 8 percent, the winemaker arrests the fermentation by adding brandy, which has an alcoholic content of 40 to 50 percent. This stops the fermentation process, and the wine retains its 5 to 8 percent sugar count, with an alcohol level in the 16 to 20 percent range. The result is a sweet but raw wine.

Port develops its distinctive flavor through an extensive aging process (it can take years). The wine is stored in charred oak barrels.

Port is essentially the wine of philosophical contemplation.

— H. Warner Allen (1881–1955)

MAKING PORT AT HOME

Home winemakers (and some commercial wineries) have developed creative ways to simplify the process of making port or portlike wines.

One popular approach is to take a sound red wine, such as a Zinfandel or a Cabernet Sauvignon, add sugar and brandy to bring the sugar level up to 8 percent and the alcoholic content to 20 percent, and then age the mixture in a charred barrel for 6 months.

The difficult part of this method is figuring out the amount of brandy needed to reach the 20 percent specified. There is a formula — the Pearson square — that assists winemakers in making this calculation.

The formula consists of six steps:

1. Draw a square and divide it into thirds vertically and horizontally.

2. Place in the upper left-hand corner of a square the alcoholic strength of the brandy to be used in fortification. It is assumed to be 40 percent, or 80 proof.

3. In the lower left-hand corner, place the alcoholic strength of the wine that is to be fortified. We assume it is 10 percent.

4. In the center of the square, place the desired alcoholic strength of the finished product. It is determined that this is to be 20 percent.

5. Subtract the center figure from the figure in the upper left-hand corner, and place the remainder in the lower right-hand corner (40 – 20 = 20).

6. Subtract the figure in the lower left-hand corner from the figure in the center of the square and place the remainder in the upper right-hand corner (20 – 10 = 10).

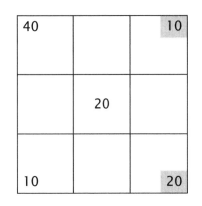

The last figure (10) is the number of parts of the 80 proof (40 percent alcohol) brandy needed to fortify 20 parts of wine of the indicated alcohol strength up to 20 percent of alcohol. Another way of putting it is that 10 gallons (37.8 L) of brandy containing 40 percent alcohol will fortify 20 gallons (75.6 L) of 10 percent wine up to an alcoholic strength of 20 percent. After the brandy is added, the whole amount will be 30 gallons of fortified wine with a strength of 20 percent alcohol.

We do have a simplified method of making port wine, still with excellent results. No additional equipment is required, but you will have to adhere to the procedures and follow the recipe exactly.

 **PORT WINE**

Just about everyone enjoys one of the most popular of all dessert wines, a good glass of port. The wine can be served with a wide assortment of desserts, including most chocolate dishes, strawberry creations, Melbas, and fruit pies. Served neat or on the rocks, port wine will enhance any event and help to stimulate conversation.

Yield: 6 gallons (23 L)

1 package (5 g) Red Star Pasteur Red yeast
1 pound (454 g) dried bananas, sliced
1 gallon (3.8 L) red grape concentrate
5 gallons (19 L) warm water
6 pounds (2.7 kg) sugar
6 ounces (170 g) dried elderberries
2 teaspoons (9.2 g) yeast nutrient
3 ounces (43 g) acid blend
5 Campden tablets or ½ teaspoon (3.1 g) potassium metabisulfite powder
Additional 6 pounds (2.7 kg) sugar to be added in two stages
2 tablespoons (37.2 g) bentonite
60 ounces (1.8 L) brandy

1. Sanitize all equipment.

2. Prepare yeast 2 days in advance.

3. Separate the dried banana slices and combine with red grape concentrate, water, sugar, elderberries, yeast nutrient, and acid blend in a 7½-gallon (28 L) carboy; mix well.

4. When must cools to 70°F (21°C), add yeast.

5. Attach rubber bung and fermentation lock filled with fresh water.

6. Stir gently once a day. In 4 to 7 days, when the specific gravity reaches 1.040, withdraw 3 cups (700 mL) of must. Dissolve an additional 3 pounds (1.4 kg) of sugar into the 3 cups (700 mL) and stir back into the primary fermentor. Wine should not be left in the primary fermentor for more than 7 days.

7. In 3 to 4 days, when specific gravity is 1.030, strain out the elderberries and bananas and siphon into another carboy. Attach lock and bung.

8. When the specific gravity is 1.010, add 3 pounds (1.4 kg) of sugar and dissolve in the primary fermentor.

9. When fermentation has stopped, place 5 crushed Campden tablets or ½ teaspoon (3.1 g) potassium metabisulfite in a glass carboy and rack the wine. Fine the wine with bentonite and then filter.

10. Sweeten to taste using a mixture of 2 parts sugar to 1 part water.

11. Add 2 ounces (60 mL) of brandy to each 750-mL (25.4 oz) bottle, fill with wine, and cork.

12. Age 1 year before tasting.

SHERRY

With a wide range of sweetness, from none at all to very sweet, sherry-fortified wines offer a unique challenge to the home winemaker. Authentic sherry is produced in Spain from grape varieties like Palomino, Pedro Ximenez, and muscatel in the region surrounding the southeastern town of Jerez.

You will never see a vintage sherry, as the process *(solera)* blends various years. When the new vintage is ready for aging, the oldest blends (usually at the bottom of a series of barrels in stacks) will be removed and bottled. A minimum of one-third the quantity is allowed for bottling each year. The bottom barrel is then refilled from the barrel above it, that barrel is filled from the one above it, and so on until the top barrel is filled with the new wine. "The old wine teaches the new wine" is the philosophy.

Some Spanish bodegas (wineries) are several hundred years old and, theoretically, when you buy a bottle of their sherry, you might be drinking wine that is as old as those bodegas.

An interesting, unexplained development occurs in Spain each year. When the vintages are complete and the wines are ready for winter storage, they are placed in wooden barrels about three-fourths full, which allows for some oxidation. During the aging period, some of the barrels develop a film and some don't. Why some do and some do not has never been understood. The wine with the film, or *flor* (flower), is considered to be the best and is designated as fino (fine). The rest of the vintage is designated

Sherry is the brightest jewel in the vinous crown of Spain. There is no wine like it.

—André L. Simon (1877–1970)

oloroso. Fino is the driest, lightest in color, and nuttiest sherry; the rest of the vintage, with the addition of caramel and sugar, is made into amontillado (semi-dry and medium in color), oloroso (darker and sweeter), and finally cream sherry (the darkest and sweetest).

For the home winemaker to attempt to make sherry as the Spaniards do is futile, but there are other ways of making sherrylike wines with less effort and good results.

The initial wine should be a fino, if possible. If it doesn't work out that way, you can then make it into an amontillado, an oloroso, or a cream sherry.

The riskiest part of sherry making is the time that the wine is exposed to air or oxygen, which it must have to give the wine its unique flavor and character. Too much exposure or contamination, however, will spoil the lot.

Another issue is that of heat and cold. In Spain, the barrels are warmed in the daytime by the sun and cool off in the evening, so the rapid changes in temperature also add to the nutty character of sherries. When you age your sherry, we recommend you keep it near a furnace, where it can be heated when the furnace goes on and cooled when it shuts itself off.

A sherry yeast is necessary to help develop the *flor*. The actions of the *flor* can be observed during the aging process if you store the wine in glass. The *flor* starts along the side of the storage vessel and emerges at the top of the wine. Initially, the *flor* appears as tiny globules floating on the surface. Eventually, they unite and form a solid film.

As time goes by, the wine will slowly clarify (beneath the *flor*) into a clear, light wine.

Fino sherry is dry and austere with a nutty character; and it makes an excellent aperitif. It's tasty on the rocks with a twist. Fortified with brandy, sherries have an alcoholic content between 17 and 20 percent and enjoy extended longevity.

FINO SHERRY

This is a challenge for any home winemaker. It is a little more time-consuming to make than is table wine, but the flavors are worthy of the effort. Sherry goes well with tapas, spicy Mexican finger foods, raw clams and oysters, and olives and nuts. A glass of sherry on a cold day will warm you and a glass before retiring helps with a good night's sleep.

Yield: 5 gallons (19 L)

- 1 package (5 g) Red Star sherry yeast
- 1 gallon (3.8 L) white grape concentrate
- 4½ gallons (17 L) water
- 5 pounds (2.3 kg) sugar
- 1 ounce (28 g) tartaric acid
- 3 Campden tablets or ¼ teaspoon (1.4 g) potassium metabisulfite powder
- 3 teaspoons (13.8 g) yeast nutrient
- 1½ teaspoons (4.2 g) grape tannin
- 2 teaspoons (10.2 g) acid blend
- 64 ounces (1.9 L) brandy
  Additional 5 pounds (2.3 kg) sugar

1. Sanitize all equipment.

2. Prepare sherry yeast 2 days in advance of use (see page 38).

3. Combine white grape concentrate, water, 5 pounds (2.3 kg) sugar, tartaric acid, Campden tablets or potassium metabisulfite, yeast nutrient, grape tannin, and acid blend in a 7-gallon (27 L) carboy and mix well.

4. Check the specific gravity of the must; it should be 1.100.

5. Take 3 cups (700 mL) of the must and set it aside.

6. Add three-fourths of the yeast starter to the must in the fermentor. Take 2 cups (475 mL) of this mixture and add to the yeast starter left in its container.

7. Stir daily. In a couple of days, fermentation will start. At that time, add the rest of the yeast starter and the additional 5 pounds (2.3 kg) of sugar, and stir vigorously.

8. Allow to ferment a week to 10 days, stirring daily.

9. Rack the wine into a sanitized 7-gallon (27 L) carboy and insert an air lock and bung.

10. Within a few months, the *flor* should appear on the surface of the carboy. If not, you will make oloroso sherry.

11. Leave the wine alone until it clears completely. Eventually, the *flor* will fall to the bottom. At this point, rack the wine into a sanitized carboy and prepare to bottle.

12. Place 2 ounces (60 mL) of brandy in each bottle and fill with the sherry. Taste in 3 months.

MADEIRA

During colonial times, the island of Madeira was a commercial focal point of many ships traveling from the Americas to Europe and from Europe to the Americas. One of the most important cargoes carried to the New World was the Madeira wines that were used for barter and trade. Because of the small size of the sailing vessels, shippers had to come up with creative methods of storing cargo. The wines, which were extremely important and profitable, took up a great deal of space, so a process was devised to concentrate the wines by "cooking" or "steaming." When they reached their destination, they could be reconstituted with the addition of water.

When the first batch reached the Americas, some eager imbibers couldn't wait for the reconstitution process. They tasted the wines in their new "cooked" state — and they loved them as they were. Hence, a new wine was born.

When the Madeiras were good, they pleased my senses, cheered my spirits, improved my moral and intellectual powers, besides enabling me to confer the same benefits on other people.

—George Saintsbury (1845–1933)

The cooking process is known as *estufa,* and is used to this day on the island of Madeira. The fully fermented wine is warmed to about 145°F (63°C) and kept at that temperature for up to 6 months, then slowly cooled to 70°F (21°C).

All Madeira wines are fortified, so their eventual alcohol count is between 17 and 20 percent of volume. Like the sherries of Spain, Madeiras range from dry to sweet. The wine varieties are named after the grapes from which they are made. The driest is Sercial, a medium-bodied wine that is excellent as an aperitif. Verdelho is medium dry and a little darker in color. Bual is medium sweet and Malmsey is a heavy dessert wine. Madeiras are similar to sherries in that they go from dry-tasting and light in color to sweet and dark.

In order to make Madeira, which isn't as difficult as many other wines, we have to create a place where we can confine the heat in order to give the wine the required Madeira flavor.

ESTUFA TIP

If you're having difficulty locating the perfect *estufa* box, check with a local furniture or department store, which might have a plentiful supply.

MAKING AN ESTUFA

Materials Needed to Make an Estufa

To make an *estufa,* you must gather the following materials:

- A large cardboard or wooden box, 24" x 28" x 36" (60 x 70 x 90 cm)
- Aluminum foil
- Wooden 2 x 3s, 2 x 4s, or bricks to put under the carboy
- Carboy
- Work light with an extension cord and cage around the bulb
- Blanket
- Thermometer

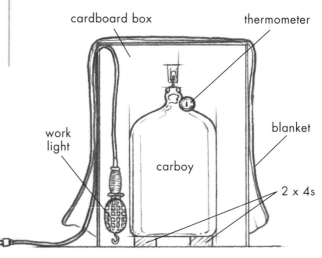

Estufa

Preparing the Box

1. Remove bottom from box.

2. On one side of box, near top, cut a hole slightly larger than the width of the work light's plug.

3. Line the interior of the box completely with aluminum foil.

Situating and Assembling the *Estufa*

1. Identify the warmest part of your cellar. This is the best location for your *estufa.*

2. Lay boards or bricks side-by-side on the cellar floor.

3. Place readied carboy on top of boards or bricks.

4. Place light inside box, and feed plug through the prepared hole. (*Note:* When the box is placed over the carboy, the light should hang a few inches from the ground.)

5. Place box over carboy, and cover box with the blanket to help retain the heat.

6. Plug in work light.

Using the *Estufa*

The ideal temperature inside the *estufa* is 110° to 125°F (43°–52°C). You must monitor the *estufa* and its temperature daily. If the temperature is too high or too low, adjust it until it falls within the ideal temperature range, then continue to monitor daily.

TEMPERATURE TIPS

Achieving and maintaining the ideal temperature in an estufa is a trial-and-error process. Begin by using a 60-watt bulb, and monitor daily.

If the temperature is too low, hang the bulb closer to the carboy. The closer the bulb is to the carboy, the warmer the contents of the carboy will get. If the temperature does not improve, try using a higher watt bulb, and repeat this testing process. You might also cover the box with an extra blanket to help improve insulation. Continue to make adjustments until the temperature falls within the ideal range.

If the temperature is too high, move the bulb farther away from the carboy. If the temperature is still too high, remove the insulating blanket from the top of the box or move the *estufa* to a cooler location in your basement. Continue to make adjustments until the temperature falls within the ideal range.

BUAL OR MALMSEY MADEIRA

This is a challenging and interesting recipe for making Madeira. The result is a wine that creates a great deal of conversation around the tasting table. The finished product makes a fine dessert wine and complements baked fruit desserts, flan or custard, ice cream (particularly vanilla), and chocolate desserts.

Yield: 6 gallons (23 L)

64 ounces (1.9 L) white grape concentrate
32 ounces (1 L) fig concentrate
12 ounces (336 g) dried bananas
5½ gallons (21 L) hot water
5 Campden tablets or ½ teaspoon (3.1 g) potassium metabisulfite powder
2 teaspoons (10.2 g) acid blend
2 teaspoons (9.2 g) yeast nutrient
1 package (5 g) Red Star sherry yeast
Simple syrup (2 parts sugar to 1 part water)
2 tablespoons (37.2 g) bentonite
64 ounces (1.9 L) brandy

1. Sanitize all equipment.

2. Mix all ingredients except the yeast, the simple syrup, and the brandy in a 7- to 10-gallon (27–38 L) container.

3. When the must cools to 70°F (21.1°C), add sufficient simple syrup to raise the specific gravity to 1.100. (Check the specific gravity before and after each adjustment.) Add the yeast and cover the container with cheesecloth or an air lock.

4. When fermentation diminishes, rack into a secondary fermentor, preferably a glass carboy.

5. After 2 weeks, read the specific gravity. If it is below 1.000, add more simple syrup to raise it to 1.010, but not any higher.

6. Test the specific gravity daily. Every time it gets below 1.000, raise it to 1.010 with simple syrup. This may have to be repeated six or seven times over the next few months.

7. When the specific gravity remains steady at 1.000 for at least a month, you will have an alcohol count of about 18 percent. Sweeten again to 1.010.

8. Put the carboy in the *estufa* and cook for 3 to 4 months, being sure to check the *estufa* and its temperature daily (see page 229).

9. After cooking, fine with bentonite and filter the wine and prepare to bottle.

10. Add 1 to 1½ ounces (30–45 mL) of brandy to each 25.4-ounce (750 mL) bottle. Fill with wine and cork.

11. Age 1 or 2 years. Taste after 1 year.

TROUBLE-SHOOTING 10

*After bread comes wine, the second
nutrient given by the Creator to sustain life
and the first to be famed for its excellence.*

—Olivier de Serres (1539–1619)

WINEMAKING SUPPLY STORES RECEIVE a fair number of calls for help. Here are just a few of some typical examples:

"The fermentation has stopped."

"My wine has turned cloudy."

"My wine smells funny."

"My wine smells like vinegar."

"Hear that noise? My bottles are exploding in the cellar!"

Each of these problems, even the last one, can be considered "common." In many instances, poor sanitation is the culprit, which is why we've stressed cleanliness throughout this book.

For example, a winemaker who is careless when it comes to selecting grapes is looking for trouble. Make sure that your grapes are clean, and throw away any rotten or moldy ones. Leaves, stems, and other foreign matter should be removed before initiating fermentation.

Your containers and equipment should be scrupulously clean before you use them (see page 28).

Sugar and acid tests are critical, and in most cases adjustments should be made prior to fermentation when needed.

Alcohol content should be at least 10 percent. If it's lower, you may have problems; low-alcohol wines are more susceptible to disease than are their higher-voltage counterparts.

Finally, even if you've done everything correctly, natural phenomena may cause a problem or two. Let's address the most common ones.

The problems that follow are divided into four categories: process, fragrance, flavor, and appearance. Some problems may fit into more than one category, but the solutions remain the same.

PROCESS

Experience is our greatest teacher, so if you encounter these common winemaking problems consider them important learning opportunities.

FERMENTATION WON'T START

There may be times when the fermentation simply will not start. Occasionally it may take several days to begin, but when nothing happens after several days, you have a problem.

Too much sugar. One of the problems might be too much sugar in your must. This can stun the yeast and inhibit the chemical action necessary for fermentation. Add water to the must and dilute it somewhat to lower the sugar. Be careful to monitor this with constant evaluations until the proper sugar level is reached. You will also have to keep track of the acid count as you dilute the must. Too much water also dilutes the acids, and you will then have to make adjustments to bring the acid counts within the desired range.

Extreme temperatures. Extreme temperatures — too high or too low — can inhibit the start of fermentation. Adjust temperature to about 68°F (20°C). Shake the must and let it sit for a couple of days. Fermentation should start within a few days.

Too much potassium metabisulfite. Too much potassium metabisulfite powder in the must can also stop fermentation. Appropriate doses will maintain the wine stability. After a few more days of just sitting there, the must should start fermenting, as the metabisulfite dissipates and lowers resistance to the fermentation.

Old yeast. Another cause could be that the yeast is too old and has lost its potency. Properly packaged yeast can and does last for several years, but there comes a time when it will lose its effectiveness. Storing yeast under refrigeration will maximize its life span, but eventually it just won't work. Get a fresh package of yeast and make a new solution. Stir it into the must and watch it ferment.

STUCK FERMENTATION

This is a common problem. Basically, four things happen when fermentation is "stuck":

1. The must stops bubbling prematurely.
2. Specific gravity remains high.
3. The conversion from sugar to alcohol is incomplete.
4. The yeast's conversion remains incomplete.

In short, your wine isn't doing anything. Common causes are a must whose temperature is too high or too low, has insufficient nutrients, or has excess sugar.

Temperature too high. Stuck fermentation may occur if the temperature of the must was too high — 85°F (29°C) or higher.

Solution. Try moving the must to a cooler

location. Wait until the temperature drops to an acceptable level, then referment (see below).

Temperature too low. If the temperature of the must drops below 60°F (16°C), you've got a problem. Try to keep the mixture between 70° and 75°F (21°–24°C).

Solution. Move the cold must to a warmer location to keep the temperature within the optimum range. Then immediately shake the must to restart fermentation.

Insufficient nutrients. Insufficient nutrients, particularly when you're making fruit wines, can cause stuck fermentation.

Solution. Add 1 teaspoon (6.2 g) of yeast nutrient per gallon (3.8 L) of your wine, and make sure that the wine's temperature does not exceed 75°F (24°C). This should be sufficient to restart fermentation.

Excess sugar. Excess sugar can stop fermentation. It will inhibit the yeast's action in the same manner as too much alcohol.

Solution. Add 1 gallon (3.8 L) of water and 1 ounce (28 g) of acid blend to each 5 gallons (19 L) of wine.

Refermenting the must. No matter the cause, you must referment every stuck fermentation. After you've determined that fermentation is stuck, try to referment the must with a new yeast starter. Check with your winemaking supply store to make sure you're using the proper yeast.

1. Sanitize all equipment.

2. Using the same yeast you used the first time, prepare a new yeast starter.

3. Draw off 1 cup (8 oz; 240 mL) of the must and mix with yeast starter until it starts to ferment.

4. Draw off 1 quart (32 oz; 960 mL) of the stuck must and mix with the yeast starter until it is all fermenting.

5. Draw off 1 gallon (3.8 L) of the stuck must; mix with yeast starter until it is all fermenting.

6. Continue to draw off large amounts of the stuck must and add to the fermenting yeast starter mix until full fermentation resumes.

ACETIC FERMENTATION

Mycoderma aceti bacteria live in the air and are ready to pounce on your wine at every opportunity. Once infected with this organism, the wine smells like vinegar and can never be cured; there is no known effective treatment. This organism converts the alcohol in wine to acetic acid, the main ingredient of vinegar. Many longtime home winemakers, when their wine is contaminated by this organism, give up and either make vinegar (which is a good alternative) or just throw away the wine.

Prevention. Minimize air contact with the wine during rackings and fill the jugs right up to the bottom of the bottle closures. Wine with too little alcohol is vulnerable to the organism and all precautions should be taken to ensure that at least 10 percent alcohol is the minimum quantity in any batch.

Suggestions for salvage. The best way to save your wine is to add 2 teaspoons (12.4 g) of potassium bitartrate to 5 gallons (19 L) of wine. Dissolve the potassium bitartrate in 1 quart (1 L) of the infected wine, then add the mixture to the main batch. Within a week, the wine should be corrected. Smell and taste the wine to determine whether it's okay. If not, repeat this practice up to five times. If it isn't cured after the fifth attempt, bottle your *vinegar*.

SHORT-LIVED CURE

Even if you're able to "save" your wine from *Mycoderma,* the cure will last for only a short time. Once bottled, the wine should be consumed within 6 months.

Exploding Bottles

There are two common causes of this messy problem:

1. Wine was bottled prior to completion of secondary fermentation.
2. Potassium sorbate wasn't added after sweetening the wine prior to bottling.

Solution. When the first shot rings out, do the following:

1. Uncork every bottle and put the contents in sanitized 5-gallon (19 L) carboys to enable the wine to complete its fermentation.
2. Check the specific gravity regularly. When the specific gravity reading stays at 1.000 or lower for a month or so, you can begin final processing.

3. If the problem was caused by incomplete secondary fermentation, rack the wine to another sanitized container when the specific gravity stabilizes at 1.000, add either 3 crushed Campden tablets or ¼ teaspoon (1.4 g) of potassium metabisulfite powder, and rebottle.

Unstabilized wine (refermentation). If you forgot to stabilize the wine by adding potassium sorbate after sweetening it, you must stabilize it after letting the wine finish its fermentation.

Solution. Follow the above instructions and let the wine finish its fermentation. When the wine is fermented (specific gravity of 1.010 or lower), add 2 teaspoons (6 g) of potassium sorbate to 5 gallons (19 L) of wine and either 3 crushed Campden tablets or ¼ teaspoon (1.4 g) of potassium metabisulfite powder.

Oxidized Wine

If a wine becomes oxidized, it's no longer good to drink. It will turn brown, impart a sour or bitter taste, and have a general funkiness about it. Unfortunately, there is no cure for an oxidized wine. Most new home winemakers, if not properly trained, will probably have an oxidized wine or two.

Prevention. Several key points will help you prevent oxidation:

◆ Bring acid counts into line before fermentation begins and watch them carefully throughout the winemaking process. Low-acid wines (which are high pH wines) are vulnerable to oxidation.

- Use Campden tablets or potassium meta-bisulfite powder properly and at the appropriate times.
- Maintain fermentation temperatures between 65° and 80°F (18°–27°C). If fermentation temperatures are above the desired range, fermentation problems and oxidation can result.

Fragrance

Your nose can be a great help to you when making wine. Notice the fragrance of the wine as you work, and recall that it should not be noxious but pleasant.

Bottle Odor

If, when pulling the cork on a bottle of wine, you get a severe odor of sulfur, it means that the wine has been oversulfited.

Excessive use of sulfur dioxide. Excessive use of sulfur dioxide (SO_2) during the secondary fermentation or at the time of bottling will give off a stench.

Solution. Decant the wine and let it sit for a couple of hours.

Prevention. Careful use of potassium metabisulfite during the winemaking process eliminates this problem: Always measure accurately.

A Flower or Geranium Smell

An excess of potassium sorbate can produce a flowery or geranium smell. Unfortunately, there is no cure for this.

Prevention. Be careful not to add too much potassium sorbate. Accuracy is important. Also, when using sorbate, always use metabisulfite. Potassium sorbate plays an important role in winemaking: It prevents your wine from refermenting after you add sugar to it. Use it the proper way and you will not have a problem.

Mustiness

On occasion, you might pull the cork from a bottle of wine only to be greeted by a musty, unpleasant odor. This unattractive smell usually results from a cork that has developed a fungus or mold. All natural corks are porous, but they should not be split, divided, or have large holes in them that provide entry to molds.

Solution. If you discover a malodorous bottle, check the rest of your bottles by pulling the corks. Sanitize inside the necks of musty bottles by wiping them thoroughly with a clean cloth and a sulfite solution consisting of 8 ounces (240 mL) of water and 1 crushed Campden tablet or ⅛ teaspoon (0.7 g) potassium metabisulfite powder. Recork with clean, new corks.

Carefully inspect new corks before use. Choose only corks without splits or holes. New plastic corks are entering the market, and these may eventually eliminate this problem.

"Rotten-Egg Syndrome"

Shades of high school chemistry! It's easy enough to recognize this problem, the wine smells like rotten eggs! This results from using overly ripe grapes that are low in acid and were sprayed with copper sulfate prior to picking. This usually happens to California grapes (vinifera).

Solution. Solving this problem, if it is discovered early, can be relatively easy. Aerate the wine, rack it again, and add either 1 crushed Campden tablet or ⅛ teaspoon (0.7 g) potassium metabisulfite powder per gallon (3.8 L) of wine. Vigorous shaking of the wine after racking will help to aerate it and eliminate the odor of rotten eggs. Repeat the above instructions six or seven times, if necessary. If this doesn't work, try baking the wine à la Madeira. Baking will definitely solve the odor problem, but you will also change the wine.

GETTING RID OF HYDROGEN SULFIDE

Frequent rackings during the early fermentation stages are a deterrent to hydrogen sulfide gas. Appropriate additions of Campden tablets or potassium metabisulfite powder are also required for an odor-free wine. Follow your recipe closely.

FLAVOR

Winemakers are often most concerned with a wine's flavor, and rightfully so. Unpleasant tastes will help you remember the solutions offered here.

EXCESS MALIC AND TARTARIC ACIDS

Excess malic and tartaric acids, due to underripe grapes, present an unpleasant and harsh wine. This is common with many eastern and northern United States and Canadian grape types.

Solution. You have two options for solving this problem: calcium carbonate and potassium bicarbonate. Calcium carbonate is best suited to work with tartaric acid rather than malic acid. You should try not to reduce the acidity by more than 0.3 to 0.4 percent. Wine stability will take longer with calcium carbonate than with potassium bicarbonate. Use calcium carbonate as soon as possible to avoid problems later. Use 1½ teaspoons (9.3 g) per gallon (3.8 L) to reduce acidity approximately 0.15 percent.

Use potassium bicarbonate if you are attempting to reduce the acid count up to 0.3 percent; if the pH is above 3.5, don't use it. An important factor is that you must cold-stabilize after adding potassium bicarbonate. About one third of the acid reduction will occur when you cold-stabilize. Use 1⅛ teaspoons (6.7 g) per gallon to lower the acidity approximately 0.1 percent, but remember to cold-stabilize after adding it to the wine.

"FUNKINESS" OR "CASKINESS"

Some barrels have essential oils in them and they can impart an odd flavor to the wine.

Solution. Rack the wine into glass carboys. Let it sit for a few weeks, then rack it again. You may need to repeat this process several times in order to solve the problem. Alternatively, blend the wine with one or more stronger-flavored wines.

Prevention. Improper sanitation is the probable cause of the problem, so devote plenty of time to preparing your barrels. Better yet, use Oak-Mor or oak chips. They're a lot cheaper than barrels, and much easier to control. Start with a small amount, as you can always add more. Keep in mind that "overoaking" can hide your wine's best characteristics.

YEASTINESS

Unless you are making a sparkling wine, a yeasty flavor is undesirable. It can be caused by young age or incorrect yeast culture.

Age. Ordinarily, yeastiness is characteristic of young wines that haven't been properly aged. Generally speaking, time will take care of this.

Wrong yeast culture. Using the wrong yeast culture can also contribute to yeastiness. Consult your winemaking supply store or an experienced winemaker before you begin to make wine.

Regular racking (see your recipe) goes a long way to eliminating yeastiness, and most wines will, in time, clarify themselves naturally.

APPEARANCE

As you become more experienced in your winemaking, your ability to judge the quality of your wine's appearance will improve. Two common cosmetic problems follow.

CLOUDINESS

Albuminous matter that remains suspended in the wine sometimes affects low-alcohol wines.

Solution. The process of removing cloudiness can be a bit expensive for the home winemaker, as a couple of liters (2 quarts) of brandy are usually required for each 5 gallons (19 L) of wine.

1. Sanitize all equipment.
2. Rack wine into a new container and add 2 liters (2 quarts) of brandy to raise alcohol count.
3. Check the alcohol count and add more brandy, if needed, to reach the 10 percent level.
4. Fine the wine (see page 13 for instructions).
5. Two weeks after fining the wine, add 1 teaspoon (6.2 g) of tartaric acid powder to the 5 gallons (19 L) of wine.
6. Filter the wine, then bottle.

TARTRATE CRYSTALS

Tartrate crystals, known as gravel or snowflakes, may appear in some white wines after they have been bottled. Although unacceptable to commercial wineries, amateur winemakers can live with this problem. These crystals are not appealing, but they aren't harmful.

Prevention. All white wines should be cold-stabilized or placed in a near-freezing environment for at least 1 month after they are fermented. However, this causes the formation of tartrate crystals. To eliminate the problem, rack the wine immediately after taking it out of the cold environment. Some home winemakers also cold-stabilize their red wines, though it really isn't necessary. The tartrate crystals that form in red wines are tiny and few.

APPENDIXES

One not only drinks wine, one smells it,
observes it, tastes it, sips it and —
one talks about it.

—King Edward VII (1841–1910)

SO MUCH CAN BE SAID ABOUT WINEMAKING that we'll conclude with a few words more. We hope you'll find the following resources helpful.

To aid you in your winemaking efforts, we've included some masters for keeping detailed winemaking records, including fermentation and bottling data. (See pages 239 and 240.) These forms will help take the guesswork out of replicating your successes. Make as many photocopies of the forms as you need.

The section on wine evaluation explains how wines are judged by winemakers and panels of experts at wine competitions. (See pages 241–244.) These criteria will help you to appraise your efforts objectively.

Though the prospect of entering a competition may seem a bit daunting for fledgling winemakers, we know quite a few people who have experienced great success within a year or two of taking up this hobby. We provide information on five major events that are open to amateurs. When you make a wine you're particularly proud of, we urge you to enter it in one or more of the competitions listed. (See pages 245–246.)

Finally, suppliers and equipment providers come and go, and there are hundreds of them throughout the United States and Canada. While not exhaustive, the list that follows is a good place to begin if local suppliers are not an option for you. (See pages 247–253.)

WINEMAKING RECORD

Date _____

Variety _____

Quantity _____

Juice/Conc./Other _____

Volume of Must _____

Origin _____

Price _____

ANALYSIS

	INITIAL	ADJUSTED	FINAL
Brix (%)			
T.A. (g/L)			
PH			
SO_2 (PPM)			
Sorbate			
Alcohol (%)			

INITIAL ADDITIVES

SO_2		Sugar	
Acid		Nutrient	
Cal. Carb.		Bentonite	
Yeast		Oak-Mor	
Water		Other	

Remarks: _____

_____

_____

_____

T.A. = total acid

FERMENTATION DATA

Days on skin ( ) Ferment temp. ( )

Days in primary
fermenter ( ) Malolactic ( )

Yeast strain ( ) Yeast lag time ( )

Date	Rack	Remarks: racking, transferring, stabilizing, filtering, additives, blending, others

BOTTLING DATA

Date bottled ( )

Number of
bottles ( ) How
labeled

Taste description: _____

_____

_____

_____

WINE EVALUATION

Wine evaluation, more commonly called *wine tasting,* is an important part of winemaking. Getting to know a wine's proper color ranges, aroma, and flavor helps the winemaker evaluate the wine's positive features and negative aspects. Wine evaluation is a rewarding, fascinating, and simple art. It requires that you use your senses of sight, smell, and taste, and then describe your impressions. This process offers an opportunity to evaluate and explore the virtues of wine and to sharpen your ability to further understand and enjoy wine. Winemakers are constantly requesting feedback on their wines in order to improve their winemaking techniques. We include this overview of wine evaluation to help you improve your creations.

APPEARANCE

Fill the glass at least one-third and hold it up to the light or against a white background. The first task here is to judge the wine's color and hue. A sound wine is clear and bright. A hazy wine means that there is probably a physical

If the first glass of wine invites a second glass—then it's a good wine.

—August Sebastiani

instability or a microbial infection. The hue can determine changes in the wine. Most white wine is usually greenish yellow or light yellow when made properly. If a white wine darkens to a deep yellow or brown, this usually means that the wine is oxidized, a common problem for many home winemakers. If a wine is oxidized, unwanted air and bacteria have made their way into the wine through sloppy handling on the part of the winemaker. The wine then turns brown and loses its freshness, balance, and flavor.

Some red wines may contain sediment, a harmless natural by-product of older red wines. Wines with sediment should be decanted before drinking. Through aging, red wines will generally lose their vibrant, ruby color and lighten to a bricklike color; in many cases, the wines also develop a brownish hue, which indicates old age.

AROMA

A major portion of wine evaluation involves a study of the wine's aroma. Twirl the wine in the glass to aerate the wine and release the aroma or bouquet. Raise the glass to your nose and inhale the aroma. You may have to perform this procedure several times before the wine "opens" up and the aroma is evident. Aroma helps to define how flowery or fruity a wine is and illustrates the positive and negative traits. The positive smells you should notice are varietal aroma (i.e., the aroma of a particular grape variety), fruitiness (i.e., tones of fruit such as apple or strawberry), and bouquet (i.e., the combination of grape aroma and wood aging). The most pronounced aromas will come from grape varieties like Niagara, Muscat, Gewürztraminer and Riesling that have strong, pleasant aromas. Red wines that have had some wood aging usually have a rounder (or more pleasing), richer smell or bouquet that derives from the wood and the aging process.

With some practice and proper instruction, you will develop a talent for identifying grape varieties through their aromas. All aromas should be pleasant. An unpleasant odor usually indicates a physical problem with the wine.

TASTE

There are four different tastes: salty, sweet, bitter, and sour. These tastes are discerned by taste buds located on the human tongue. Sweet buds are located on the front of the tongue; bitter on the back of the tongue; sour on the sides of the tongue, and saltiness on the center of the tongue. These taste receptors are connected by nerves to the cortex, or outer layer of the brain, where taste sensations are recorded.

There is little, if any, salt in wine, and of the other three tastes only sweetness is pleasant by itself. Sweetness is apparent when there is residual sugar present, for example in ports or Sauternes.

Bitterness indicates a high degree of tannin in the wine. Tannin, an ingredient from the grape skins, is extremely important in red wines. It has a puckish, astringent flavor when the wine is young, but as red wine matures and ages, tannins soften and add a rounder finish to the wine.

The sourness, or acidity, of wine is due to the presence of tartaric and malic acids that are necessary ingredients for white wines. An overabundance of acidity makes a wine taste unpleasant and tart. Not enough acidity makes a wine taste flabby and bland. When the acids are in balance with the alcohol, the wine has a lively, fresh taste. If any of the ingredients are in excess, the wine is considered out of balance and will taste bitter, stale, and unattractive. Strive for a balance of tastes, as balance ensures a quality wine.

HOW TO TASTE WINE

In order to extract the flavors or tastes of a wine, draw a small amount of wine into the mouth and run the liquid over the top of the tongue to properly register the tastes. Slurping is socially acceptable in this situation, as it helps to highlight the flavors. You need not swallow the wine to evaluate it. Most wine judges spit out the wine when they are finished with it. Swirl the wine around your mouth and draw in a little air to help the tasting process.

WHAT TO TASTE FOR

Balance in a wine is a high priority when evaluating it. It should have a pleasant, well-rounded taste with none of the ingredients overpowering any of the others. Your mouth or palate should also be able to determine the "weight" of the wine and decide whether it is light-bodied, medium-bodied, or full-bodied. A long, lingering finish of the wine and a pleasant aftertaste are signs of high quality wine.

When to Taste

If possible, wine should be evaluated early in the morning before you have saturated the mouth with foods that may impart lingering flavors capable of affecting the way a wine tastes. You should be well rested and in good health.

When Not to Taste

In some cases, it's better to leave wine tasting to another day. Don't taste wine under the following circumstances:

- **If you have a bad cold or flu or a digestive disorder.** Each of these conditions can negatively impact your ability to taste.
- **If you are on medication.** Mixing medication and alcohol can cause severe adverse reactions. *Never* taste wine when on medication.
- **If you are extremely tired or run down.** Fatigue can cause your senses to be less acute.
- **If you have only a short period of time.** Attempting to evaluate too many wines within a few hours can cause fatigue of the palate and eventually you will temporarily lose the ability to taste.

Wine Evaluation by Number

The University of California at Davis, Department of Viticulture and Enology (America's most famous wine college), developed a numerical system for evaluating wines that has become an industry standard. The system is based on 20 points, with 20 points being the highest possible rating and 0 points the lowest possible rating. There are five categories of wine evaluation used. Each category has a different number of maximum points that may be scored, as shown in the chart on page 244.

Wines that earn from 18 to 20 points are considered extraordinary; 15 to 17 excellent; 12 to 14 good; 9 to 11 commercially acceptable; 6 to 8 deficient; and 0 to 5 poor and objectionable. The American Wine Society uses the University of California, Davis, wine evaluation scale for its Amateur Wine Competition and its extensive Commercial Competition.

Some groups have modified this scoring system to suit their needs; we've heard that some competitions use a 10-point system and others a 100-point system. There is no one mandatory evaluation system, but most of the premier agencies conducting national and international wine judging competitions are using the 20-point system explained above.

UNIVERSITY OF CALIFORNIA, DAVIS, WINE EVALUATION SCALE

CATEGORY	SCORE	DESCRIPTION
Appearance	0 points	Objectionable (cloudy and/or off-color)
	1 point	Poor (slight haze or slight off-color)
	2 points	Good (clear with characteristic color)
	3 points	Excellent (brilliant with outstanding characteristic color)
Aroma and bouquet	0 points	Objectionable (offensive odor)
	1 point	Poor (off-odors)
	2 points	Deficient (no perceptible aroma or bouquet or with slight off-odors)
	3 points	Acceptable (slight aroma and bouquet, pleasant)
	4 points	Good (characteristic aroma, distinguished bouquet)
	5 points	Excellent (characteristic aroma, complex bouquet, well balanced)
	6 points	Extraordinary (unmistakable characteristic aroma of grape variety or wine type, outstanding)
Taste and texture	0 points	Objectionable (offensive flavors and texture)
	1 point	Poor (disagreeable flavors, poorly balanced, and unpleasant texture)
	2 points	Deficient (undistinguished wine with more pronounced faults)
	3 points	Acceptable (undistinguished wine but pleasant; may have minor off-flavors; may be slightly out of balance and/or somewhat thin or rough)
	4 points	Good (characteristic grape variety or wine type flavor; good balance; smooth; may have minor imperfections)
	5 points	Excellent (excellent but not overwhelming)
	6 points	Extraordinary (unmistakable characteristic flavor of grape variety or wine type; outstanding balance; smooth, full-bodied, and overwhelming)
Aftertaste	0 points	Objectionable (unpleasant aftertaste)
	1 point	Poor (little or no distinguishable aftertaste)
	2 points	Good (pleasant aftertaste)
	3 points	Excellent (lingering outstanding aftertaste)
Overall impression	0 points	Poor
	1 point	Good
	2 points	Excellent

COMPETITIONS

Many home winemakers are content with making their wine and enjoying it with friends and relatives. But there are many others who are extremely competitive in nature and so proud of their wines that they enter them in competitions. Just as commercial wineries can gain prestige and credibility with each medal earned, so can home winemakers.

The American Wine Society

The American Wine Society conducts an amateur competition as part of its annual November conference. Only members may enter the competition. Each year, more than 500 wines are entered. The American Wine Society boasts more than 5,000 members, of whom approximately 25 percent are home winemakers.

> **American Wine Society**
> 3006 Latta Road
> Rochester, NY 14612-3298
> Phone: 716-225-7611
> E-mail: angel1910@aol.com
> Web site: www.vicon.net/~aws

Purdue University

Purdue University conducts the largest amateur wine competition in the United States as part of the Indiana State Fair each summer. Entries are encouraged from home winemakers throughout North America. Purdue University also sponsors a commercial wine competition and an amateur label competition. For entry information contact:

> Competition Director
> **Purdue University**
> Department of Food Science, Smith Hall
> W. Lafayette, IN 47907-1180
> Phone: 317-494-6704 / Fax: 317-494-7953

InterVin International

InterVin International is an organization with offices in Canada and the United States. Initially, InterVin held only commercial competitions but it has recently begun conducting amateur wine competitions each spring. The entry fee is higher than most amateur wine competitions, but the group claims to hold the largest competition in North America. For details and entry affidavits contact:

> **InterVin International**
> 441 Sprucewood Terrace
> Williamsville, NY 14221-1910
> Phone: 716-614-2456 / Fax: 416-429-0382

> Canadian office:
> P. O. Box 488
> Don Mills, ON M3C RT2
> Phone: 416-429-6523 / Fax: 416-429-0382

AMERICAN WINE SOCIETY, PITTSBURGH CHAPTER

The Pittsburgh Chapter of the American Wine Society, in concert with Country Wines, a wine supply store, sponsors an amateur wine competition in conjunction with a day of seminars and wine tastings. Entries from other regions are welcomed for this annual event.

Country Wines
3333 Babcock Boulevard
Pittsburgh, PA 15237
Phone: 412-366-0151
E-mail: info@countrywines.com

AMENTI DEL VINO

One of the oldest amateur wine competitions is held in Connecticut each fall. Sponsored by Amenti del Vino and the Connecticut chapters of the American Wine Society, the competition features a postcompetition awards banquet. Any home winemaker can enter. Entries usually include wines from five to seven Northeast states each year. Amenti del Vino also conducts a commercial competition each summer for international entries.

Connecticut Amateur Wine Competition
Amenti del Vino
57 East Main Street
Mystic, CT 06355
Phone: 860-536-0249 / Fax: 860-536-7224

What contemptible scoundrel stole the cork from my lunch?

—W. C. Fields

SUPPLIERS AND EQUIPMENT

The most important part of home winemaking is starting with good grapes or juice. It is difficult, if not impossible, to make good wine from poor grapes, so you must find quality ingredients.

If you live near commercial wineries, you might be able to negotiate a contract to buy some of their quality grapes. If you have the wherewithal, you might even be able to grow your own. However, most home winemakers must buy grapes from local or regional distributors. In some instances, there will be no competition and you'll have no choice but to take what they offer at their price. Where there's a will there's a way.

If you band together with other home winemakers, either through a local wine club or by seeking each other out, you can try to negotiate directly with a grape source by buying in quantity. For tips on identifying the best suppliers, consult longtime home winemakers and local wine clubs.

California is the major supplier of grapes to home winemakers, and many California packers ship to every region of the United States and Canada. The California suppliers have established a system of grape picking and packing for shipment. Called *house pack,* in this system grape picking is supervised in the field and poor grapes are bypassed. The grapes, all of comparable quality, are then taken to a warehouse where they are packed by variety and weighed precisely. Twigs and leaves are removed before weighing, and the grapes are placed in boxes to prevent crushing in transit.

Another system, called *field pack,* is less desirable, as the grapes are packed in the field, many times with twigs and leaves and rotten or unripened grapes. If possible, always buy grapes that are *house packed.*

EQUIPMENT

In addition to being the largest grape broker and distributor in the eastern part of the United States, the Prospero Equipment Company of Pleasantville, New York, is a major equipment distributor and imports foreign winemaking equipment. Prospero also sells grapes to regional distributors throughout the eastern United States and Canada.

Prospero Equipment Company
134 Marble Street
Pleasantville, NY 10570
Phone: 914-769-6252
Fax: 914-769-6786
E-mail: prospero@cloud9.net

You can't make good wine from bad grapes.

—Peter Mondavi, Jr.

Local and Regional Sources

The local or regional wine supply source is another important link in the quality winemaking process. You must have faith and confidence in your suppliers and rely on their integrity for guidance and instruction. Many suppliers are combination outlets featuring both winemaking and beer-making supplies. That's fine, as long as they offer you reliable, consistent service and information.

There are literally hundreds of outlets in the United States and Canada. Businesses change addresses, close, expand, and merge with other companies, so some of the suppliers listed here might not be available when you contact them.

We have found that the most reliable national source of home winemaking supplies is Presque Isle Wine Cellars. Founded in 1964, this business continues to satisfy thousands of home winemakers throughout the United States and Canada. They maintain an excellent catalog and offer competitive pricing that in some cases may be lower than your local supply house. Presque Isle offers information on supplies, grapes, juices, and equipment.

Presque Isle Wine Cellars
9440 W. Main Road (US Rte 20)
Near East, PA 16428
Phone: 814-725-1314
Fax: 814-725-2092
E-mail: prwc@erie.net
Web site: www.erie.net/~prwc

Other Suppliers

United States

Arbor Home Beermaking & Winemaking Supplies
23 E. Main Street
East Islip, NY 11730
Phone: 516-277-3004
Fax: 516-277-3027

Bacchus & Barleycorn, Inc.
6633 Nieman Road
Shawnee, KS 66204
Phone: 913-962-2501
Fax: 913-962-0008

Pat Baker
Box 41
Westmoreland, NH 03467
Phone: 603-399-8361

Barleywine
110 E. 25th Street
Joplin, MO 64804
Phone: 417-626-9463
Fax: 417-626-9923

Beer & Wine By U
1456 N. Greenbriar Road
Evansville, IN 47715
Phone: 317-848-6218

Beer & Wine Craft
371 Lynden-Birch Bay Road
Lynden, WA 98264
Phone: 360-354-3735

Beer & Winemaking Cellar
14411 Greenwood Avenue N.
Seattle, WA 98133
Phone: 206-365-7660

Chicagoland Winemakers, Inc.
689 W. North Avenue
Elmhurst, IL 60126
Phone: 708-834-0507

Corrado's Wine Grapes, Inc.
1578 Main Avenue
Clifton, NJ 07011
Phone: 201-340-0628/0848
Fax: 201-340-2052

Country Wines
3333 Babcock Boulevard
Pittsburgh, PA 15237
Phone: 412-366-0151

Crosby & Baker, Ltd.
3912 Shirley Drive
Atlanta, GA 30336
Phone: 404-505-0002
Fax: 404-505-7942

Crosby & Baker, Ltd.
999 Main Road, Box 3409
Westport, MA 02790
Phone: 508-636-5154

Defalco's Wine Cellars
5611 Morningside Drive
Houston, TX 77005
Phone: 713-523-8154
Fax: 713-523-5284

**Delta Packing Company
of Lodi, Inc.**
5950 East Kettleman Lane
Lodi, CA 95240
Phone: 209-334-1023

**Edmund's Beer &
Winemaking Supply**
220 E. 8th Street
Wyoming, PA 18644
Phone: 717-691-6282

Fall Bright
9750 Hyatt Hill #16
Wayne, NY 14893
Phone: 407-292-3995

The Flying Barrell
111 S. Carroll Street
Frederick, MD 21702
Phone: 301-663-4491

Foxwood Farm & Vineyard, Inc.
83 W Johnston Lane
Cape May Court House, NJ 08210
Phone: 609-463-8266

Fruit O' the Vine
2616 McDonald Road
Tyler, TX 75701
Phone: 903-593-4688

Fulkerson's
5576 Route 14
Dundee, NY 14837
Phone: 607-243-7883

**Grande Home Beer &
Winemaking Supplies**
4641 Warner Road
Garfield Heights, OH 44125
Phone: 216-883-5590

The Grape & Granary, Inc.
1302 E. Tallmadge Avenue
Akron, OH 44310
Phone: 330-633-7223
Fax: 330-633-6794

**Great Fermentations
of Indiana**
1712 E. 86th Street
Indianapolis, IN 46240
Phone: 317-848-6218

Great Fermentations of Marin
136 Bellam Road
San Rafael, CA 94901
Phone: 415-459-2520
Fax: 415-459-3001

Home Winemaking Shop
22836 Ventura Boulevard
Woodland Hills, CA 91364
Phone: 818-884-8586

G. W. Kent, Inc.
3667 Morgan Road
Ann Arbor, MI 48108
Phone: 313-572-1300
Fax: 313-572-0097

Lamanuzzi & Pantaleo
11767 Road 27½
Madera, CA 93637
Phone: 559-432-3170

The Liquor Collection
1050 Ala Moana Street
Waimanali, HI 96795
Phone: 808-259-6884
Fax: 808-259-6755

Maltose Express
391 Main Street
Monroe, CT 06468
Phone: 203-452-7332

Maryland Wine Cellars
9120 Main Street
Ellicott City, MD 21043
Phone: 410-465-1926
Fax: 410-465-5790

M & R Packing Company
33 E. Tokay Street
Lodi, CA 95240
Phone: 209-369-2725

Neptune's Homebrew & Wine Supplies
121½ E. Callender Street
Livingston, MT 59047
Phone: 406-222-9146

New Grapes on the Block
16069 Manchester Road
Ellisville, MO 63011
Phone: 314-256-3332

Niebert's Spielgrund Wine & Gift Shop
3528 E. Market Street
York, PA 17402
Phone: 717-755-3384
Fax: 717-755-1248

The Purple Foot, Inc.
3167 S. 92nd Street
Milwaukee, WI 53227
Phone: 414-327-2130
Fax: 414-327-6682

The Purple Foot Down East, Inc.
Box 116, Main Street
Woldoboro, ME 04572
Phone: 207-832-6286

F. H. Steinbart Company
234 SE 12th Street
Portland, OR 97214
Phone: 503-232-8793
Fax: 503-238-1649

Triboro Fruit
2500 South Fowler
Fresno, CA 93725
Phone: 559-486-4141

Vinotheque U.S.A., Inc.
24 St. Martin, Bldg. 2
Marlboro, MA 02790
Phone: 800-481-8466
Fax: 800-635-0035

Vintages Wine & Coffee
11804 Springfield Pike
Cincinnati, OH 45246
Phone: 513-671-2085

The Wine & Beer Barrel
Ridge Road & Rte 202
Chaddsford, PA 19317
Phone: 610-558-BEER

The Wine Boutique, Inc.
2701 Monroe Street, Ste. 240
Madison, WI 53711
Phone: 608-232-3911

Wine & Cake Hobbies
6527 Tidewater Drive
Norfolk, VA 23509
Phone: 757-857-0245
Fax: 757-857-4743

Wine Craft of Atlanta
5920 Roswell Road, C-205
Atlanta, GA 30328
Phone: 404-252-5606

Wine Hobby, U.S.A.
401 Route 206 South
Somerville, NJ 08876
Phone: 908-874-4141

The Wine Press & Hops
50 State Street
Pittsford, NY 14534
Phone: 716-381-8092

The Wine Works
5275 W. Alameda
Denver, CO 80219
Phone: 303-936-4422

The Winemaker's Loft
830 East Main Street Rear
Follansbee, WV 26037
Phone: 304-527-0600

Winemaker's Pantry
4599 Park Boulevard
Pinellas Park, FL 34665
Phone: 813-546-9117

The Winemaker Shop
5356 W. Vickory
Fort Worth, TX 76107
Phone: 817-377-4488
Fax: 817-732-4327

Canada

Bacchus Productions, Inc.
2 Bloor Street West, Ste. 100-370
Toronto, ON M4W 3R6
Phone: 416-429-3050
Fax: 416-429-2529

Can'an Cork
5519A 137th Avenue
Edmonton, AB T5A 3L4
Phone: 403-473-4598

Canmore Wine Mine
108 Coyote Way
Canmore, AB T1W 1C2
Phone: 403-678-6901

Chernick Wine & Beer Supplies
5203 42nd Street
Ponoka, AB T4J 1C9
Phone: 403-783-3890
Fax: 403-783-6949

Coastal Winemakers, Inc.
2546 B King George Highway
White Rock, BC V48 5E7
Phone: 604-538-0286
Fax: 604-538-0348

Corkscrew Emporium
#105, 1221 Kingsway Avenue SE
Medicine Hat, AB T1A 2Y2
Phone: 403-526-1920

Cowichan Valley Vines to Wines, Inc.
11-850 Shawingan Mill Bay Road
Mill Bay, BC V0R 1L0
Phone: 250-741-4647
Fax: 250-743-4657

Eastern Beer & Wine Supplies Ltd.
22 Glendale Avenue, Unit #4
Lower Sackville, NS B4C 3M1
Phone: 902-864-0100
Fax: 902-864-5628

Glass O' Wine
678 Columbia Street
New Westminister, BC V3M 1A9
Phone: 604-540-6440

Grape Expectations Wine Emporium, Inc.
#238-215 Port Augusta Street
Comox Centre Mall
Comox, BC V9M 3M9
Phone: 250-339-2555
Fax: 250-339-2841

Grapefully Yours
431 Front Street
New Westminister, BC V3L 1A4
Phone: 604-521-3660

Grapes 4 U Enterprises, Inc.
404-4955 River Road
Delta, BC V4K 4V9
Phone: 604-878-0966
Fax: 604-940-8807

The Home Vintner
#4, 4404 14th Street NW
Calgary, AB T2K 1J5
Phone: 403-284-0486
Fax: 403-284-0503

Island Wine Works, Inc.
9A-1150 N. Terminal Avenue
Nanaimo, BC V9S 5L6
Phone: 604-754-5116

Just Fine Wine
2639 Kingsway Avenue
Port Qoquitlam, BC V3C 1T5
Phone: 604-944-7818

Kamil Juices
199 Victoria Road S
Guelph, ON N1E 6T9
Phone: 519-824-1624
Fax: 519-824-0808

MC Wines the Winemaker
1470 Pemberton Avenue
North Vancouver, BC V7P 2S1
Phone: 604-987-4464
Fax: 604-987-4313

Mosti-Mondiale, Inc.
6865 Route 132
Ville Ste-Catherine, QC J0L 1E0
Phone: 514-926-1955
Fax: 514-926-1956

Niagara Vine Products Ltd./Vineco International
27 Scott Street W, P.O. Box 578
St. Catherine, ON L2R 6W8
Phone: 905-685-9342
Fax: 905-685-9551

Private Vintners
4191 203rd Street
Langely, BC V3A 1T9
Phone: 604-532-0941

Rainbow Winemakers
2702 Clarke Street
Port Moody, BC V3H 1Z1
Phone: 604-931-4720
Fax: 604-931-4736

R. J. Grape Products
1570 King Street E
Kitchener, ON N2G 2P1
Phone: 519-743-3755
Fax: 519-743-4613

Valley Wines
105 — 2866 Mt. Lehman Road
Abbotsford, BC V8W 2N6
Phone: 604-864-0180

Vintner's Choice
10A 7100 50th Avenue
Red Deer, AB T4N 6A5
Phone: 403-340-1518
Fax: 403-346-6065

Wine Art, Inc.
55 Clegg Road
Markham, ON L6G 1B9
Phone: 905-477-9463
Fax: 800-461-2129

Wine Art, Inc.
#120 6080 Russ Baker Way
Richmond, BC V7B 1B4
Phone: 604-278-2332

The Wine Baril
591 Archibald Avenue
Winnipeg, MB R2J 0X7
Phone: 204-237-3936

The Wine Barrel
644 Broughton Street
Victoria, BC V8W 1C9
Phone: 604-388-0606

The Wine Maker
1736A Island Highway
Victoria, BC V9B 1H8
Phone: 604-474-4405

**Winemaker Wine
Company, Ltd.**
3630 Brentwood Road NW, 322
Calgary, AB T2L 1K8
Phone: 403-282-9810
Fax: 403-282-1149

The Wine 'n Beer Company
150 Hespeler Road
Cambridge, ON N1R 6V6
Phone: 519-622-9288

Winexpert, Inc.
710 South Service Road
Stoney Creek, ON L8E 5S7
Phone: 905-643-9158
Fax: 905-643-9161

Woodstock Wines
3902 Glenroy Road, RB #1
Apple Hill, ON K0C 1B0
Phone: 613-525-5171
Fax: 613-525-0085

GLOSSARY

Acetic acid. A major reason for spoiled wine; an organic acid that is a chief ingredient of vinegar.

Acidity, fixed Natural acids, usually tannic and tartaric, that add pleasant tartness to wine.

Alcohol. An important by-product of fermentation; yeasts in combination with sugar located in juice transform into carbonic gas and alcohol.

Amelioration. Winemaker's terminology referring to the adding of sugar, acid, and water to properly balance juice or wine.

Appetizer wine. Usually a dry wine to be consumed before dinner to stimulate the appetite.

Aroma. The smell or fragrance that comes from the grape or fruit.

Astringency. The puckery taste imparted by tannins in wine.

Balling. A scale graduation for a hydrometer, or saccharometer, used in reading the specific gravity of liquids or their sugar content; same as Brix.

Bentonite. A powdery clay used as a fining agent.

Blending. The mixing of two or more wines to achieve a better product or to enhance or improve a wine.

Body. The substance or depth of a wine. Light wines lack body, whereas most hearty wines have heavy or "chewy" body.

Bottle sickness. A temporary situation usually developing right after being bottled. Some call the condition *bottle shock*. It usually clears up within a month or so.

Bouquet. The fragrance of a wine produced by the combination of its volatile acids and its essential oils with the alcohol.

Brix. A scale graduation for a hydrometer, or saccharometer, used in reading the specific gravity of liquids or their sugar content; same as Balling.

Burette. A graduated glass tube used in the titration process.

Burgundy. A generic term used to describe wines made from the Burgundy region of France. The reds are usually heavy bodied.

Cap. When making red wine, the grapes are crushed and all of the ingredients are placed in a fermentor. As fermentation begins, the skins, pulp, and seeds from the grapes rise to the surface, forming this. In France, it is known as the *chapeau.*

Capsules. Closures for the tops of wine bottles usually made from plastic, metal foil, paper, or wax.

Carbon dioxide (CO_2). A gas given off by fermenting grape juice.

Carboy. Large glass jug ranging in size from 1 gallon (3.8 L) to 15 gallons (56.8 L).

Cask. A barrel-like container for wine use; usually made of wood.

Caskiness. A flavor imparted to wine by certain essential oils that remain in a cask if it is not properly cleaned.

Cellar. An area where wine is stored.

Chablis. A light, dry white wine from the Burgundy region of France. Often used as a generic term for many white wines made in the Burgundian style.

Champagne. A sparkling wine made in a well-defined region of France, using specific grapes and secondary fermentation.

Character. Wine — possessing the proper color, bouquet or aroma, and taste — thought to be the ideal essence of a wine, will be described as having this.

Chateau bottled. Wine bottled at the winery, chateau, bodega, or estate where the grapes were grown and the wine was made.

Claret. A red table wine from the Bordeaux region of France; commonly, a dry, light-bodied red wine.

Clean. A wine that leaves a pleasant aftertaste and has no off-odors.

Cloudy. A state often characteristic of wines of low alcohol content in which some albuminous substance refuses to settle.

Cold-stabilize. The process of placing wine in a cool or cold area in order to crystallize the tartrates in the wine, so they can be removed by racking.

Colloidal suspension. A state that exists in liquids when albuminous particles remain suspended.

Cordial. A sweet, aromatic beverage, usually with high alcoholic content; also known as a *liqueur.*

Corkiness. A flavor imparted to wine by a defective cork or closure.

Corks. Wine bottle stoppers made from the bark of a tree known as the cork oak; the best corks come from Spain.

Cooperage. A term used for barrels or casks.

Cream of tartar. A white, crystalline deposit that settles out from wines during cold stabilization as the temperature is lowered.

Cuvée. A French word literally meaning "tub-full." A blend of wines prepared for champagne production.

Decant. The pouring of clean wine from a bottle into another container and leaving the sediment behind.

Demijohn. A large glass bottle holding from 5 to 10 gallons (19–38 L).

Dinner wine. All still wines with less than 14 percent alcohol by volume; usually dry; also known as *table wine*.

Deposit. The normal sediment of fine particles precipitated by wine as it matures in the bottle.

Dessert wine. Usually the name given to sweet or semisweet wines; usually fortified with brandy containing up to 22 percent alcohol like sherries and port wines.

Disgorging. The act of removing sediment after bottle fermentation of the champagne-type and sparkling wines.

Dry. The opposite of *sweet* in wine terminology when all of the fermentable sugars have been consumed.

Essential oils. Volatile oils that give distinctive odor or flavor to fruit, plants, and flowers. In wines they combine with alcohol to determine its bouquet.

Estufagem. A method of cooking wines developed in Madeira and still used today. Wines are steamed for six or more months at temperatures approaching 110°F (43°C) or more.

Fermentation. The chemical process in which sugar in a liquid is broken down by yeasts into alcohol, carbonic gas, and some by-products. The process changes grape juice into wine.

Fermentation lock. A bottle-sealing device that allows carbon dioxide gas to escape the bottle while not allowing any air into the container.

Fermentor. A container in which grape juice or must is held to undergo a primary fermentation.

Fine. To clarify wine by adding a fining agent such as bentonite, gelatin, or egg whites.

Fino. A type of dry, delicate, light sherry.

Flabby or **flat.** A wine with a low alcohol content is described thus.

Flowery. The characteristics of flowers evident in some young wines.

Fortified wine. A wine whose alcoholic content has been raised up to 20 percent or more by the addition of brandy or other spirits.

Foxy. A taste quality associated with native American grape varieties like Concord; some drinkers like this quality but most find it undesirable.

Fox grape. Grapes that are of the species *Vitus labrusca* and considered to be the native American varieties.

Free run. Juice flowing from the first pressing of the grapes.

Fruity. A term used to indicate the flavor or aroma of the grape in the finished wine.

Gallon. A liquid measure containing 128 ounces (3.8 L).

Generic. The names of wines taken from geographic regions like Burgundy, Chablis, Champagne, Rhine, Bordeaux, and more.

Greenness. An excess of malic acid and tartaric acid due to early picking of unripened grapes causes this harshness.

Harshness. A condition due to a lack of age; it usually disappears when the wine is aged.

Hock. An English abbreviation for the German Hochheimer; a type of Rhine wine.

Hybrid. A cross between two different grape varieties.

Hydrometer. An instrument, similar to the saccharometer, for measuring the density of liquids.

Isinglass. Used for the fining of white wines; made into gelatin from certain fish parts for fining purposes.

Isobarometric pressure. Term used when making sparkling wines, either by the "transfer" process or by the "Charmat" or "bulk" process. "Filtered and bottled in an isobarometric line" means that pressure is kept constant using inert gas and thereby eliminating air contact.

Keg. A small cask.

Lees. The sediment found at the bottom of a carboy or wine cask.

Malic acid. An acid occurring in certain fruits like apples and grapes.

Malolactic culture. A special yeast strain developed to initiate a secondary fermentation to convert malic acid to lactic acid.

Marc. The skins or husks and seeds that remain after the pressing of the grapes.

Mold. A fungus that sometimes appears in wines as a result of insufficient alcohol and/or sanitation procedures.

Must. Grape juice that is not yet wine.

Noble rot. A mold that develops in some years; it can be a boon for some areas and grapes and a devastating development for others. The mold penetrates the grape and leaves a high concentration of sugar in the shriveled grape. Some varieties thrive on this event, like the Sauternes of France, the Tokays of Hungary, and the heralded Auslese varieties of Germany. Other varieties are ruined.

Oxidation. When wine comes in contact with oxygen, chemical changes occur and cause white wine to turn brown and eventually deteriorate.

Parts per million (ppm). A term used in winemaking to designate small quantities; 1 pound of any ingredient in 1 million pounds of water yields 1 ppm of the ingredient.

Pasteurization. The process, discovered by Pasteur, of arresting ferments in wine, beer, milk, and other liquids by heating for a period of time to a temperature between 144°F and 149°F (62°C–65°C).

Pips. Seeds.

Piquant. The right amount of balance and acidity in wine.

Pomace. Crushed fruit or grapes after the juice has been extracted.

Port. A heavy, sweet wine from the Douro region of Portugal made by arresting the fermentation by adding brandy when the residual sugar is between 6 and 8 percent. Sweet wine with up to 20 percent alcohol; usually long aged for complexity.

Racking. The siphoning or pumping of wine from one container to another container, leaving the lees behind.

Red dinner wine. Usually dry and rich, highly acidic, and well suited to many red meats, pastas, and stews.

Rhine wines. Named after the light, spicy wines of the Rhine River region in Germany.

Rosé. A wine pink in color and light in body; pleasant to drink.

Saccharometer. An instrument used to measure the sugar content of liquids.

"Round." Term used to describe a well-balanced wine.

Sauternes. Usually a white dessert wine; semisweet and sweet; originally from France but copied in other regions of the world.

Sec. The French word for "dry."

Sediment. The natural deposit developed as wine ages.

Sekt. The German term for "sparkling wine."

Sherry. A fortified wine of Spain, made from dry to sweet; made in other areas using the name generically.

Siphon. Usually a tube used to transfer wine from one container to another from a higher level into a lower level.

Soft. A wine that is balanced, has low acidity and is easy to drink.

Soften. To lower the harsh acids in wine in order to bring the wine into balance. A soft wine is a low-astringency wine, sometimes called *smooth.*

Solera. The method of making Spanish sherries by blending older wines with younger wines; there is never a sherry vintage year.

Sour. A description of a vinegary or spoiled wine.

Sparkling wine. A wine with bubbles and effervescence like champagne.

Spigot. A faucet, usually connected at the bottom of a cask, used to draw wine from a barrel.

Still wine. A nonsparkling wine with less than 14 percent alcohol.

Stuck wine. A wine that has stopped fermenting before all of the sugar has been consumed.

Sweet wine. A wine with at least 3 percent sugar after fermentation.

Sulfiting. The adding of potassium metabisulfite or sodium metabisulfite to a must.

Sulfur dioxide (SO_2). Sulfur dioxide, used in wines, kills bacteria, yeasts, and fungi that can be harmful to wine. Undesirable microbes are eliminated, and wine browning is eliminated with the proper use of sulfur dioxide.

Sweetness. The taste sensation derived mainly from fructose and glucose; sweet wines have 3 percent sugar or more.

Tannin. Tannin, derived from the grape skins, stems, and pips, imparts astringency to wine and lends longevity.

Tartness. A pleasant fruit-acid balance and flavor in wines: also known as *being crisp.*

Tartaric acid. The most important fixed acid in wine, its purified form is known as *cream of tartar.*

Tartrate. Potassium bitartrate, or tartrate, is the potassium half-salt of tartaric acid — a major acid ingredient in wine; also known as *cream of tartar.* Tartrate is usually removed from most wine.

Tawny. The description of older wines, which develop a brownish red color; also used to describe a type of port.

Tokay. A sweet, fortified Hungarian wine made from the Tokay grape.

Varietal wine. A wine named after the principal grape variety it contains; for a wine to be considered varietal in the United States, the same grape variety must constitute at least 75 percent wine in the bottle.

Vermouth. A wine flavored with a variety of botanicals and herbs; it can be dry or sweet and either white or red and is usually fortified.

Vinification. Converting grape juice to wine.

Vinosity. Having a winelike quality and deriving its character from a combination of bouquet, flavor, and structure or body.

Vintage. Wine made from the particular year stated on the label.

Vintage year. Usually a year of exceptional quality.

Vintner. One who sells wine.

Viticulture. The science of vine production.

White dinner wine. Still white wines suited to many dishes and containing less than 14 percent alcohol; they can be dry or semidry.

Wine conditioner. A combination of liquid sugar, potassium sorbate, and potassium metabisulfite. It is used to sweeten wine just before bottling. The chemicals in it guarantee that the sugar won't ferment again in the bottle.

Woody. A noticeable woodlike flavor imparted by long aging in wooden barrels or spicing with wood chips.

Yeast inoculation. The process of adding yeast to a grape or fruit juice in order to initiate fermentation to convert the juice into wine and alcohol.

Yeasty. A characteristic of wines that have an aroma or taste of yeast.

INDEX

Note: Page numbers in *italic* refer to illustrations; those in **boldface** refer to charts.

A

Acetic fermentation, 233–34
Acid blends, 12, 37
Acids, balancing, 36–38, **37**
Acid test
  equipment for, 6–7
  importance of, 231
  for red wine, 23, 163
  for white wine, 22–23,
    127–28
Aerating, 20
Aging
  concentrate or kit wines, 43
  fruit wines, 200
  red wines, 20, 167
Alcohol content, 21–22, 35–36,
  231
Alicante-Bouschet, from
  grapes, 168–69
Appearance
  evaluating, 241
  troubleshooting, 237
Apple wine
  from juice, 201
  from whole fruit, 202

Aroma, evaluating, 241–42
Aurora, from grapes, 131–32
Auslesen. *See* Johannisberg
    Riesling

B

Baco Noir, from grapes, 169–70
Balling scale. *See* Brix scale
Banana wine, 203
Barbera
  from concentrate, 57
  from grapes, 171–72
  from juice, 97–98
Barolo, from concentrate, 58
Basket presses
  described, 8–9, 9, 126–27
  using, 19
Bentonite, 13
Blackberry wine, 204
Bladder presses, 8, 127
Blaufrankisch
  from grapes, 183–84
  from juice, 99–100
Blends. *See also specific wines*
  kit wines, 31–32, **32**

red wines, 166
  white wines, 130
Blueberry wine, 205
Bordeaux bottles, 10–11, *10*
Bottle brushes, 5, *5*
Bottle closures
  described, 7, 9, *9*
  using, 25
Bottles
  cleaning, 10
  exploding, 234
  odor from, 235
  types of, 7, 10–11, *10*
Bottle sterilizer/rinser, 8, *8*
Bottling. *See also* Corking
    machines; Corks
  basic procedures, 25
  concentrate wines, 43
  grape wines, 130, 166
  juice wines, 74
  kit wines, 30
Brix scale
  defined, 22
  desirable range on, 36
  raising, 37

Bual or Malmsey Madeira, 230
Burgundy
    bottles for, 10–11, *10*
    from concentrate, 64

C

Cabernet Franc
    blending, 166
    from grapes, 172–73
    from juice, 100–101
Cabernet Sauvignon
    blending, 166, 184, 193
    from concentrate, 59
    from grapes, 174–75
    from juice, 102–3
Campden tablets, 12. *See also*
    Potassium metabisulfite
Cap, defined, 164
Carboy bungs, 6, *6*
Carboys, 5, *5*
Carignane
    from grapes, 175–76
    from juice, 103–4
"Caskiness," in flavor, 236–37
Cayuga, from grapes, 132–33
Chablis, from concentrate, 53
Chambourcin, from grapes,
    177–78
Champagne
    commercial production of,
        216–17
    making at home, 218–20
    recipe for, 221–22
Champagne method, 216
Chardonnay. *See also specific*
        types

from grapes, 134–35
from juice, 75–76
Charmat process, 217
Chauche Gris. *See* Grey Riesling
Chenin Blanc
    blending, 130
    from concentrate, 44
    from grapes, 135–36
    from juice, 76–77
Cherry wine, 206
Clarifying
    concentrates, 42–43
    juices, 74
Clearing, 29–30
Cloudiness, 30, 237
Colombard. *See* French Colom-
    bard
Competitions, 245–46
Compost, 127
Concentrates
    advantages of, 33
    defined, 34
    purchasing, 34
    recipes for, 43–69
    winemaking with, 34–43
Concord
    from concentrate, 69
    from grapes, 178–79
Corking machines, 9, *9*, 25, 30
Corks, 7, 9, *9*, 25, 30, 74
Cranberry wine, 207
Crown capper, *219*
Crushers, 8, *8*, 123, 126, 198
Crushing
    red grapes, 162–63
    white grapes, 126

D

Definitions, 254–59
Defrosting, juice, 73
Delaware, from grapes, 137–38
Disgorging, 216
Drifine isinglass, 13
Dutchess, from grapes, 138–39

E

Emerald Riesling, from concen-
    trate, 45
Entre-Deux-Mers, 90
Equipment
    advanced, 7–9
    basic, 4–7
    for concentrates, 34
    for fruit, 198
    for grapes, 123, 161
    for juices, 72
    for kit wines, 27–28
    for Madeira, 228–29, 228
    purchasing, 3–4
    sanitizing, 15, 21, 28, 35
    setting up, 15
    suppliers of, 247–53
Estufa, 228–29, 228
Evaluation. *See* Wine tasting

F

Fermaid, 12–13
Fermentation
    basic process, 17
    for concentrates, 39–42
    for grapes, 128–29, 163–64
    for juices, 73
    for kit wines, 29

Fermentation *(continued)*
  secondary, 17, 18–19
  troubleshooting, 232–34
Fermentation locks, 5, *5*
Fermentors, 5, *5*
Fining agents
  for concentrates, 42–43
  for grapes, 129
  types of, 13
Fino Sherry, 226–27
Flavor, troubleshooting,
  236–37
Flies, on fruit, 199
Flor, 225
Flower smells, 235
Fortified wines
  Madeira, 227–30
  port, 222–24
  sherry, 225–27
Fragrance, troubleshooting,
  235–36
Freezing, juice, 70–71
French Colombard
  from concentrate, 46
  from grapes, 140–41
  from juice, 78–79
Fruit
  buying, 198–99
  recipes for, 201–14
  winemaking with, 199–200
Fruit crushers, 126
Fruit wholesalers, 124
Fruity-style wines
  red, 165
  white, 129

Fumé Blanc. *See* Sauvignon
  Blanc
Funnels, 6, *6*

G
Gamay
  from grapes, 180–81
  from juice, 105–6
Gamay Beaujolais, from concentrate, 60
Garganega grapes, 93–94
Gelatin, 13
German-style bottles, 10–11, *10*
Gewürztraminer
  blending, 130
  from concentrate, 47
  fruity-style, 129
  from grapes, 141–42
  from juice, 79–80
Glossary, 254–59
Grapes, red
  buying, 161–62
  characteristics of, 162
  recipes for, 167–97
  varieties of, 162
  winemaking with, 162–67,
    231
Grapes, white
  buying, 123–24
  characteristics of, 128
  recipes for, 130–60
  varieties of, 125
  winemaking with, 126–30,
    231
"Gravel," 237

Graves, 90
Grenache
  from grapes, 181–82
  from juice, 106–7
Grey Riesling
  from concentrate, 48
  from grapes, 143–44
Growers, buying grapes from,
  124

H
Health benefits of wine, 3
Hydrogen sulfide gas, 236
Hydrometer jars, 6, *6*
Hydrometers
  described, 6, *6*
  using, 17–18, 19, 21–22

I
Ingredients, quality of, 11–12,
  14. *See also specific*
  ingredients

J
Johannisberg Riesling
  from concentrate, 49
  from grapes, 144–45
  from juice, 81–82
Juices
  choosing, 71–72
  commercial preservation of,
    70–71
  recipes for, 75–121
  winemaking with, 72–74

K

Kits
  blending, 31–32, **32**
  items in, 27
  selecting, 26–27
  winemaking with, 28–30

L

Labels, 30–31
Labrusca grapes, 56, 137–39, 147
Lemberger
  from grapes, 183–84
  from juice, 99–100
Liebfraumilch, from concentrate, 50
Liqueur de tirage, 217

M

Madeira, 227–30
Malic acid, 236, 242
Malolactic cultures, 164
Malvoisie. *See* Pinot Gris
Measuring cups, 6, *6*
Melbec, from grapes, 184–85
Merlot
  blending, 166, 193
  from concentrate, 61
  from grapes, 186–87
  from juice, 108–9
Méthode champenoise, 216
Mission grapes, 161, 162
Morio Muskat, from juice, 82–83

Muller-Thurgau, fruity-style, 129
Muscat, from grapes, 146
Must, defined, 16
Mustiness, 235
Mycoderma aceti, 233–34

N

Napa Gamay. *See* Gamay
Niagara
  from concentrate, 56
  from grapes, 147–48
Numerical scale, for wine evaluation, 243, **244**

O

Oaking, 24–25
Orange wine, 208
Oxidized wine, 234

P

Pasteurization, of juice, 71
Patience, 2, 15, 200
Peach wine, 209
Pearson square, 223, 223
Pectic enzyme, 13
Petite Sirah
  from concentrate, 62
  from grapes, 189–90
  from juice, 111–12
Petit Verdot, from grapes, 190–91
pH, 38
Pinot Blanc
  blending, 130

from concentrate, 51
from grapes, 149–50
from juice, 84–85
Pinot Chardonnay, from concentrate, 52
Pinot Grigio. *See* Pinot Gris
Pinot Gris
  from grapes, 150–51
  from juice, 85–86
Pinot Noir
  blending, 166
  from concentrate, 63
  from grapes, 187–88
  from juice, 109–10
Plum wine, 211
Pomace, 127
Port, 222–24
Potassium metabisulfite. *See also* Stabilizing procedures
  adding, 16, 18, 19, 130
  described, 12
  fermentation problems and, 232
  for fruity-style wines, 129
  importance of, 14
Potassium sorbate, 18
Presses
  buying, alternatives to, 123
  types of, 8–9, 9, 126–27
  using, 19
Pressing
  red grapes, 164–65
  white grapes, 126–27
Process, troubleshooting, 232–34

R

Racking
  basic procedure, 24
  concentrates, 39
  juices, 74
  red wines, 19–20, 165
  white wines, 18, 129
Rapidase vino super, 13
Raspberry wine, 212
Ratchet presses. *See* Basket
  presses
Ravat 51, from grapes, 152–53
Record keeping
  forms for, 239–40
  need for, 43, 73
Red wines. *See also specific
  wines or ingredients*
  acid test for, 23
  blending, 166
  Brix range for, 36
  fruity-style, 165
  serving, 167
  vs. white, 15–16
  winemaking basics, 18–20
Refermentation, 130, 234
Rhubarb wine, 213
Riddling, 216
Riddling rack, *219*
Riesling. *See also specific types*
  blending, 130
  fruity-style, 129
Rioja. *See* Spanish Rioja
"Rotten-egg syndrome," 235–36
Ruby Cabernet
  from concentrate, 66
  from grapes, 192–93

from juice, 112–13
Rulander. *See* Pinot Gris

S

Saccharometers. *See* Hydrometers
Saint-èmilion, from juice, 94–95
Sal soda, 13
Sangiovese
  from grapes, 193–94
  from juice, 114–15
Sanitation
  of bottles, 10
  of equipment, 21, 28, 35
  importance of, 2, 123
  problems and, 231
Sauvignon Blanc
  blending, 130, 155
  from concentrate, 54
  from grapes, 153–54
  from juice, 87–88
Scheurebe, from juice, 88–89
Sekt, 216–17
Semillon
  blending, 130
  from grapes, 155–56
  from juice, 90–91
Seyval Blanc
  from grapes, 156–57
  from juice, 91–92
Sherry, 225–27
Silica gel, 13
Silvaner. *See* Sylvaner
Siphons, 5, *5, 39*
"Snowflakes," 237
Soave, from juice, 93–94

Soda ash, 13
Spanish Rioja, from concentrate, 65
Sparkling wines
  commercial production of,
  215–17
  recipe for, 221–22
  types of, 217–18
Specific gravity, 17–18, 19,
  21–22, 164
Spoons, 5, *5*
Stabilizing procedures
  concentrates, 42
  grapes, 128
  juices, 74
  kit wines, 29–30
Stemmer-crushers, 126
Stoppers. *See* Carboy bungs;
  Corks
Storage, of red wines, 19–20
Strawberry wine, 214
Sugar
  adding, 18, 36, 130, 199, 217
  excess, 232–33
Sugar content
  of grapes, 16, 124
  numerical scale for, 22
Sugar test
  basic procedure, 21–22
  for concentrates, 35–36
  for grapes, 127–28, 163
  importance of, 231
Sulfiting
  defined, 29
  juice, 71
  wine, 42

Sulfur dioxide, 16
Suppliers, 247–53
Supplies, 12–13
Sylvaner
    fruity-style, 129
    from grapes, 158–59
Syrah
    blending, 166
    from grapes, 195–96
    from juice, 115–16

T

Tannin, natural grape, 12, 242
Tartaric acid, 22, 236, 242
Tartrate crystals, 18, 237
Taste, evaluating, 242–43
Tasting, during production, 18.
    See also Wine tasting
Temperatures
    for estufa, 229
    fermentation and, 232–33
Thermometers, floating, 6, 23
Thompson Seedless grapes,
    122, 125
Tomato wine, 210
Transfer process, 216–17
Trebbiano, from juice, 94–95
Troubleshooting
    appearance, 237
    common problems, 231
    flavor, 236–37
    fragrance, 235–36
    process, 232–34

U

Ugni Blanc, from juice, 94–95
University of California wine
    evaluation scale, 243, **244**

V

Valpolicella, from juice, 117–18
Vidal Blanc
    from grapes, 159–60
    from juice, 96–97
    Vignoles. *See* Ravat 51
    Vino Blanc, from concentrate,
    55
    Vinometer, 7, 7

W

Water, 28
White Riesling. *See* Johannis-
    berg Riesling
White wines. *See also specific
    wines or ingredients*
acid test for, 22–23
blending, 130
Brix range for, 36
fruity-style, 129
vs. red, 15–16
winemaking basics, 17–18
Winemaking
    basic procedure, 15–20
    history of, 3
    steps in, 2
    tips for, 14–15

Winemaking stores, 125,
    247–53
Winepresses. *See* Presses
Wine tasting
    appearance, 241
    aroma, 241–42
    numerical system of, 243,
    244
    taste, 242–43
Wine thief, 8, *8*

Y

Yeast
    adding, 17
    fermentation problems and,
    232
    flavor affected by, 237
    hydrating, 38
    types of, 13, 38–39, **40–42**
Yeast inoculation, 42
Yeast nutrient, 12–13

Z

Zinfandel
    blending, 166
    from concentrate, 67
    from grapes, 196–97
    from juice, 118–19
Zinfandel Blush
    from concentrate, 68
    from juice, 120–21

OTHER STOREY TITLES YOU WILL ENJOY

Cider: Making, Using, and Enjoying Sweet and Hard Cider by Annie Proulx and Lew Nichols. This new edition of the cider maker's bible covers everything from growing the trees and harvesting, to step-by-step instructions for making basic cider as well as sparkling cider blends and cider-based recipes. Information on finding and using cider-making materials and equipment is also included. 224 pages. Paperback. ISBN 0-88266-969-9.

Homemade Root Beer, Soda & Pop by Stephen Cresswell. This is the only book on the market reviving the traditional American activity of brewing old-fashioned drinks like sarsaparilla and birch beer. 128 pages. Paperback. ISBN 1-58017-052-8.

Making Wild Wines and Meads: 125 Unusual Recipes Using Herbs, Fruits, Flowers & More by Pattie Vargas and Richard Gulling. With more than 40 new recipes, this fully revised edition of the Storey classic Country Wines is a comprehensive, inspiring how-to guide new winemakers. Simple instructions allow anyone to create luscious honey meads, refreshing coolers and punches, and elegant wines without expensive equipment or elaborate calculations. 176 pages. Paperback. ISBN 1-58017-182-6.

From Vines to Wines: The Complete Guide to Growing Grapes and Making Your Own Wine by Jeff Cox. Everything readers need to know to grow their own grapes and make homemade wine. Topics include choosing a vineyard site; constructing trellises; planting, pruning, and harvesting grapes; plus pressing, fermenting, aging, and bottling wine. This updated edition offers new trellising systems, winemaking techniques, and wine-tasting tips. 256 pages. Paperback. ISBN 1-58017-105-2.

These books and other Storey books are available at your bookstore,
farm store, garden center, or directly from Storey Books,
210 MASS MoCA Way, North Adams, MA 01247, or by calling
800-441-5700. Or visit our Web site at www.storey.com